-build zone

2.

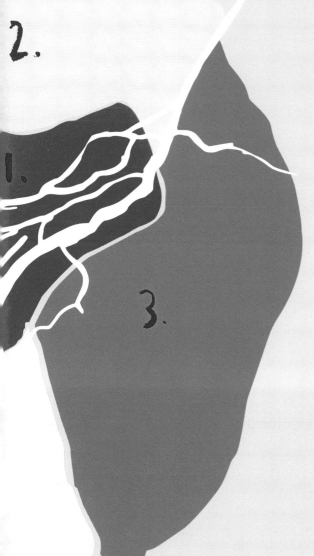

1.

3.

N W 1

New Wanlockhead
Scotland's highest village

1. old wanlockhead
2. green belt
   inc. sky farm etc
3. beverly hills
4. commercial Zone
5. Industrial zone
6. slums

IDP: 2043

IDP: 2043

Barroux, Hannah Berry, Kate Charlesworth, Dan McDaid,
Pat Mills, Denise Mina, Will Morris, Adam Murphy,
Mary Talbot and Irvine Welsh

FREIGHT
BOOKS

Second edition September 2014

Freight Books
49-53 Virginia Street
Glasgow, G1 1TS
www.freightbooks.co.uk

A CIP catalogue reference for this book is available from the British Library

ISBN 978-1-908754-63-9
eISBN 978-1-908754-64-6

Design by Freight
Printed and bound in the Czech Republic by PB Print UK

the publisher acknowledges investment from
Creative Scotland toward the publication of this book

IDP: Internally Displaced People

Man Cursing the Sea

Someone
just climbed to the top of the cliff
and started cursing the sea:

Stupid water, stupid pregnant water,
slimy copy of the sky,
hesitant hoverer between the sun and the moon,
pettifogging reckoner of shells,
fluid, loud-mouthed bull,
fertilizing the rocks with his blood,
suicidal sword
splintering itself on any promontory,
hydra, fragmenting the night,
breathing salty clouds of silence,
spreading jelly-like wings
in vain, in vain,
gorgon, devouring its own body,

water, you absurd flat skull of water—

Thus for a while he cursed the sea,
which licked his footprints in the sand
like a wounded dog.

And then he came down
and stroked
the small immense stormy mirror of the sea.

There you are, water, he said,
and went his way.

- Miroslav Holub

Intensive Care. Translated by Stuart Friebert and Dana Habova.
@1996 Oberlin College Press.

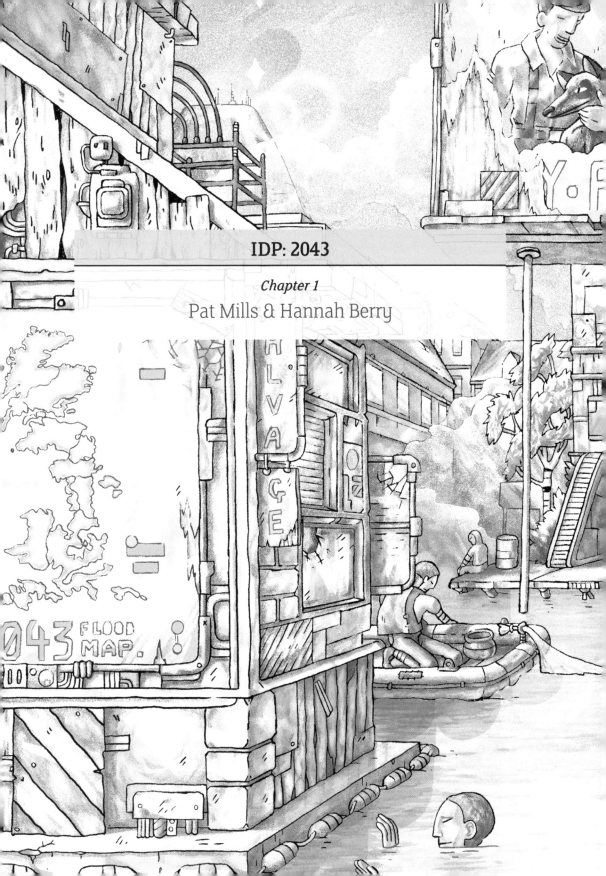

IDP: 2043

Chapter 1

Pat Mills & Hannah Berry

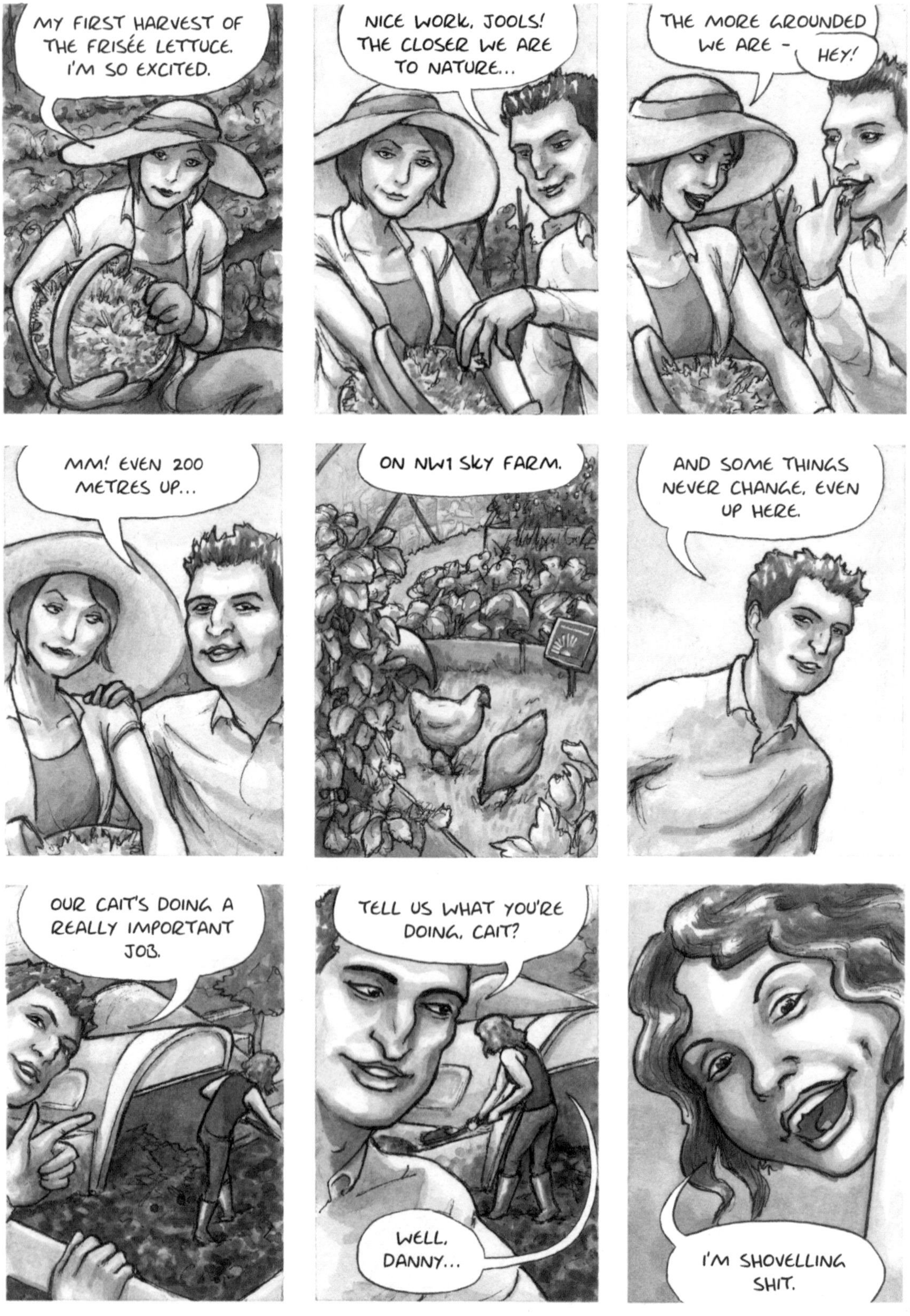
MY FIRST HARVEST OF THE FRISÉE LETTUCE. I'M SO EXCITED.
NICE WORK, JOOLS! THE CLOSER WE ARE TO NATURE...
THE MORE GROUNDED WE ARE -
HEY!
MM! EVEN 200 METRES UP...
ON NW1 SKY FARM.
AND SOME THINGS NEVER CHANGE, EVEN UP HERE.
OUR CAIT'S DOING A REALLY IMPORTANT JOB.
TELL US WHAT YOU'RE DOING, CAIT?
WELL, DANNY...
I'M SHOVELLING SHIT.

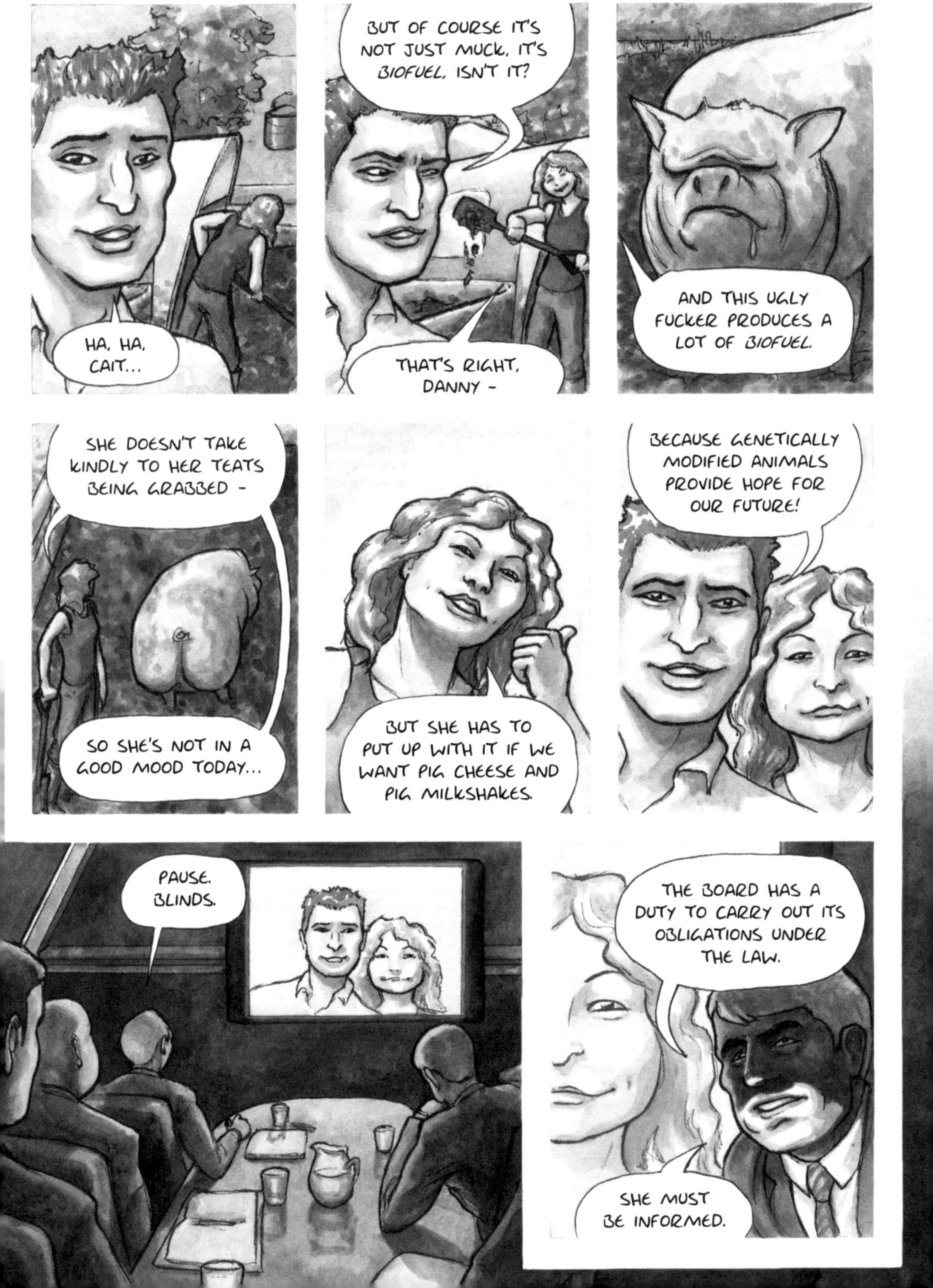
HA, HA, CAIT...
BUT OF COURSE IT'S NOT JUST MUCK, IT'S *BIOFUEL*, ISN'T IT?
THAT'S RIGHT, DANNY -
AND THIS UGLY FUCKER PRODUCES A LOT OF *BIOFUEL*.
SHE DOESN'T TAKE KINDLY TO HER TEATS BEING GRABBED -
SO SHE'S NOT IN A GOOD MOOD TODAY...
BUT SHE HAS TO PUT UP WITH IT IF WE WANT PIG CHEESE AND PIG MILKSHAKES.
BECAUSE GENETICALLY MODIFIED ANIMALS PROVIDE HOPE FOR OUR FUTURE!
PAUSE. BLINDS.
THE BOARD HAS A DUTY TO CARRY OUT ITS OBLIGATIONS UNDER THE LAW.
SHE MUST BE INFORMED.

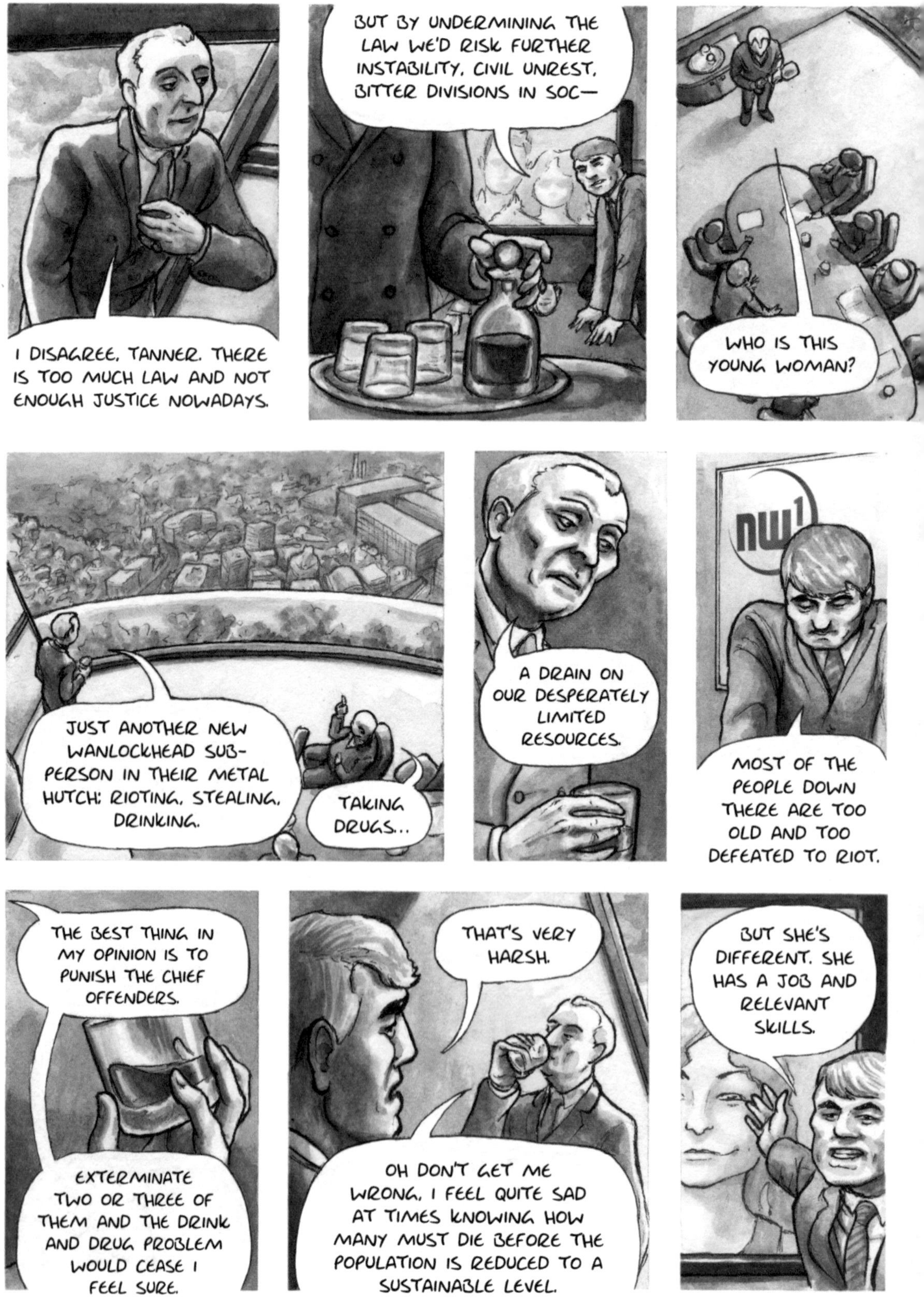
I DISAGREE, TANNER. THERE IS TOO MUCH LAW AND NOT ENOUGH JUSTICE NOWADAYS.
BUT BY UNDERMINING THE LAW WE'D RISK FURTHER INSTABILITY, CIVIL UNREST, BITTER DIVISIONS IN SOC—
WHO IS THIS YOUNG WOMAN?
JUST ANOTHER NEW WANLOCKHEAD SUB-PERSON IN THEIR METAL HUTCH: RIOTING, STEALING, DRINKING.
TAKING DRUGS...
A DRAIN ON OUR DESPERATELY LIMITED RESOURCES.
nw1
MOST OF THE PEOPLE DOWN THERE ARE TOO OLD AND TOO DEFEATED TO RIOT.
THE BEST THING IN MY OPINION IS TO PUNISH THE CHIEF OFFENDERS.
EXTERMINATE TWO OR THREE OF THEM AND THE DRINK AND DRUG PROBLEM WOULD CEASE I FEEL SURE.
THAT'S VERY HARSH.
OH DON'T GET ME WRONG, I FEEL QUITE SAD AT TIMES KNOWING HOW MANY MUST DIE BEFORE THE POPULATION IS REDUCED TO A SUSTAINABLE LEVEL.
BUT SHE'S DIFFERENT. SHE HAS A JOB AND RELEVANT SKILLS.

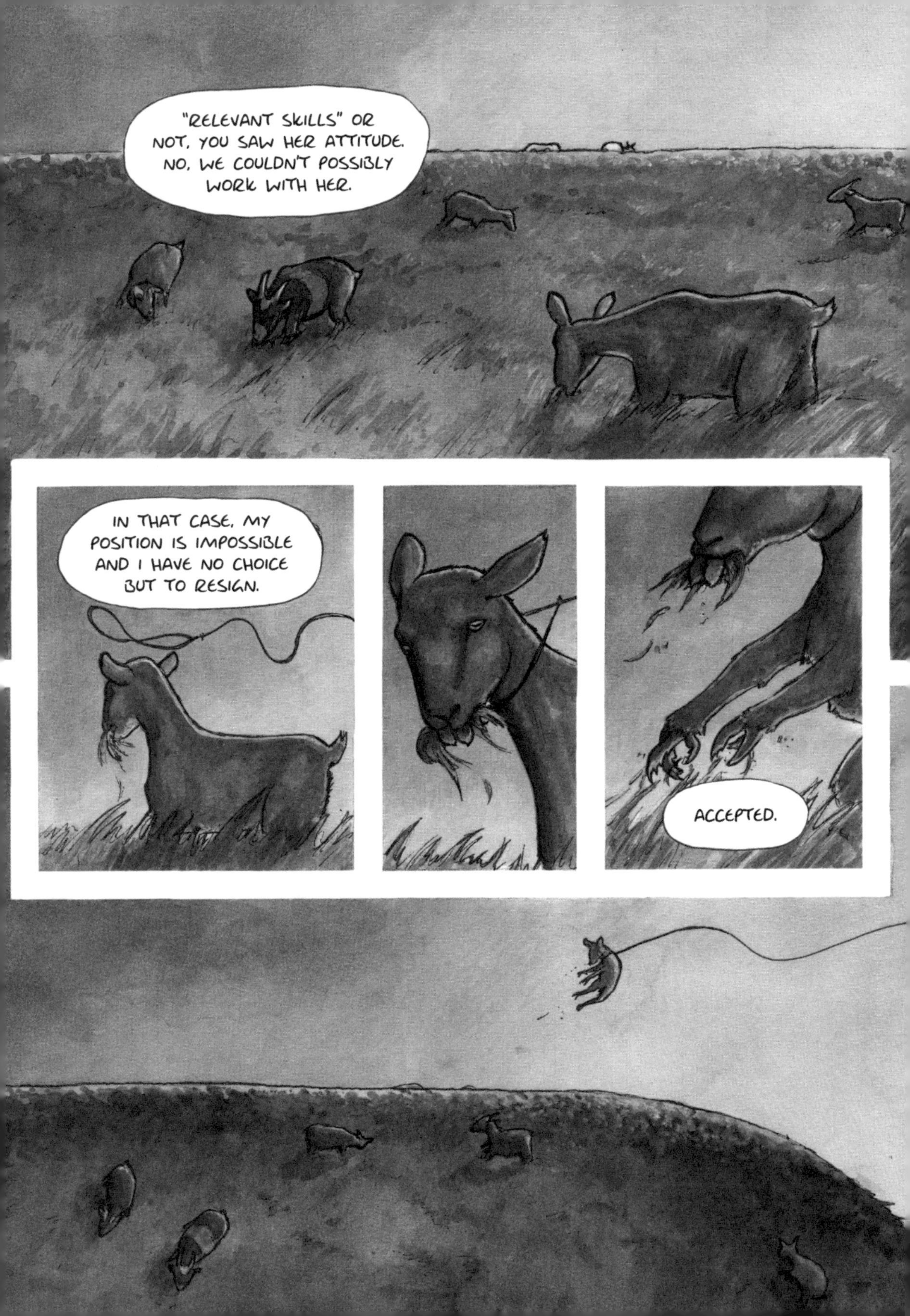
"RELEVANT SKILLS" OR NOT, YOU SAW HER ATTITUDE. NO, WE COULDN'T POSSIBLY WORK WITH HER.
IN THAT CASE, MY POSITION IS IMPOSSIBLE AND I HAVE NO CHOICE BUT TO RESIGN.
ACCEPTED.

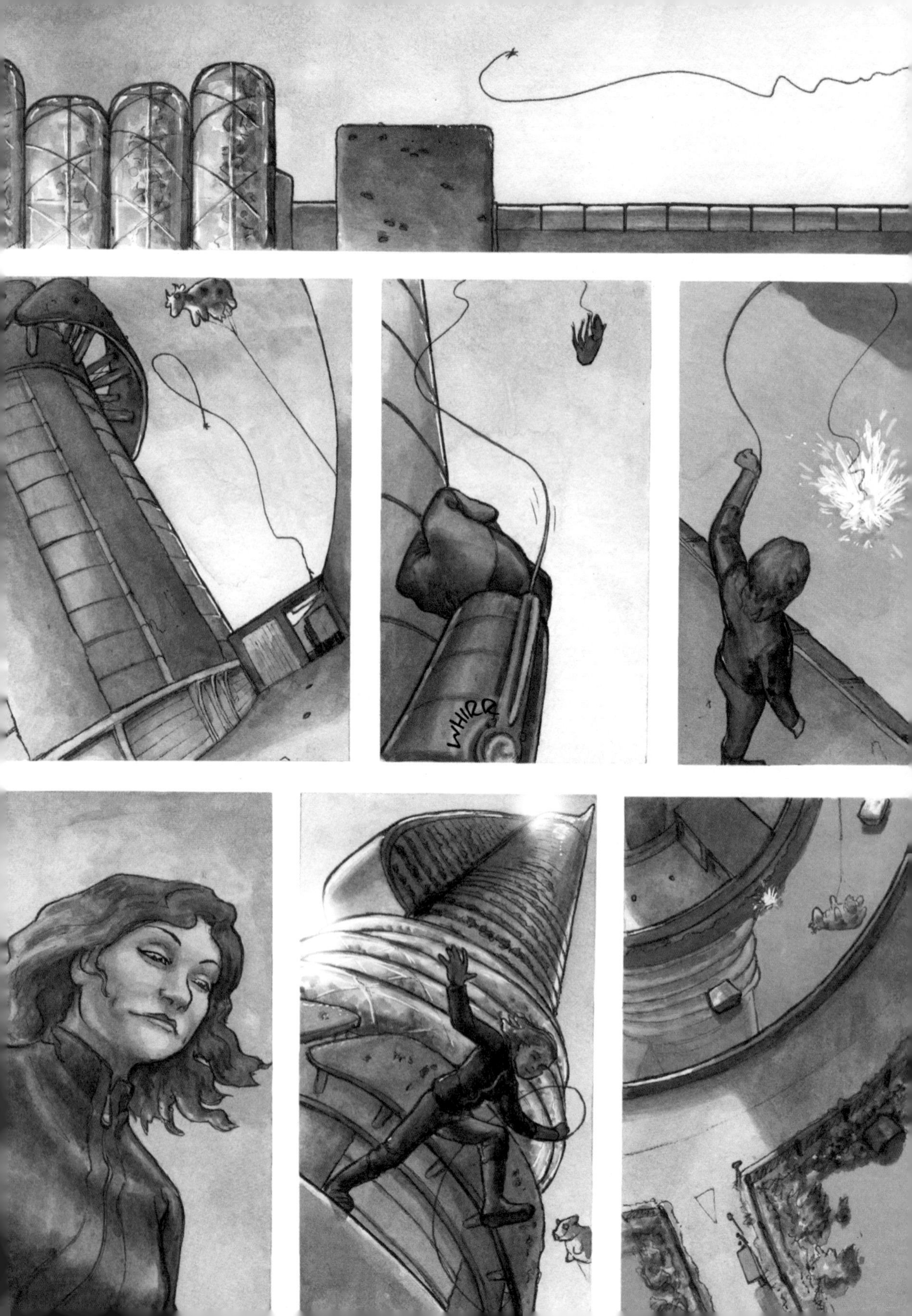
WHIRR

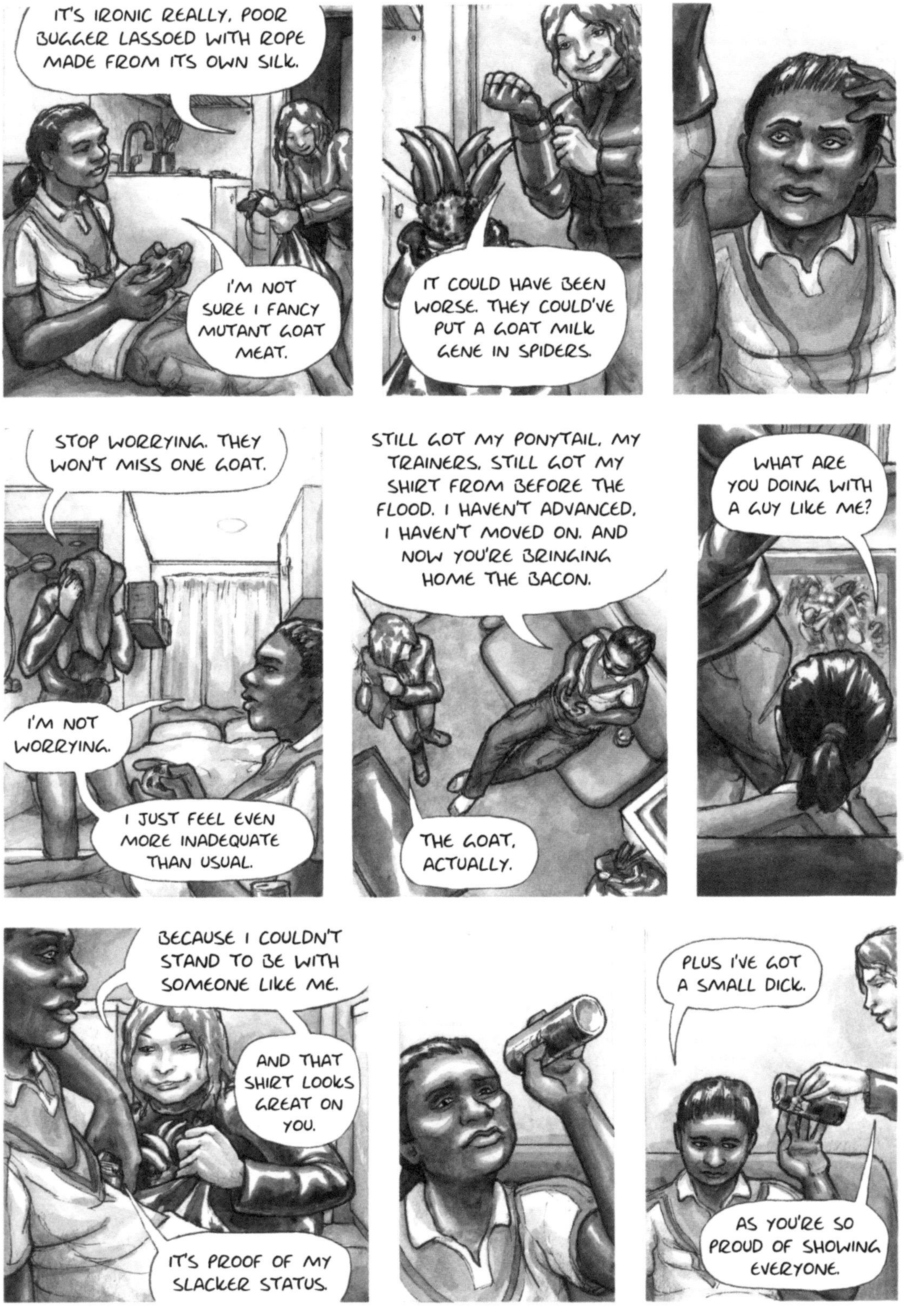
IT'S IRONIC REALLY. POOR BUGGER LASSOED WITH ROPE MADE FROM ITS OWN SILK.
I'M NOT SURE I FANCY MUTANT GOAT MEAT.
IT COULD HAVE BEEN WORSE. THEY COULD'VE PUT A GOAT MILK GENE IN SPIDERS.
STOP WORRYING. THEY WON'T MISS ONE GOAT.
I'M NOT WORRYING.
I JUST FEEL EVEN MORE INADEQUATE THAN USUAL.
STILL GOT MY PONYTAIL, MY TRAINERS, STILL GOT MY SHIRT FROM BEFORE THE FLOOD. I HAVEN'T ADVANCED, I HAVEN'T MOVED ON. AND NOW YOU'RE BRINGING HOME THE BACON.
THE GOAT, ACTUALLY.
WHAT ARE YOU DOING WITH A GUY LIKE ME?
BECAUSE I COULDN'T STAND TO BE WITH SOMEONE LIKE ME.
AND THAT SHIRT LOOKS GREAT ON YOU.
IT'S PROOF OF MY SLACKER STATUS.
PLUS I'VE GOT A SMALL DICK.
AS YOU'RE SO PROUD OF SHOWING EVERYONE.

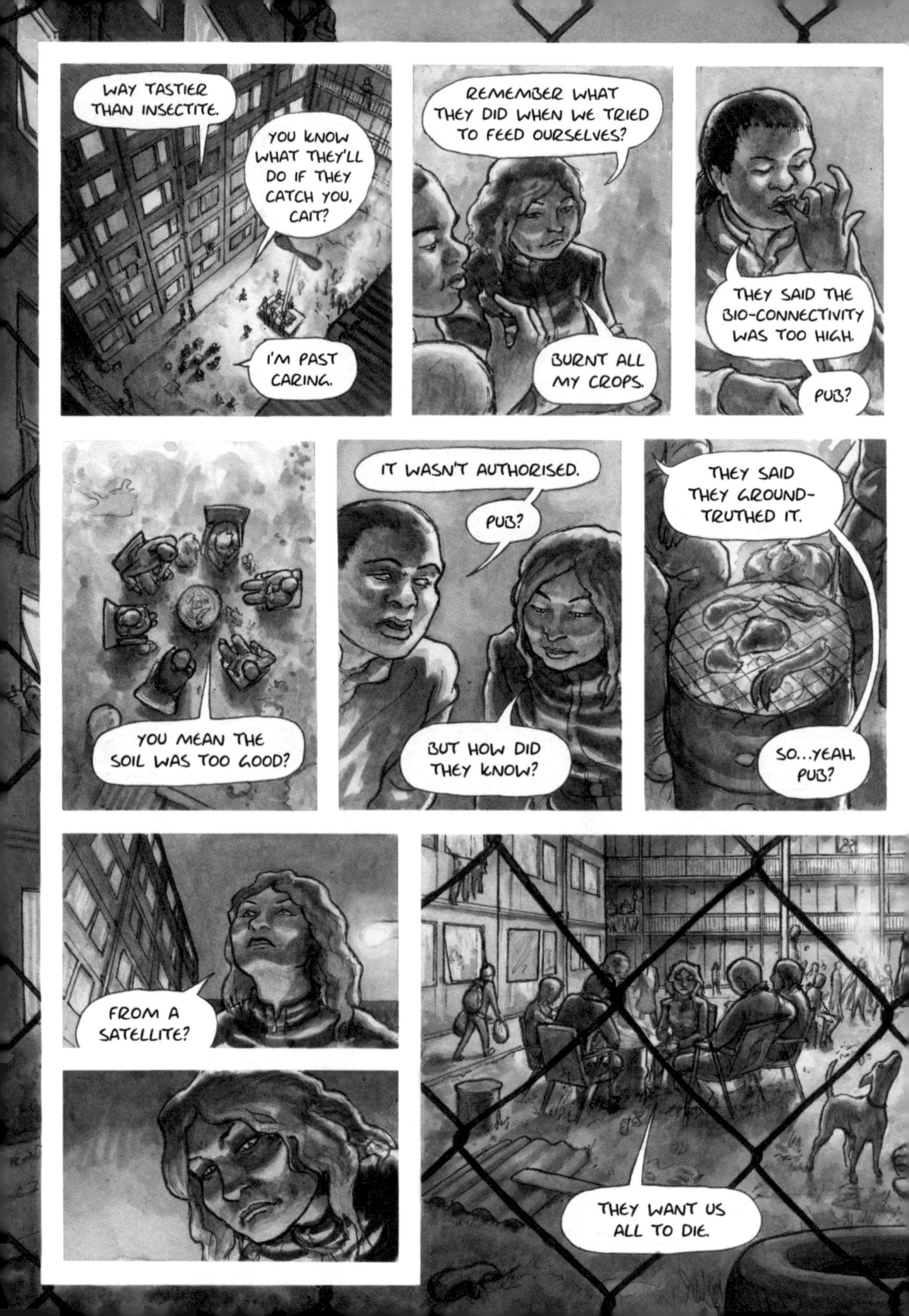
WAY TASTIER THAN INSECTITE.
YOU KNOW WHAT THEY'LL DO IF THEY CATCH YOU, CAIT?
I'M PAST CARING.
REMEMBER WHAT THEY DID WHEN WE TRIED TO FEED OURSELVES?
BURNT ALL MY CROPS.
THEY SAID THE BIO-CONNECTIVITY WAS TOO HIGH.
PUB?
YOU MEAN THE SOIL WAS TOO GOOD?
IT WASN'T AUTHORISED.
PUB?
BUT HOW DID THEY KNOW?
THEY SAID THEY GROUND-TRUTHED IT.
SO...YEAH. PUB?
FROM A SATELLITE?
THEY WANT US ALL TO DIE.

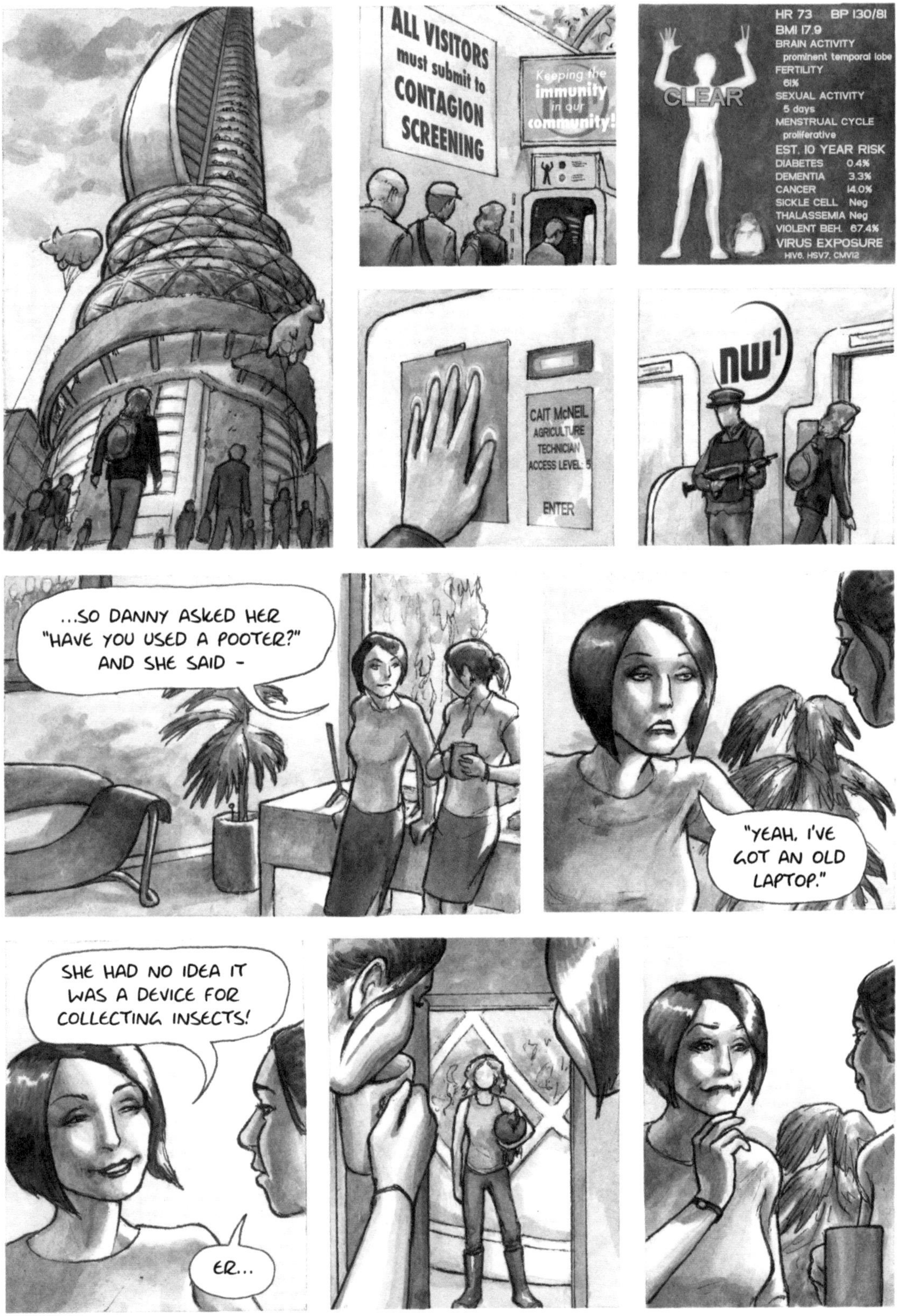
ALL VISITORS must submit to CONTAGION SCREENING
Keeping the immunity in our community!
HR 73 BP 130/81
BMI 17.9
BRAIN ACTIVITY
prominent temporal lobe
FERTILITY
61%
CLEAR
SEXUAL ACTIVITY
5 days
MENSTRUAL CYCLE
proliferative
EST. 10 YEAR RISK
DIABETES 0.4%
DEMENTIA 3.3%
CANCER 14.0%
SICKLE CELL Neg
THALASSEMIA Neg
VIOLENT BEH. 67.4%
VIRUS EXPOSURE
HIV6, HSV7, CMV12
CAIT McNEIL
AGRICULTURE
TECHNICIAN
ACCESS LEVEL: 5
ENTER
nw1
...SO DANNY ASKED HER "HAVE YOU USED A POOTER?" AND SHE SAID -
"YEAH, I'VE GOT AN OLD LAPTOP."
SHE HAD NO IDEA IT WAS A DEVICE FOR COLLECTING INSECTS!
ER...

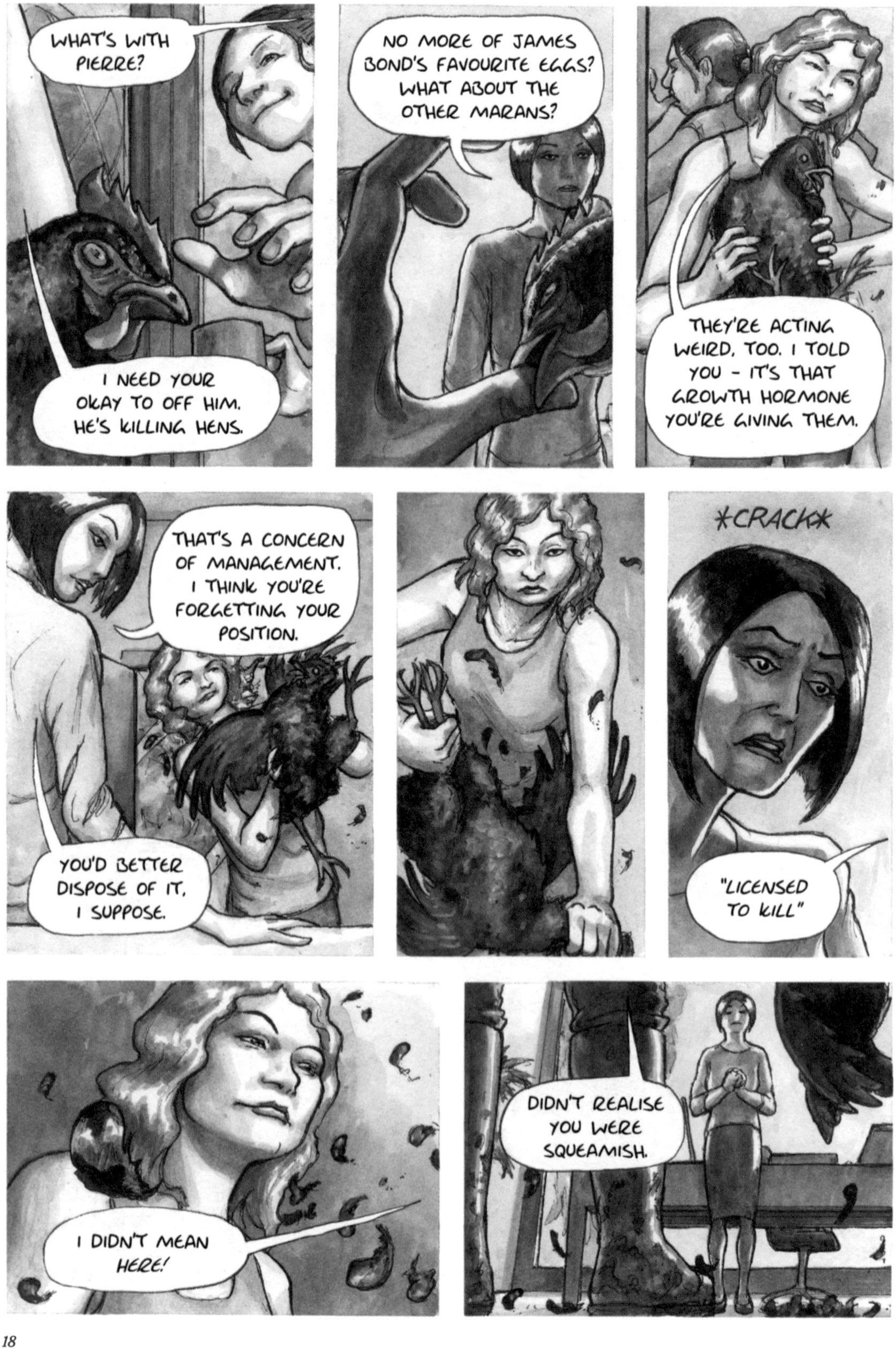
WHAT'S WITH PIERRE?
I NEED YOUR OKAY TO OFF HIM. HE'S KILLING HENS.
NO MORE OF JAMES BOND'S FAVOURITE EGGS? WHAT ABOUT THE OTHER MARANS?
THEY'RE ACTING WEIRD, TOO. I TOLD YOU - IT'S THAT GROWTH HORMONE YOU'RE GIVING THEM.
THAT'S A CONCERN OF MANAGEMENT. I THINK YOU'RE FORGETTING YOUR POSITION.
YOU'D BETTER DISPOSE OF IT, I SUPPOSE.
CRACK
"LICENSED TO KILL"
I DIDN'T MEAN HERE!
DIDN'T REALISE YOU WERE SQUEAMISH.

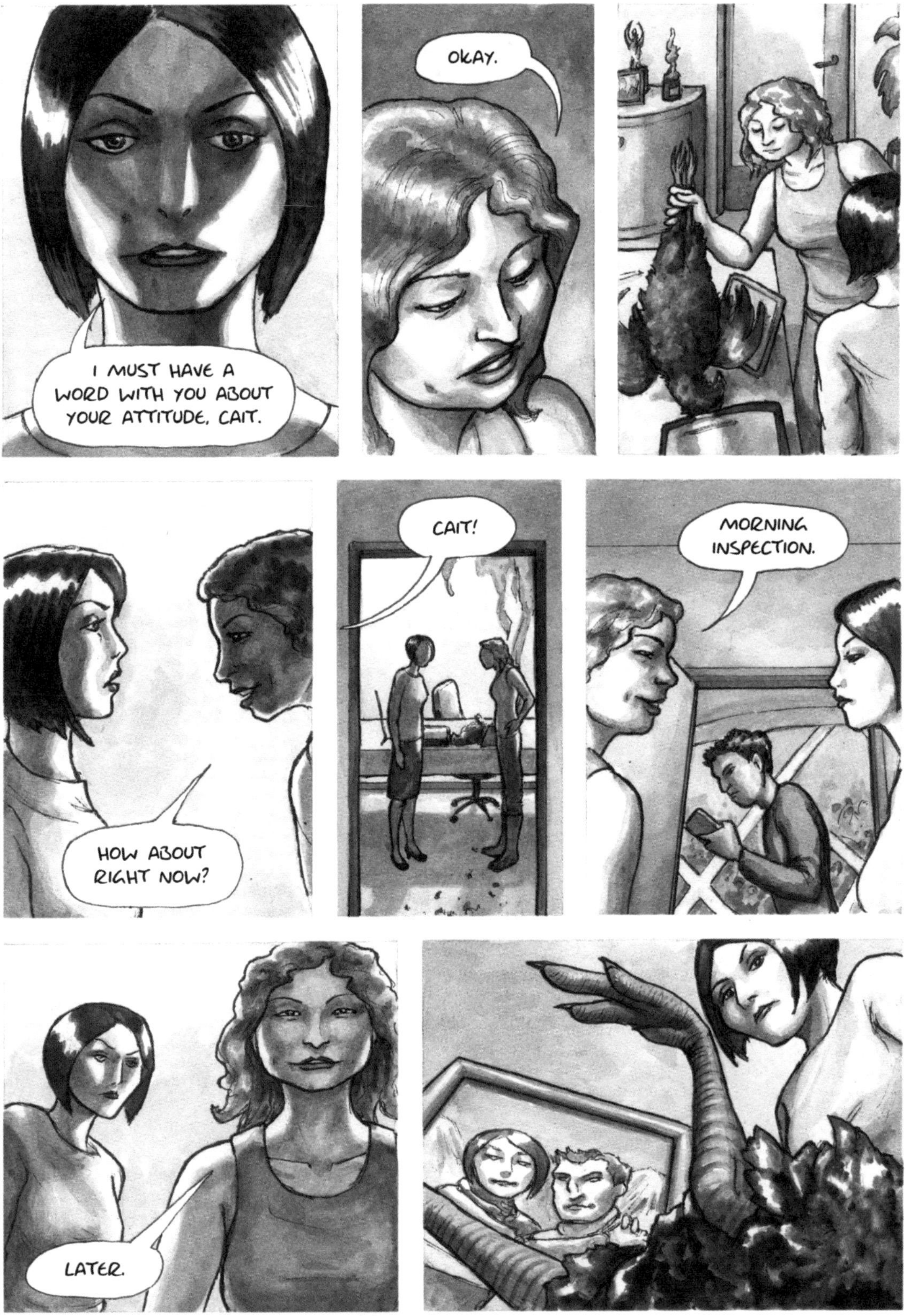
I MUST HAVE A WORD WITH YOU ABOUT YOUR ATTITUDE, CAIT.
OKAY.
HOW ABOUT RIGHT NOW?
CAIT!
MORNING INSPECTION.
LATER.

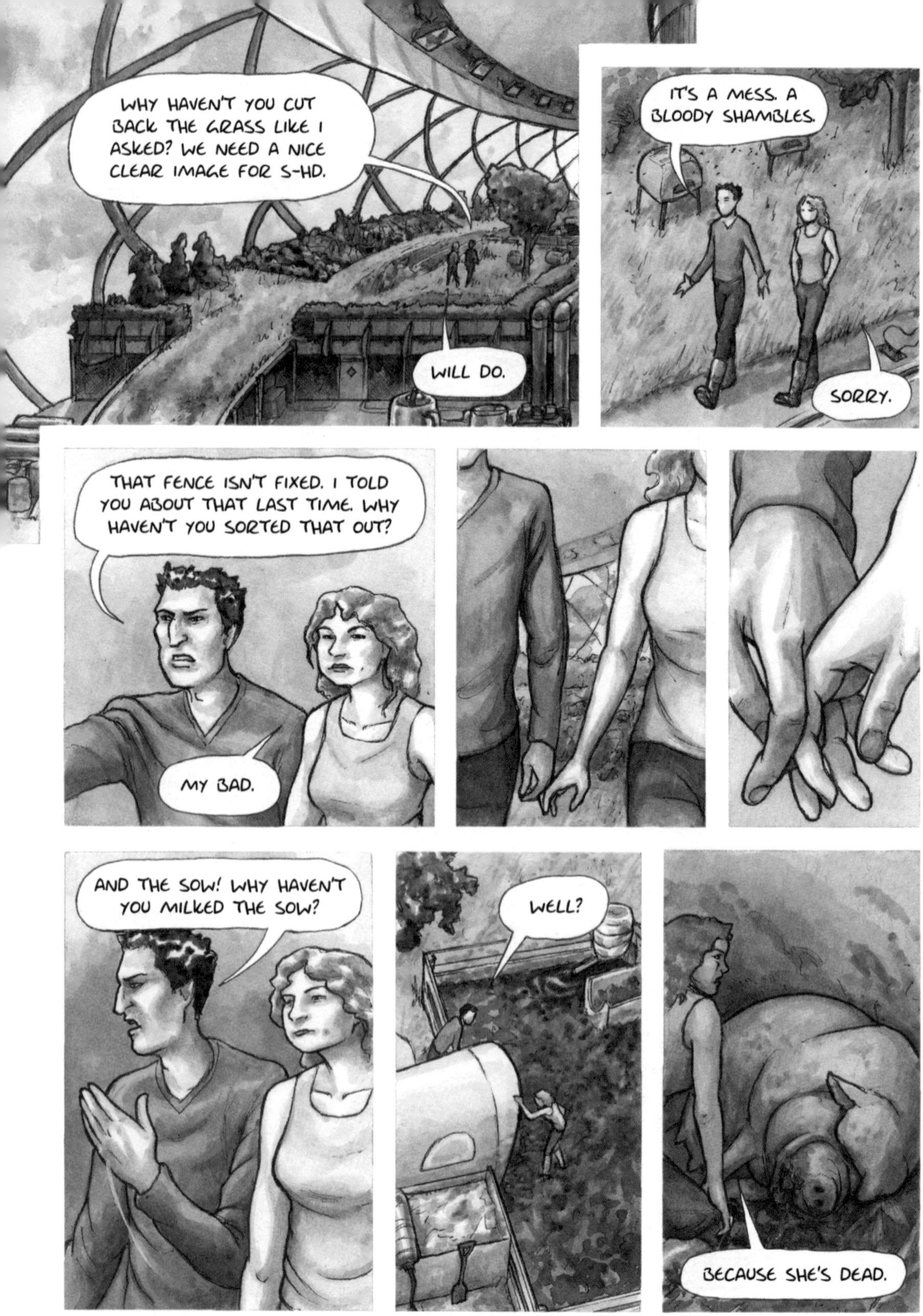
WHY HAVEN'T YOU CUT BACK THE GRASS LIKE I ASKED? WE NEED A NICE CLEAR IMAGE FOR S-HD.
WILL DO.
IT'S A MESS. A BLOODY SHAMBLES.
SORRY.
THAT FENCE ISN'T FIXED. I TOLD YOU ABOUT THAT LAST TIME. WHY HAVEN'T YOU SORTED THAT OUT?
MY BAD.
AND THE SOW! WHY HAVEN'T YOU MILKED THE SOW?
WELL?
BECAUSE SHE'S DEAD.

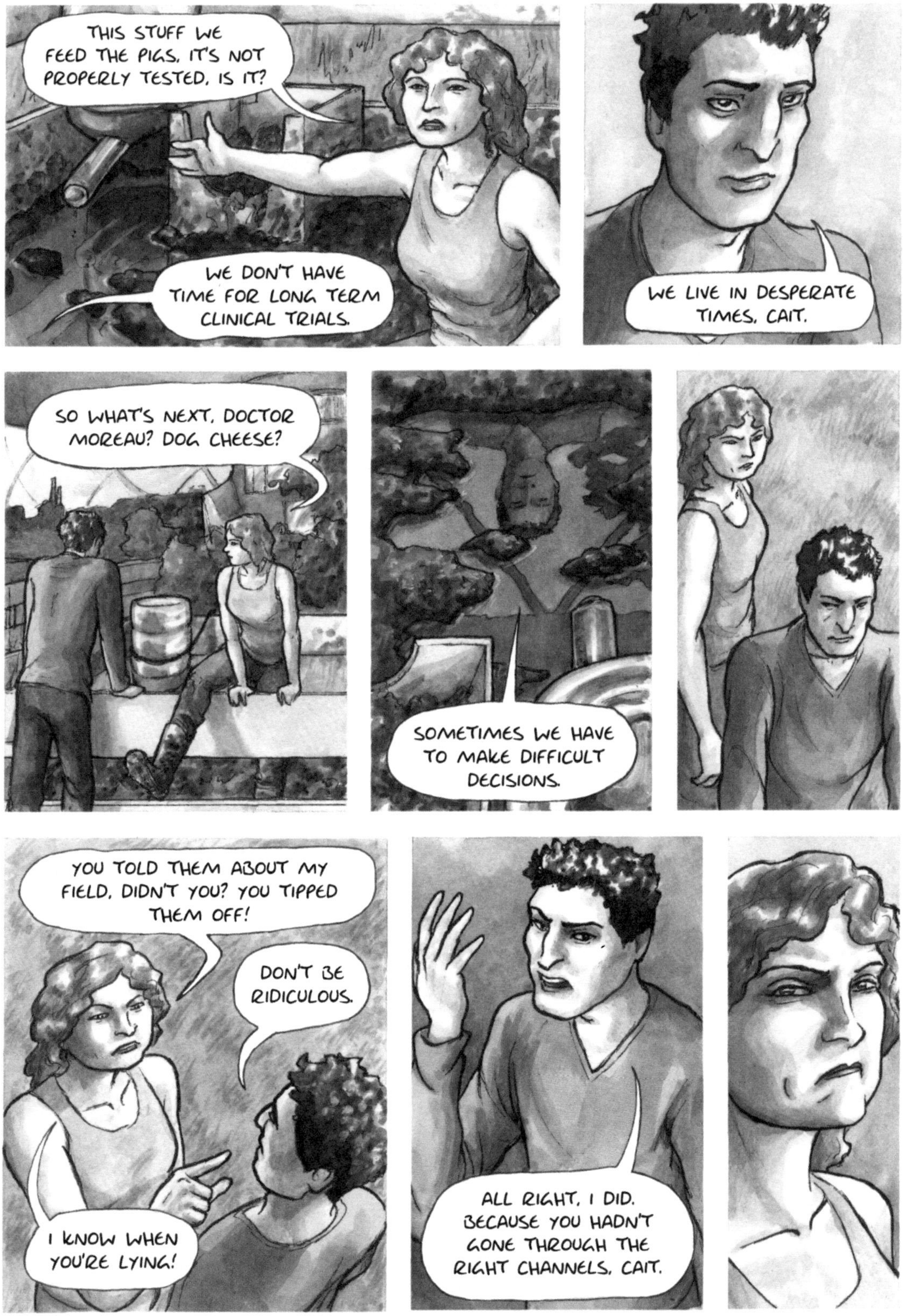
THIS STUFF WE FEED THE PIGS, IT'S NOT PROPERLY TESTED, IS IT?
WE DON'T HAVE TIME FOR LONG TERM CLINICAL TRIALS.
WE LIVE IN DESPERATE TIMES, CAIT.
SO WHAT'S NEXT, DOCTOR MOREAU? DOG CHEESE?
SOMETIMES WE HAVE TO MAKE DIFFICULT DECISIONS.
YOU TOLD THEM ABOUT MY FIELD, DIDN'T YOU? YOU TIPPED THEM OFF!
DON'T BE RIDICULOUS.
I KNOW WHEN YOU'RE LYING!
ALL RIGHT, I DID. BECAUSE YOU HADN'T GONE THROUGH THE RIGHT CHANNELS, CAIT.

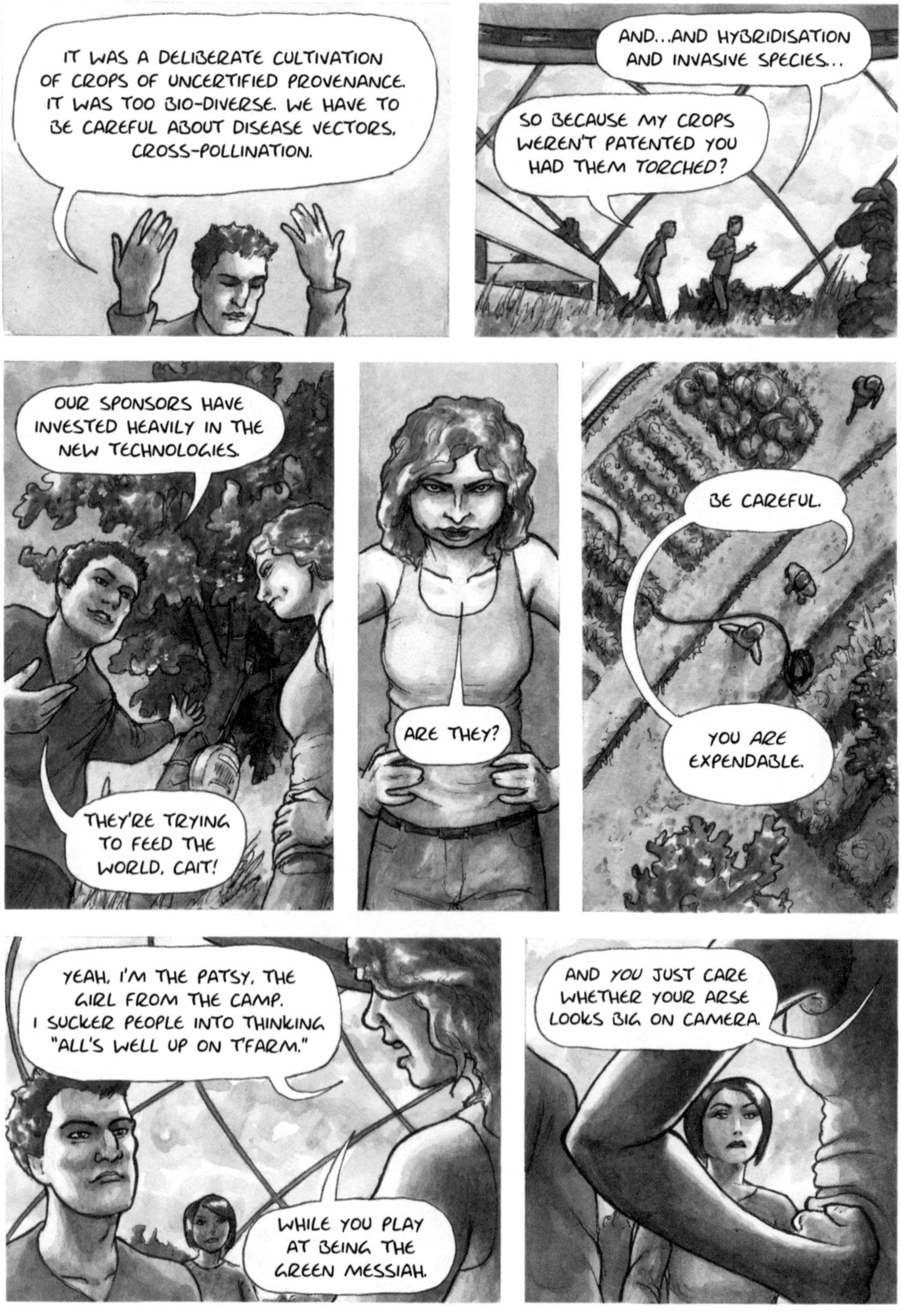
IT WAS A DELIBERATE CULTIVATION OF CROPS OF UNCERTIFIED PROVENANCE. IT WAS TOO BIO-DIVERSE. WE HAVE TO BE CAREFUL ABOUT DISEASE VECTORS, CROSS-POLLINATION.
AND...AND HYBRIDISATION AND INVASIVE SPECIES...
SO BECAUSE MY CROPS WEREN'T PATENTED YOU HAD THEM TORCHED?
OUR SPONSORS HAVE INVESTED HEAVILY IN THE NEW TECHNOLOGIES.
THEY'RE TRYING TO FEED THE WORLD, CAIT!
ARE THEY?
BE CAREFUL.
YOU ARE EXPENDABLE.
YEAH, I'M THE PATSY, THE GIRL FROM THE CAMP. I SUCKER PEOPLE INTO THINKING "ALL'S WELL UP ON T'FARM."
WHILE YOU PLAY AT BEING THE GREEN MESSIAH.
AND YOU JUST CARE WHETHER YOUR ARSE LOOKS BIG ON CAMERA.

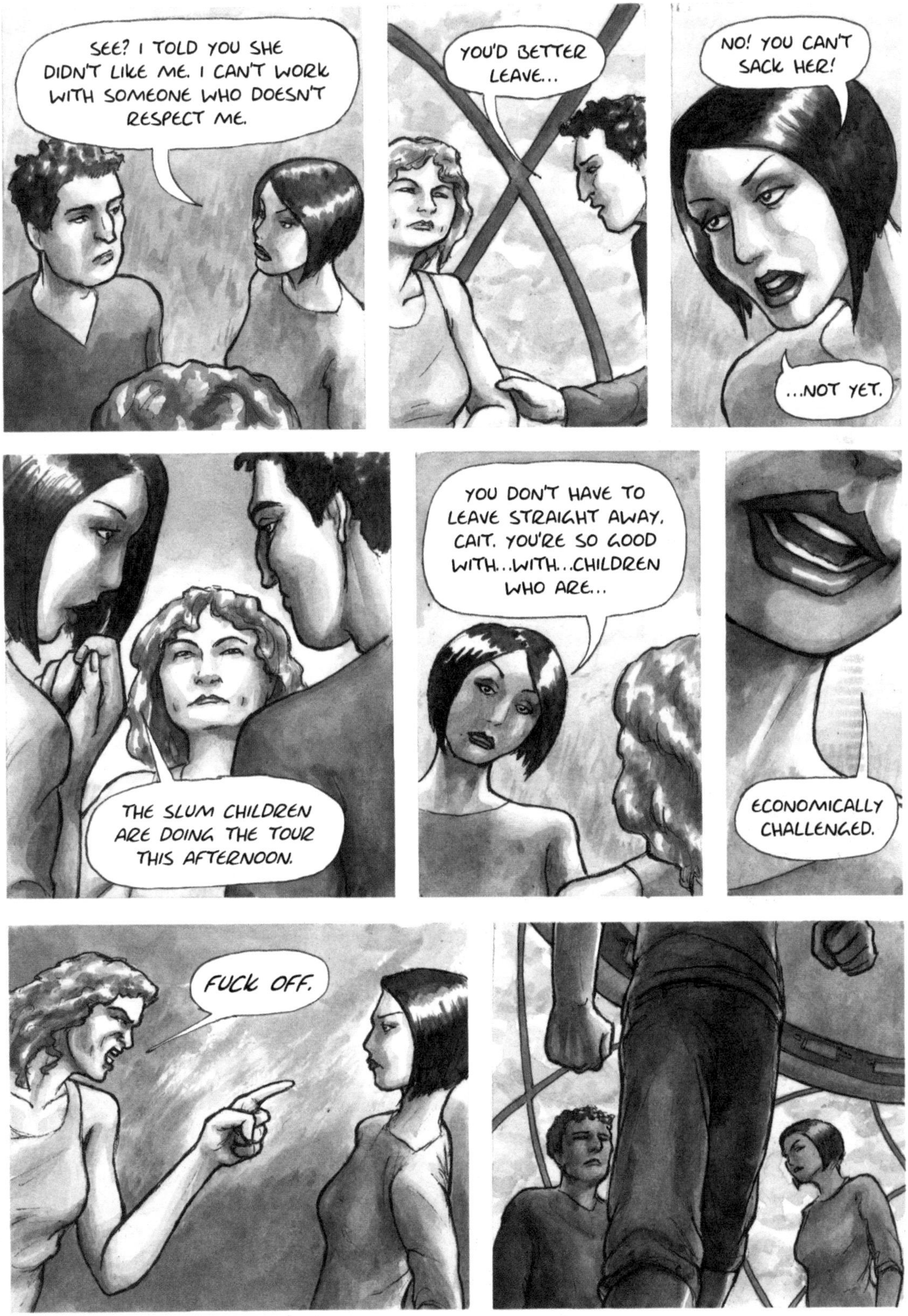
SEE? I TOLD YOU SHE DIDN'T LIKE ME. I CAN'T WORK WITH SOMEONE WHO DOESN'T RESPECT ME.
YOU'D BETTER LEAVE...
NO! YOU CAN'T SACK HER!
...NOT YET.
THE SLUM CHILDREN ARE DOING THE TOUR THIS AFTERNOON.
YOU DON'T HAVE TO LEAVE STRAIGHT AWAY, CAIT. YOU'RE SO GOOD WITH...WITH...CHILDREN WHO ARE...
ECONOMICALLY CHALLENGED.
FUCK OFF.

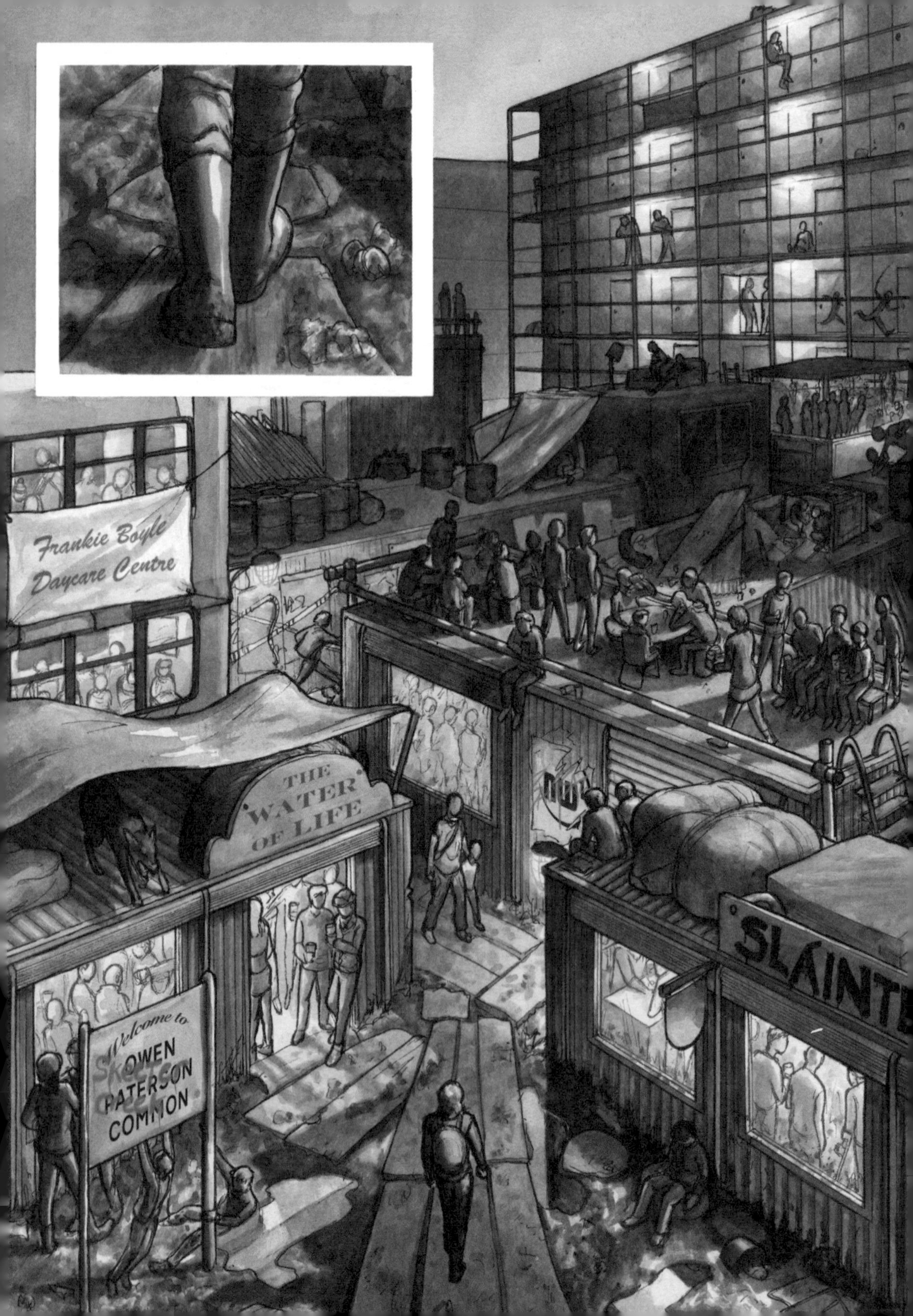
Frankie Boyle
Daycare Centre
THE
WATER
OF LIFE
Welcome to
OWEN
PATERSON
COMMON
SLAINTE

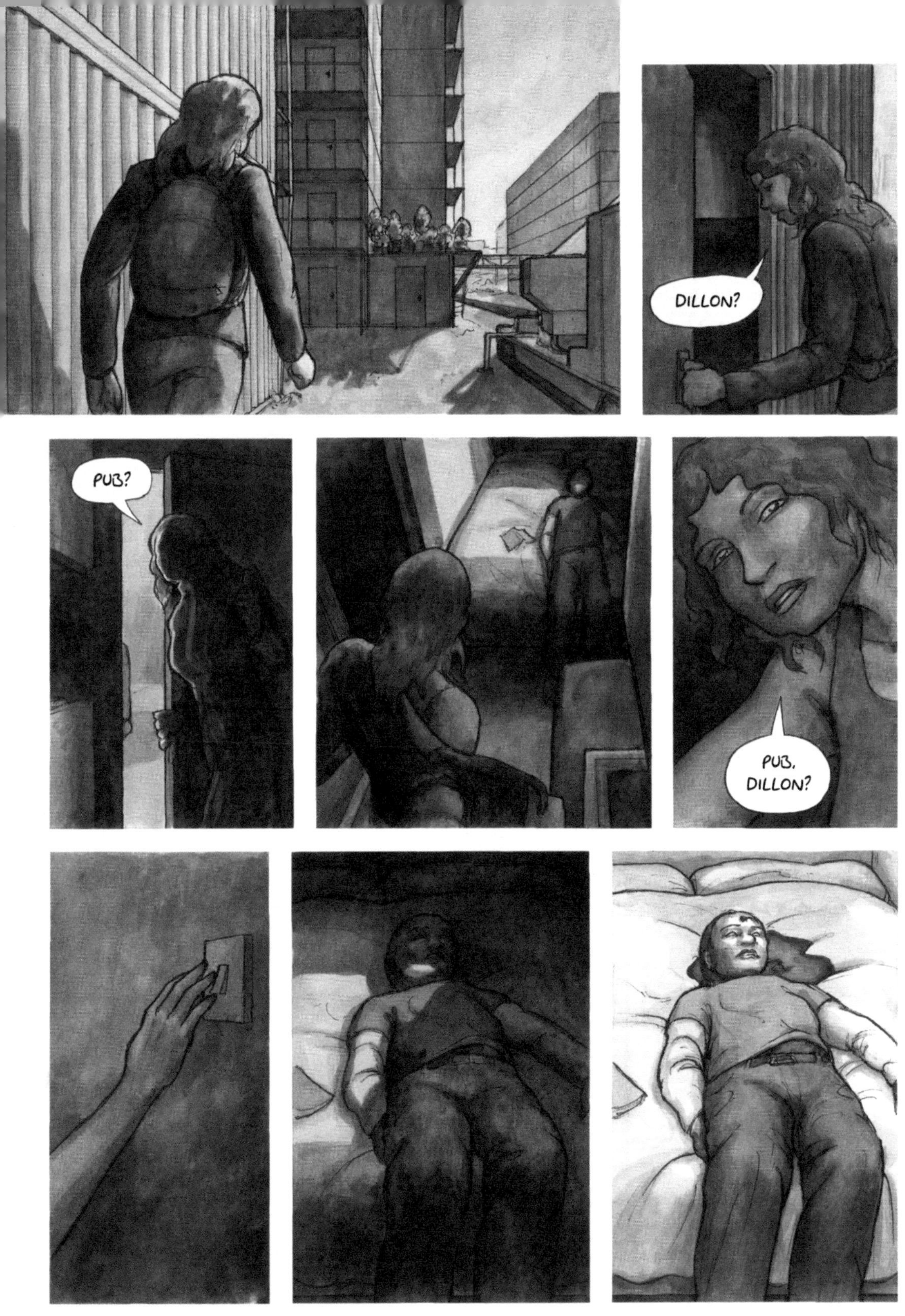
DILLON?
PUB?
PUB, DILLON?

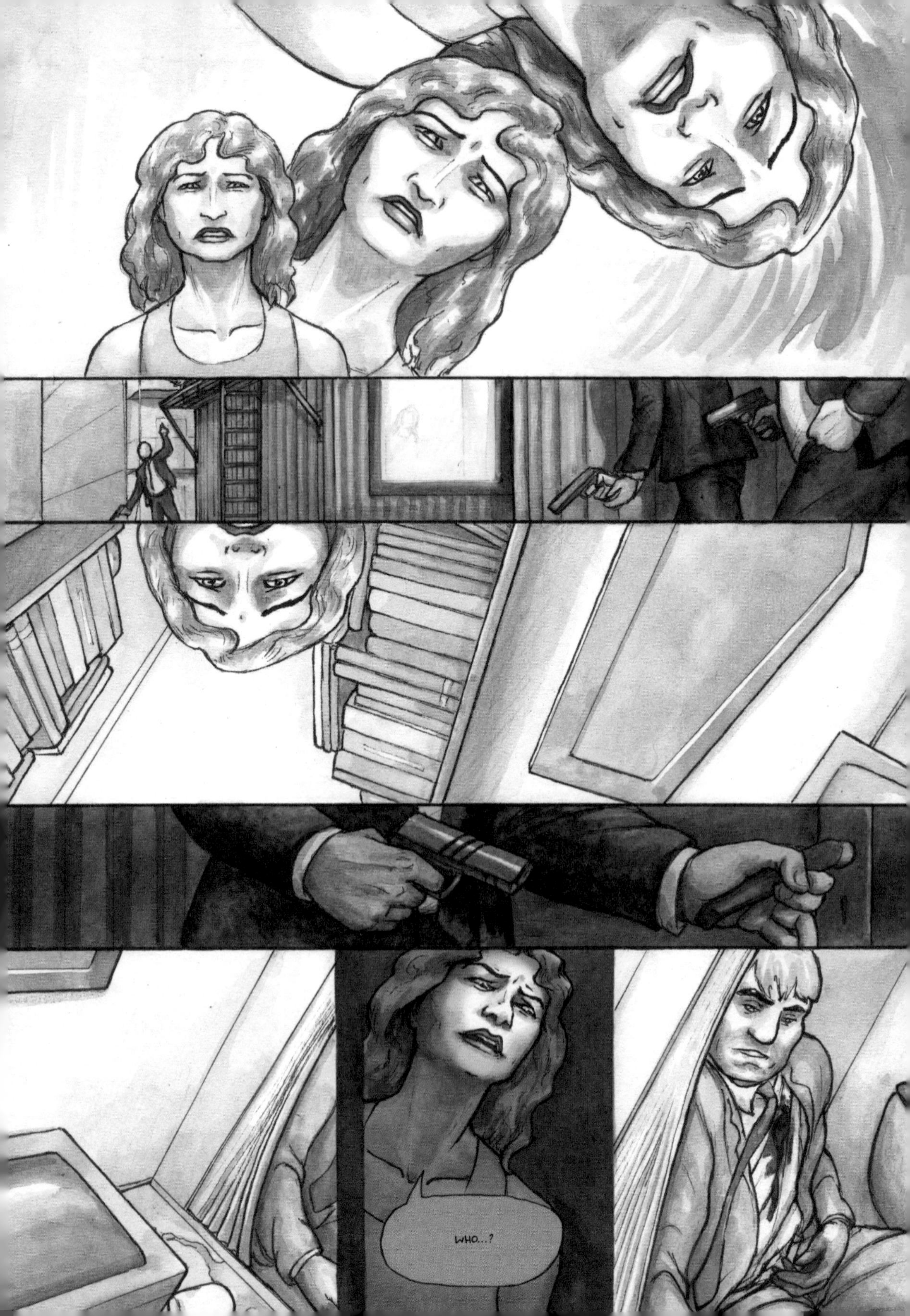
WHO...?

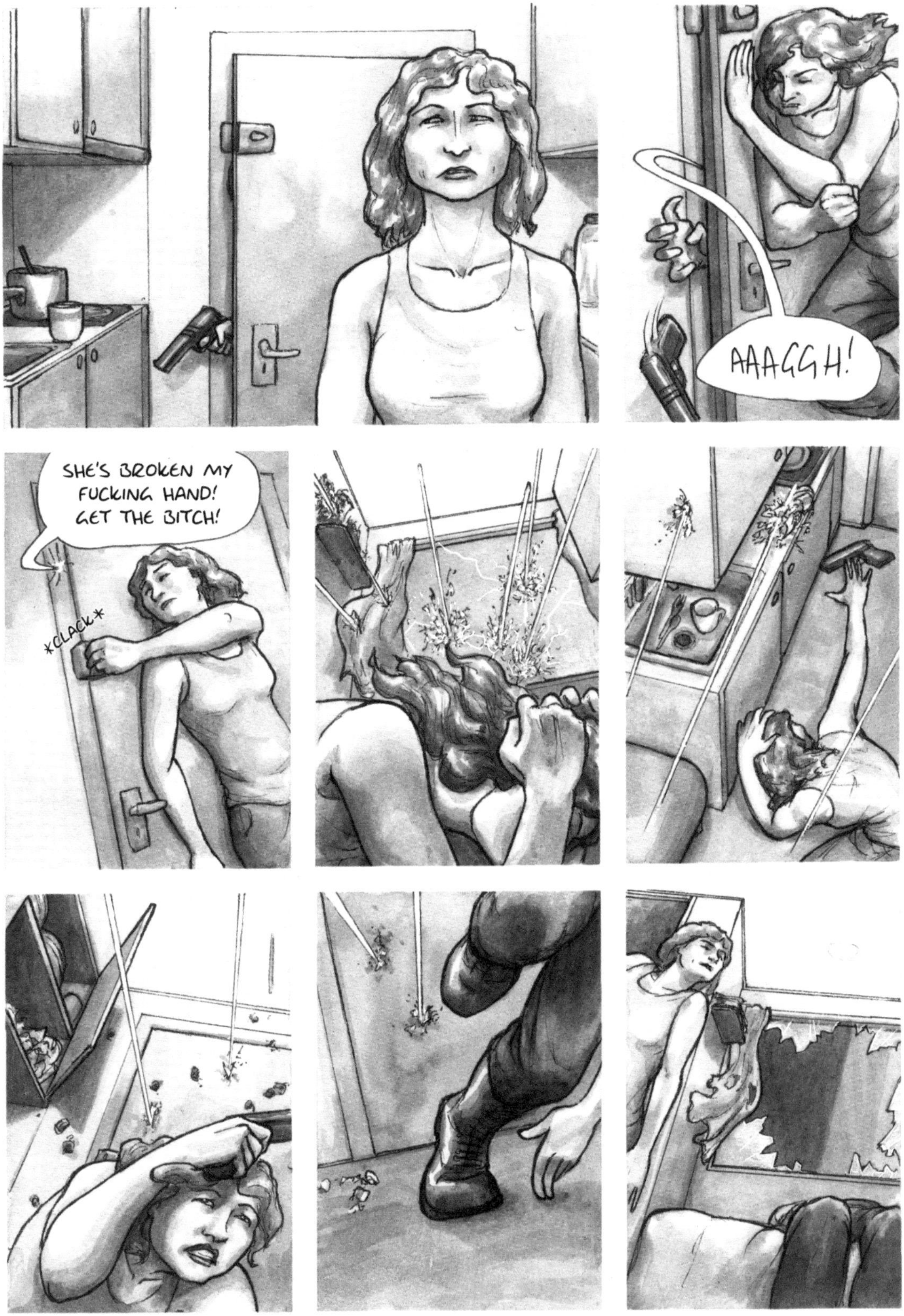
AAAGGH!
SHE'S BROKEN MY FUCKING HAND! GET THE BITCH!
CLACK

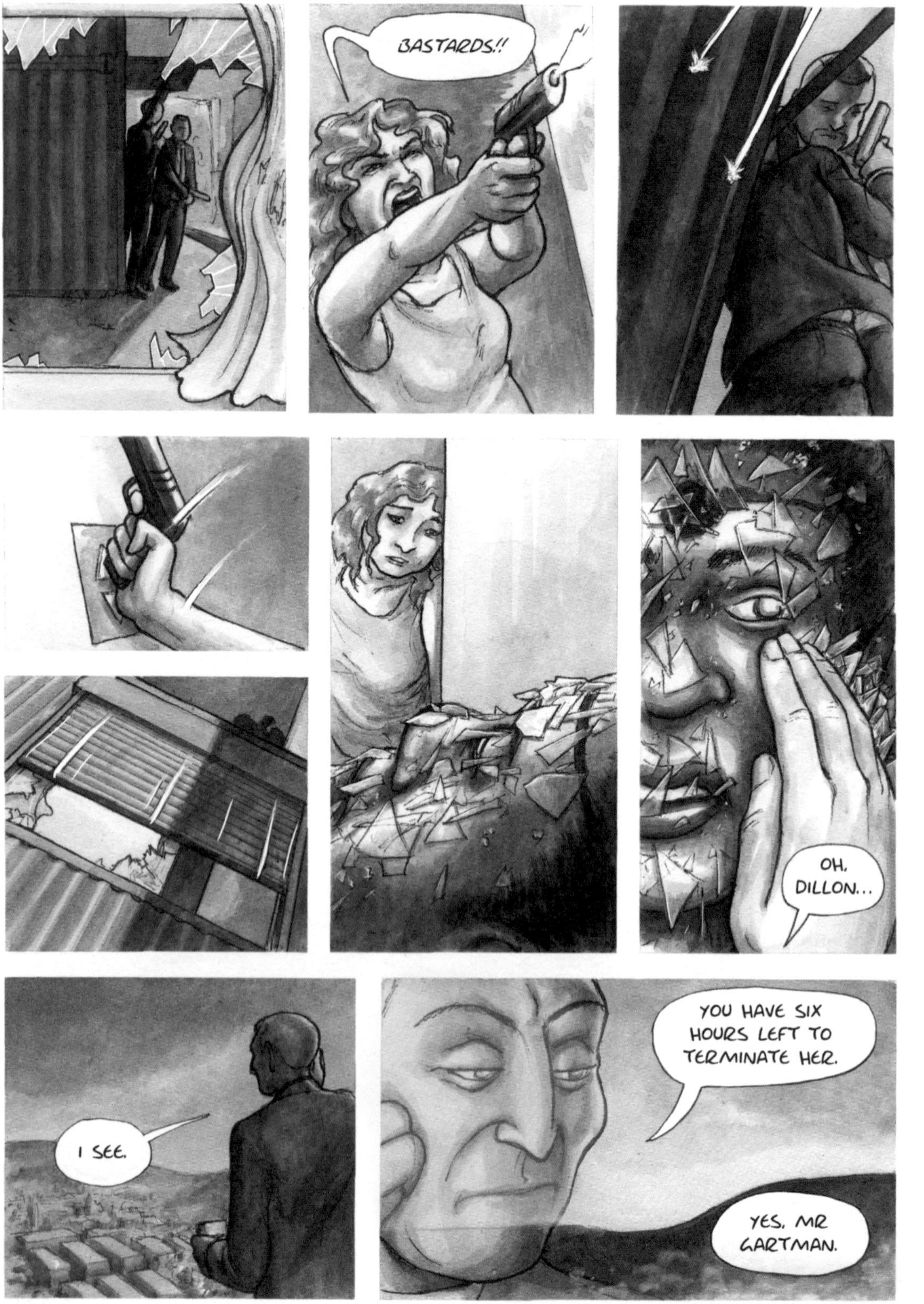
BASTARDS!!
OH, DILLON...
I SEE.
YOU HAVE SIX HOURS LEFT TO TERMINATE HER.
YES, MR GARTMAN.

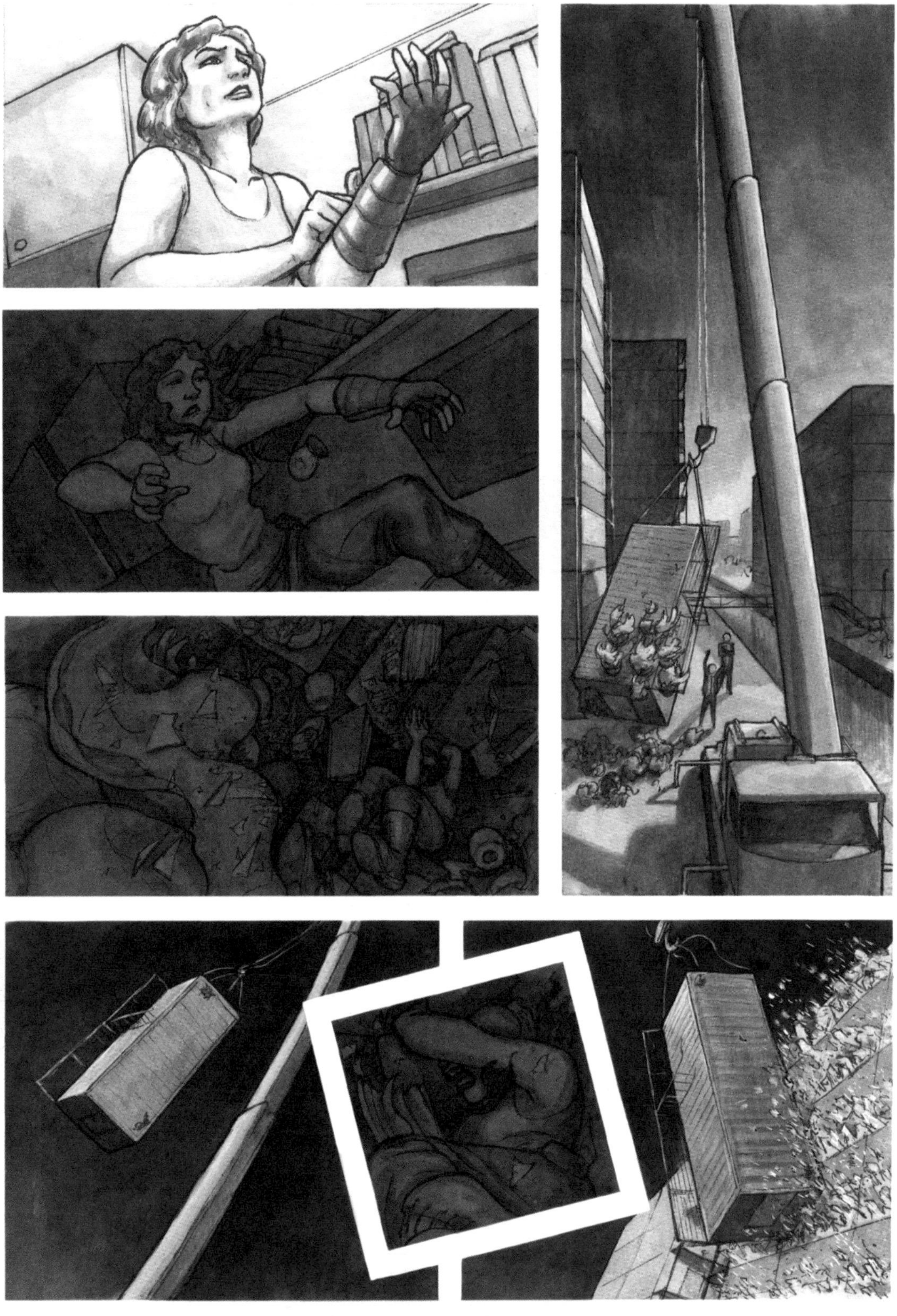

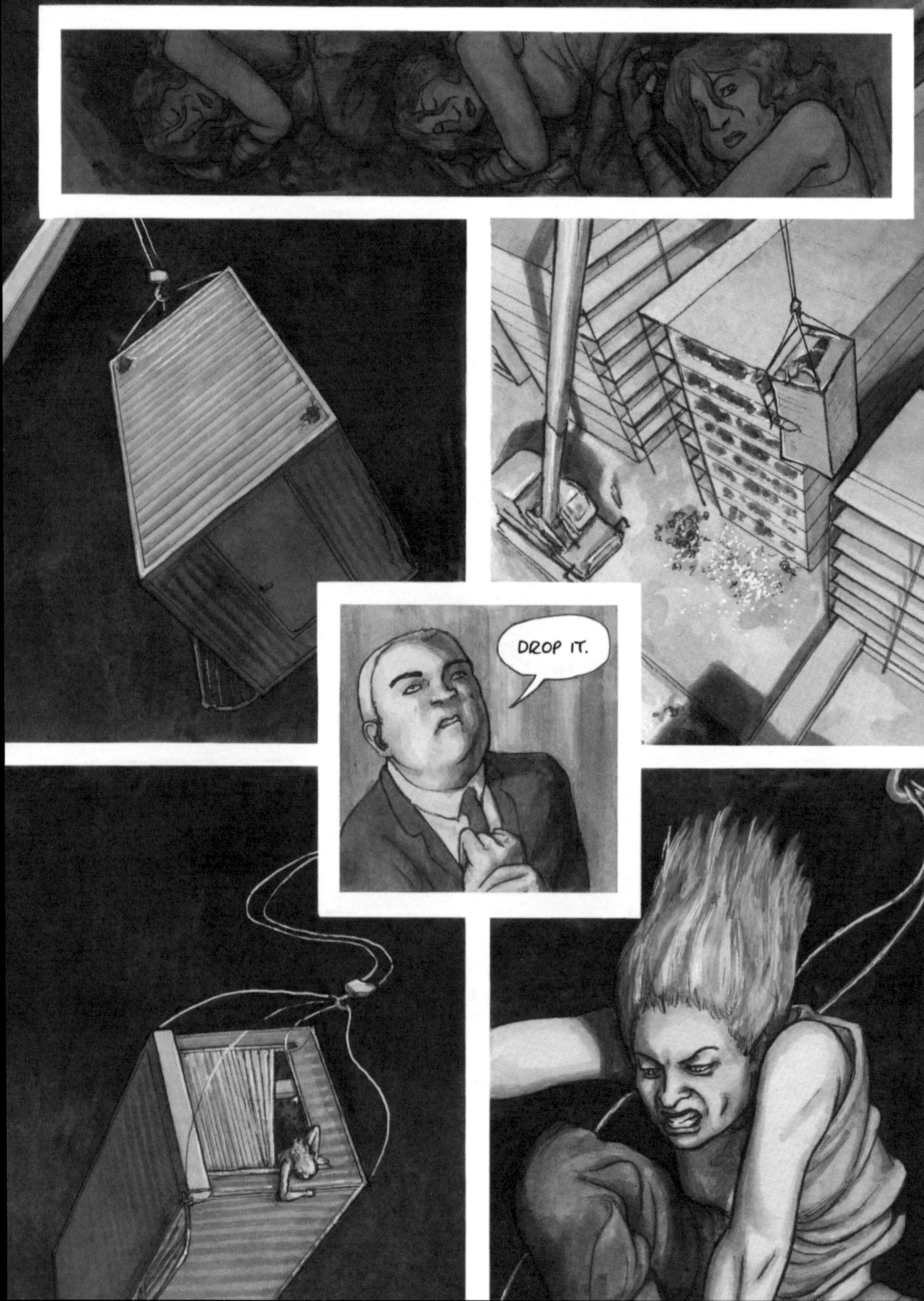
DROP IT.

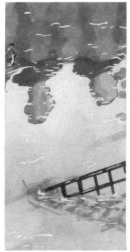

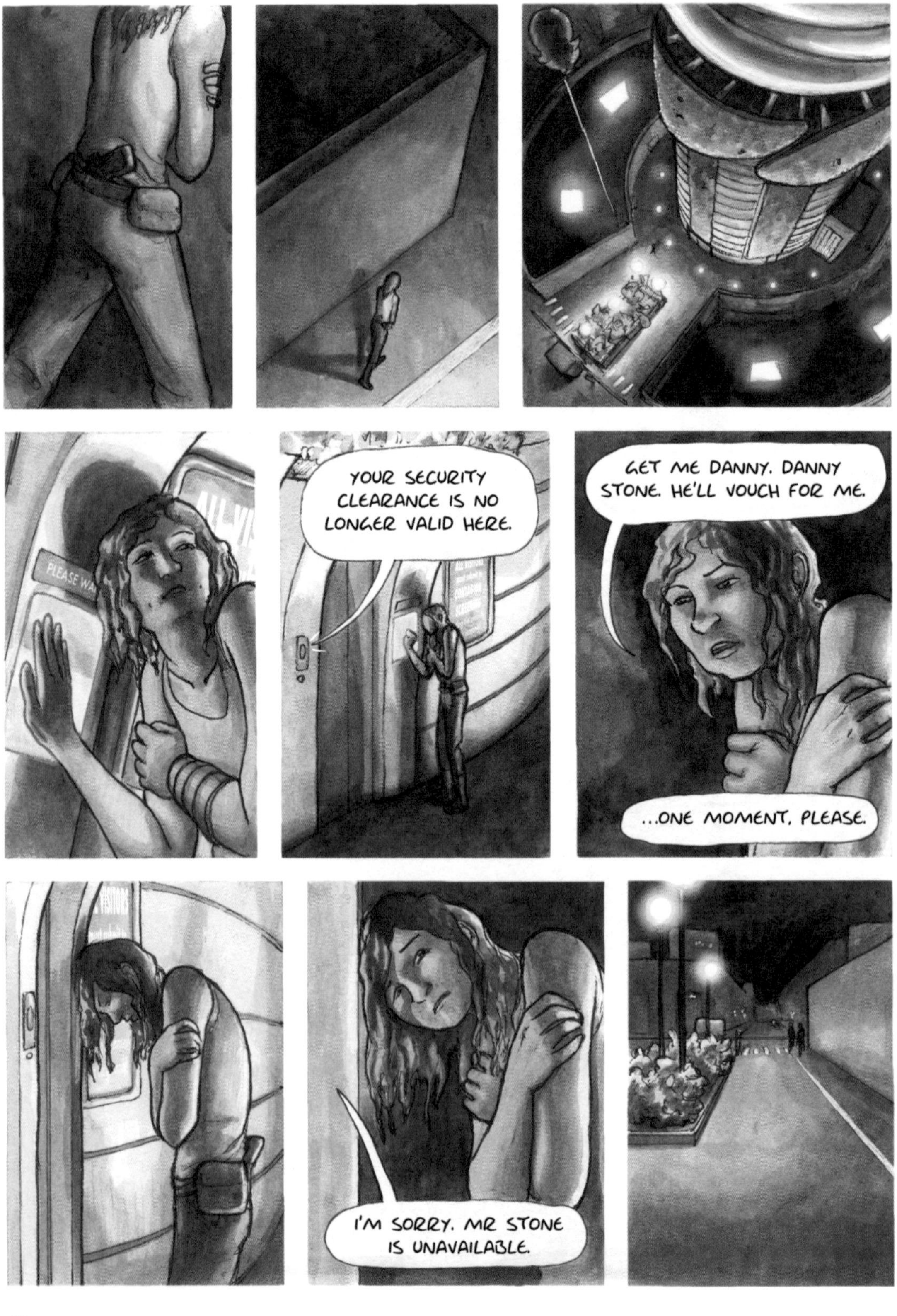
PLEASE WA
YOUR SECURITY CLEARANCE IS NO LONGER VALID HERE.
GET ME DANNY. DANNY STONE. HE'LL VOUCH FOR ME.
...ONE MOMENT, PLEASE.
I'M SORRY. MR STONE IS UNAVAILABLE.

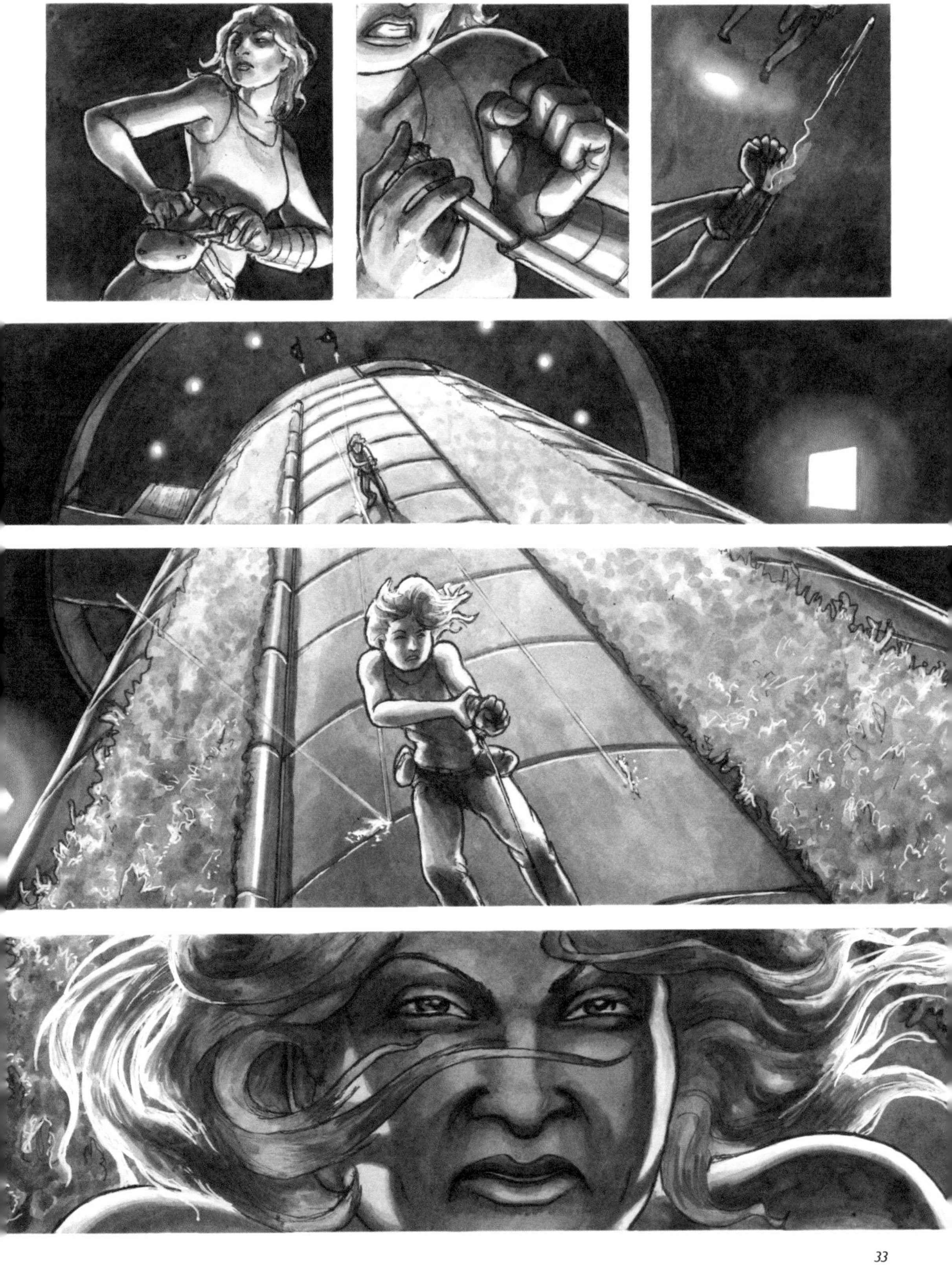

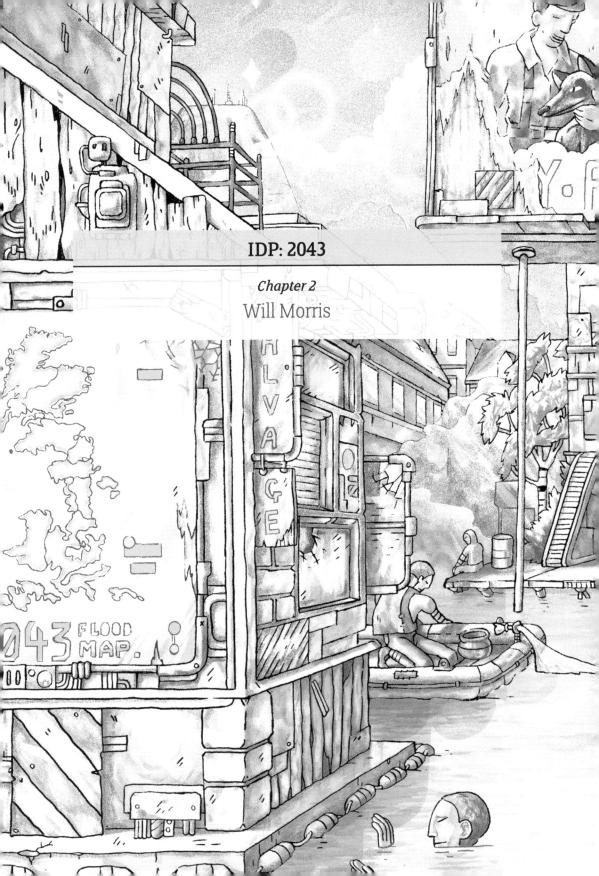

IDP: 2043

Chapter 2
Will Morris

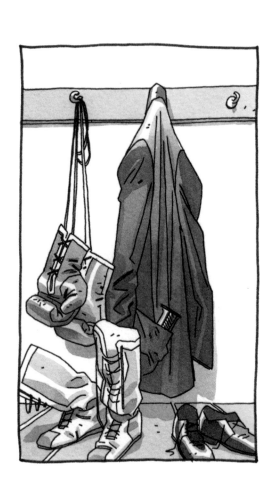

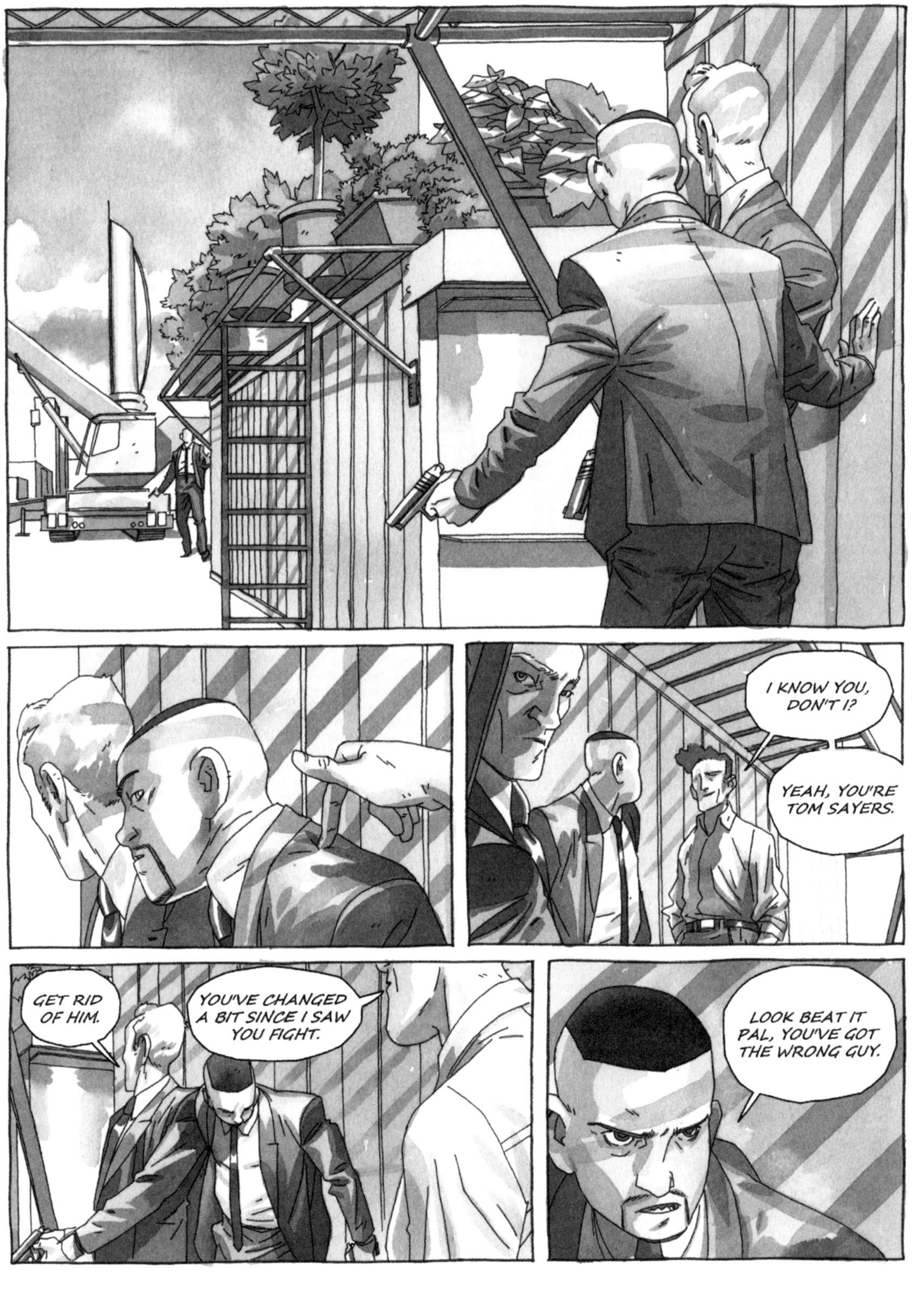
I KNOW YOU, DON'T I?
YEAH, YOU'RE TOM SAYERS.
GET RID OF HIM.
YOU'VE CHANGED A BIT SINCE I SAW YOU FIGHT.
LOOK BEAT IT PAL, YOU'VE GOT THE WRONG GUY.

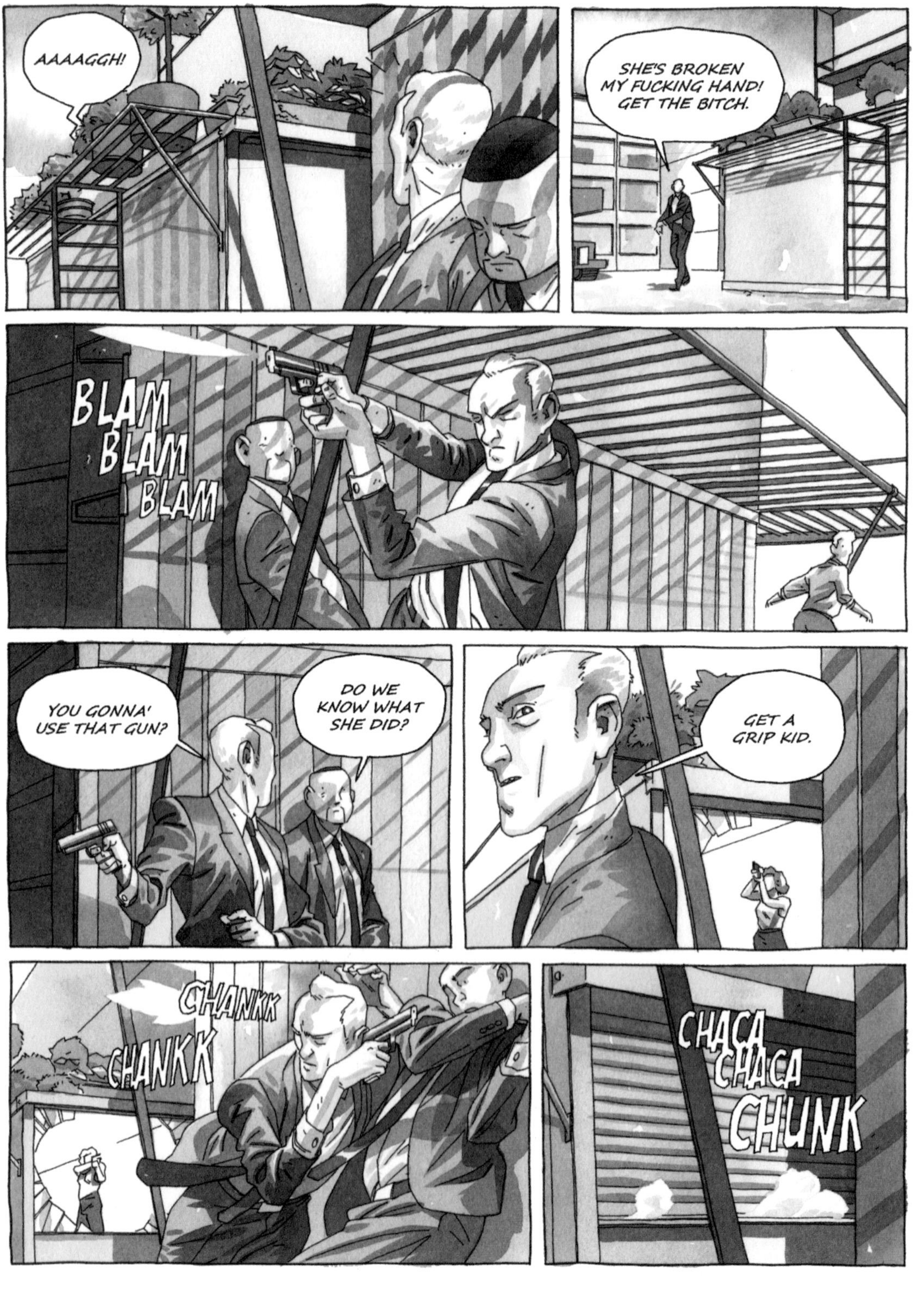
AAAAGGH!
SHE'S BROKEN MY FUCKING HAND! GET THE BITCH.
BLAM BLAM BLAM
YOU GONNA' USE THAT GUN?
DO WE KNOW WHAT SHE DID?
GET A GRIP KID.
CHANKK CHANKK
CHACA CHACA CHUNK

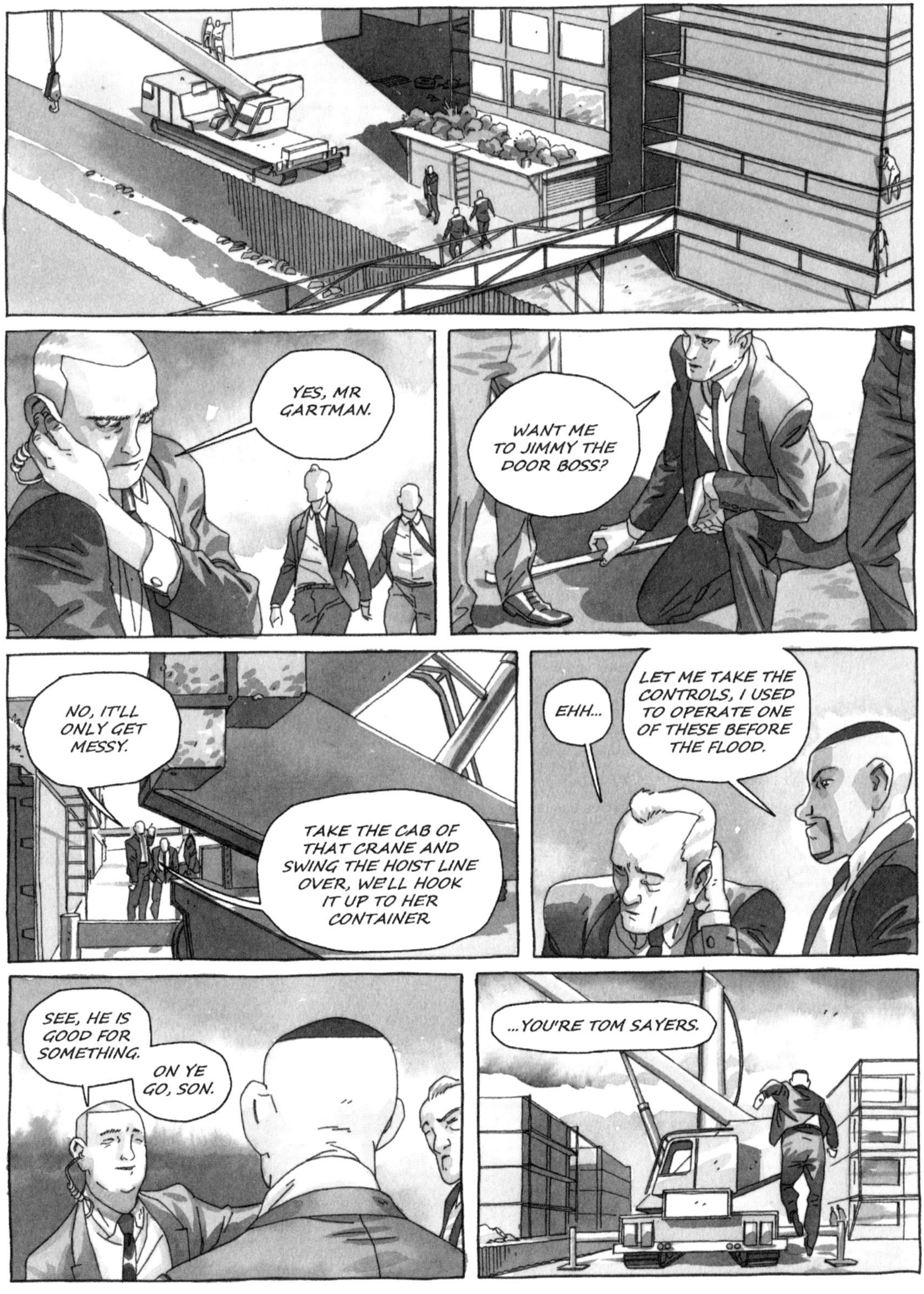
YES, MR GARTMAN.
WANT ME TO JIMMY THE DOOR BOSS?
NO, IT'LL ONLY GET MESSY.
TAKE THE CAB OF THAT CRANE AND SWING THE HOIST LINE OVER, WE'LL HOOK IT UP TO HER CONTAINER
EHH...
LET ME TAKE THE CONTROLS, I USED TO OPERATE ONE OF THESE BEFORE THE FLOOD.
SEE, HE IS GOOD FOR SOMETHING.
ON YE GO, SON.
...YOU'RE TOM SAYERS.

"THE CATAMARAN, NOW APPR-OACHING PLATFORM 3 IS THE 9:15 TO EDINBURGH, CALTON ISLAND."

DESTINATION?

NINE

TEN

NO PLACE IN PARTICULAR.

PLATFORM 14

ADULT CHILD
ONE NIL
23 MAR 42 PRICE: NIL
FROM: NEW WANLOCKHEAD
TO: NO PLACE
RTN

SEV

DESTINATION?

NIN

TEN

NO PLACE SPECIAL.

NINE

TEN

DESTINATION?

UH, TICKET FOR THE BOUT, PLEASE?

THE BOUT, SIR?

AYE, Y'KNOW, THE BOXING.

I'M SORRY SIR, BUT YOU MUST KNOW THAT GATHERINGS OUTSIDE OF THE CITY TOWER ARE BANNED.

IF IT'S ACTION YOU'RE LOOKING FOR YOU MIGHT TRY BARTLETT'S CIRCUS.

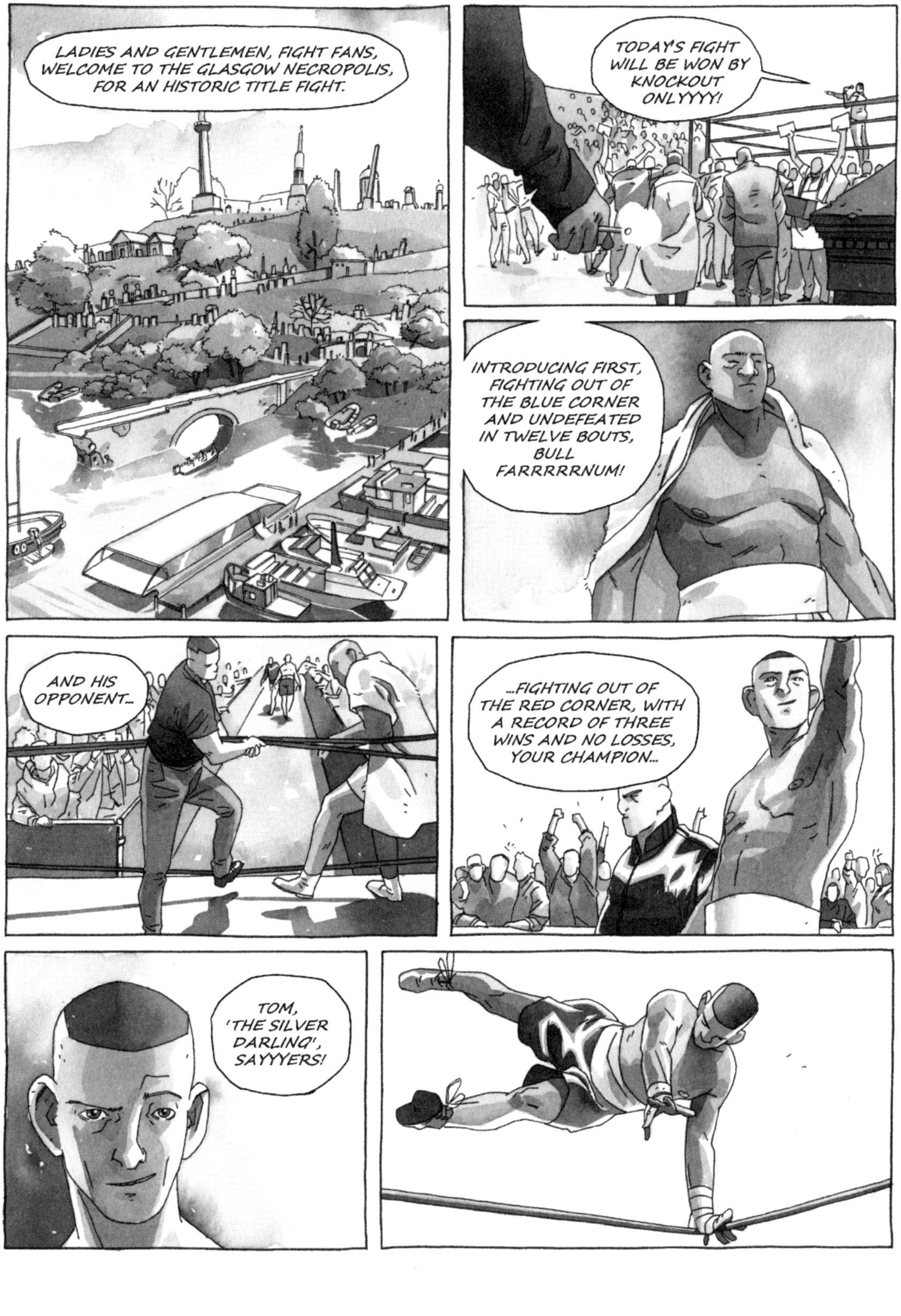
LADIES AND GENTLEMEN, FIGHT FANS, WELCOME TO THE GLASGOW NECROPOLIS, FOR AN HISTORIC TITLE FIGHT.
TODAY'S FIGHT WILL BE WON BY KNOCKOUT ONLYYYY!
INTRODUCING FIRST, FIGHTING OUT OF THE BLUE CORNER AND UNDEFEATED IN TWELVE BOUTS, BULL FARRRRRNUM!
AND HIS OPPONENT...
...FIGHTING OUT OF THE RED CORNER, WITH A RECORD OF THREE WINS AND NO LOSSES, YOUR CHAMPION...
TOM, 'THE SILVER DARLING', SAYYYERS!

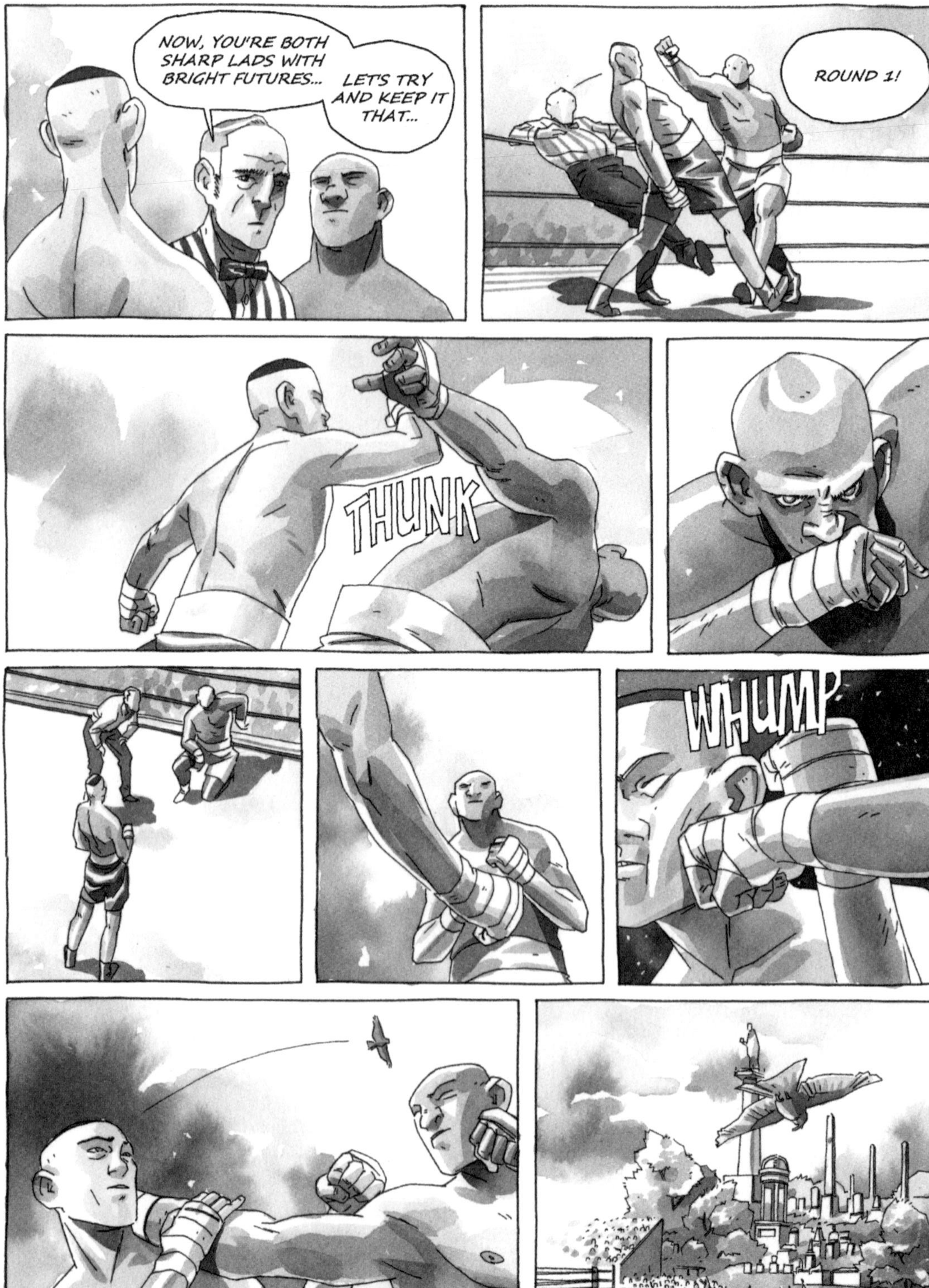
NOW, YOU'RE BOTH SHARP LADS WITH BRIGHT FUTURES...
LET'S TRY AND KEEP IT THAT...
ROUND 1!
THUNK
WHUMP

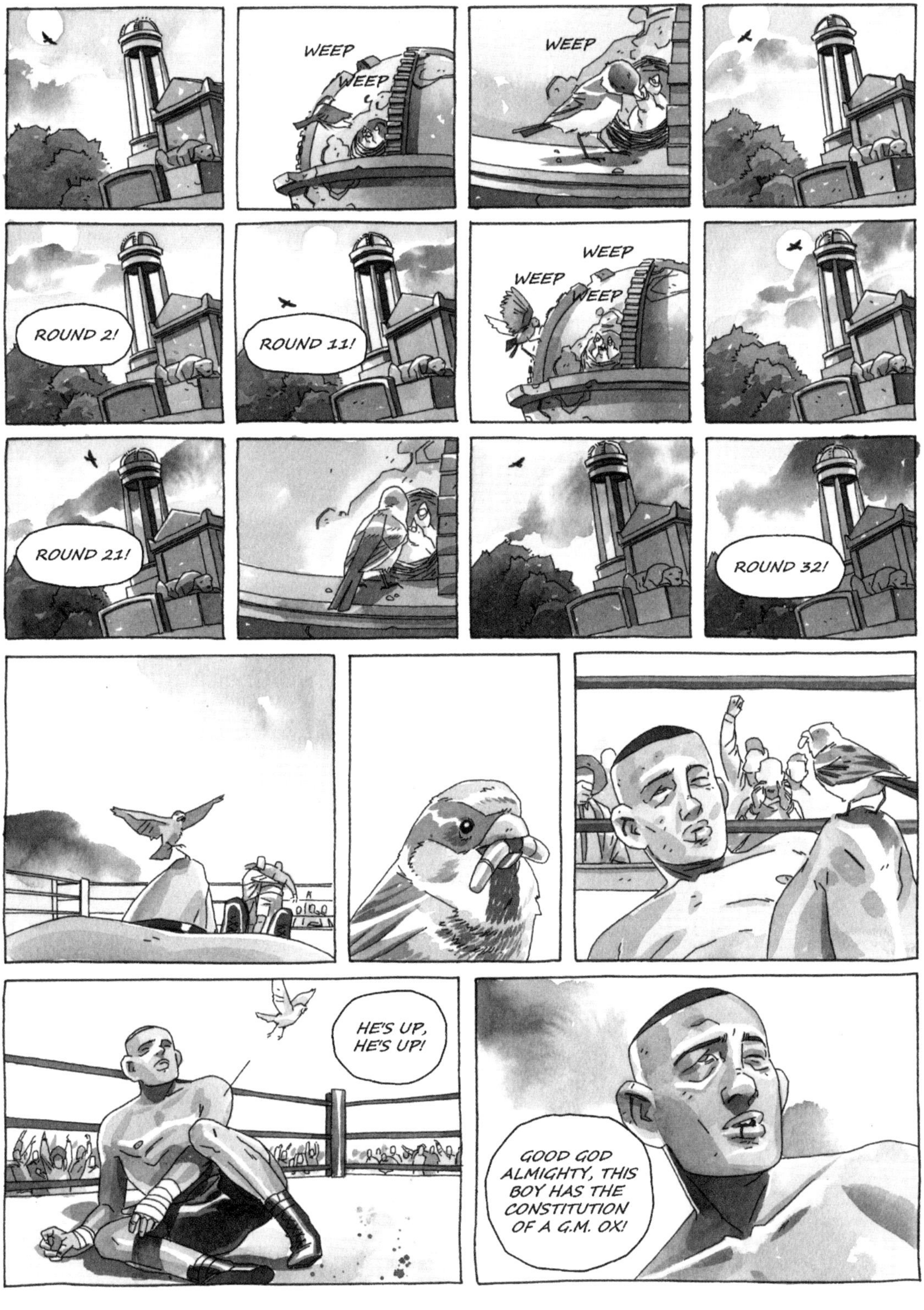
WEEP
WEEP
WEEP
ROUND 2!
ROUND 11!
WEEP
WEEP
WEEP
ROUND 21!
ROUND 32!
HE'S UP, HE'S UP!
GOOD GOD ALMIGHTY, THIS BOY HAS THE CONSTITUTION OF A G.M. OX!

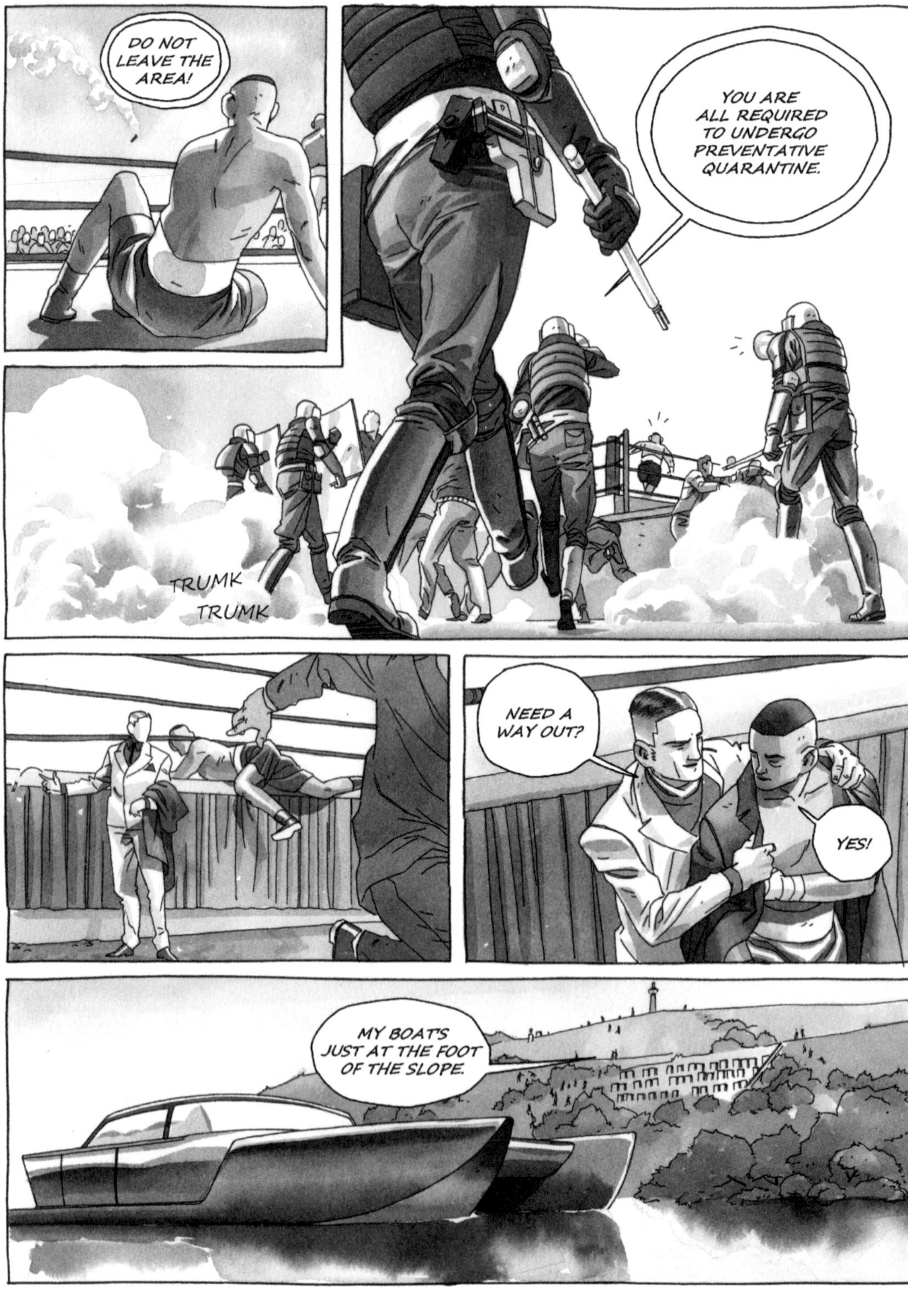
DO NOT LEAVE THE AREA!
YOU ARE ALL REQUIRED TO UNDERGO PREVENTATIVE QUARANTINE.
TRUMK
TRUMK
NEED A WAY OUT?
YES!
MY BOAT'S JUST AT THE FOOT OF THE SLOPE.

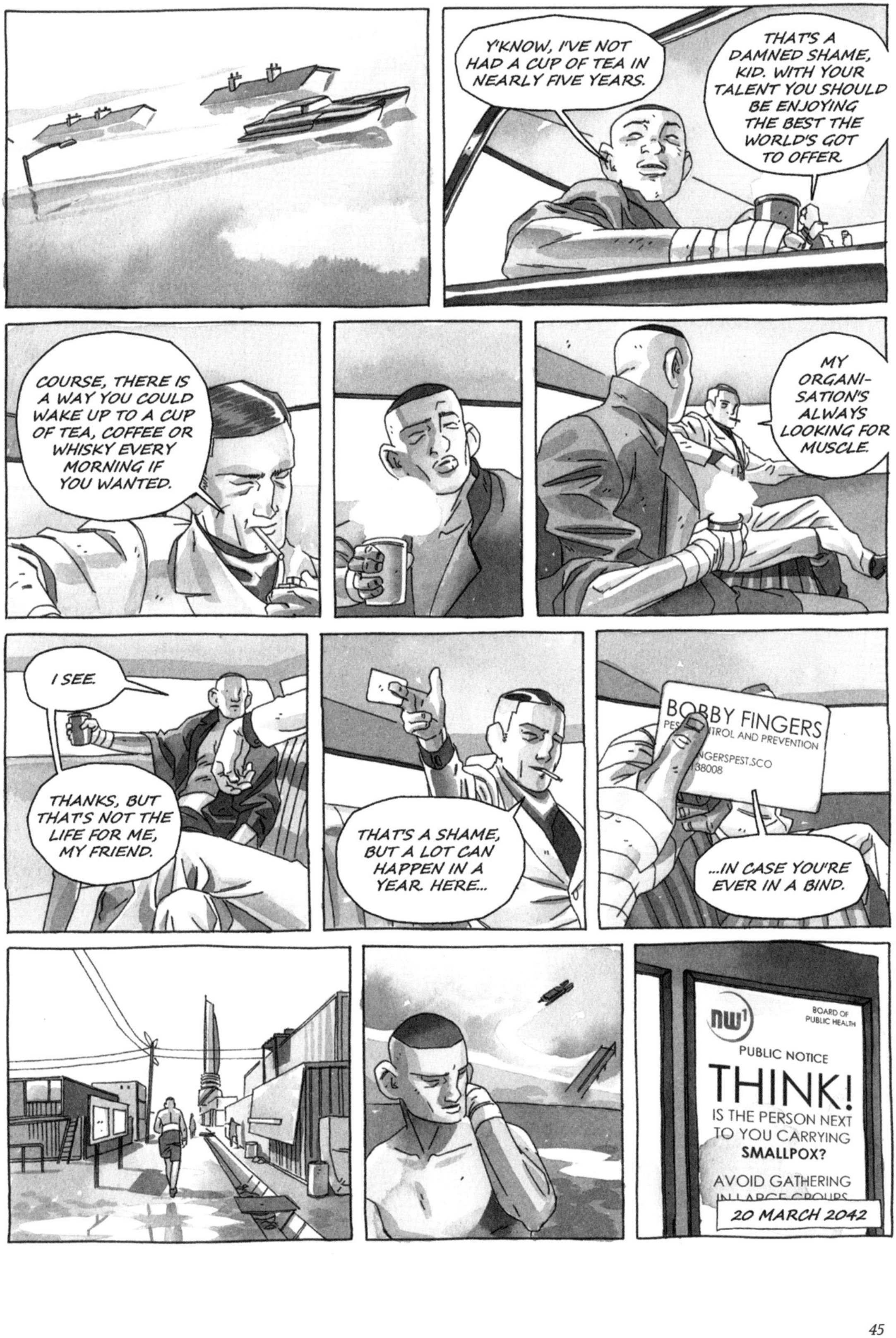
Y'KNOW, I'VE NOT HAD A CUP OF TEA IN NEARLY FIVE YEARS.
THAT'S A DAMNED SHAME, KID. WITH YOUR TALENT YOU SHOULD BE ENJOYING THE BEST THE WORLD'S GOT TO OFFER.
COURSE, THERE IS A WAY YOU COULD WAKE UP TO A CUP OF TEA, COFFEE OR WHISKY EVERY MORNING IF YOU WANTED.
MY ORGANI-SATION'S ALWAYS LOOKING FOR MUSCLE.
I SEE.
THANKS, BUT THAT'S NOT THE LIFE FOR ME, MY FRIEND.
THAT'S A SHAME, BUT A LOT CAN HAPPEN IN A YEAR HERE...
BOBBY FINGERS
...IN CASE YOU'RE EVER IN A BIND.
nw1
BOARD OF PUBLIC HEALTH
PUBLIC NOTICE
THINK!
IS THE PERSON NEXT TO YOU CARRYING SMALLPOX?
AVOID GATHERING
20 MARCH 2042

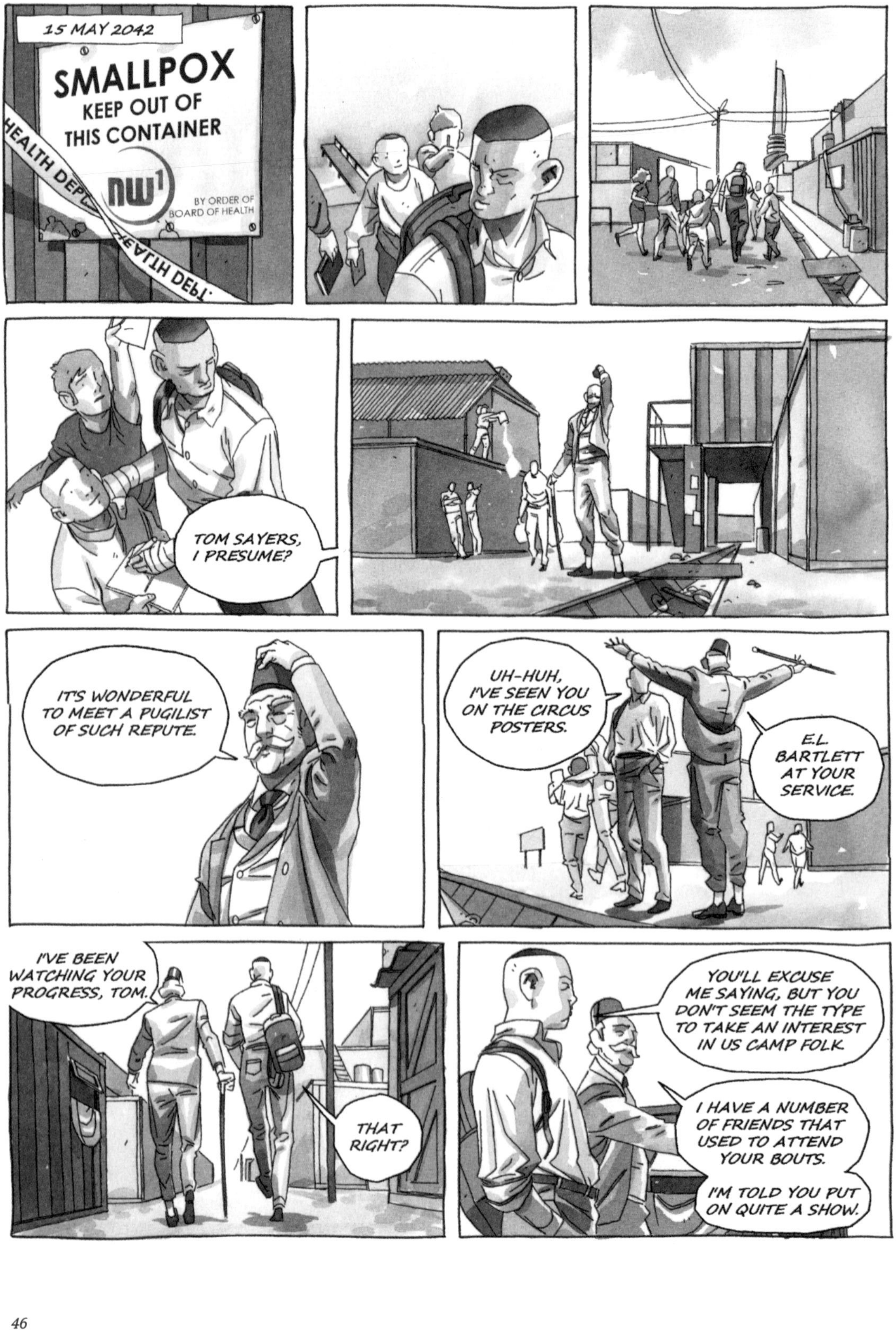
15 MAY 2042
SMALLPOX
KEEP OUT OF
THIS CONTAINER
NW1
BY ORDER OF
BOARD OF HEALTH
HEALTH DEPT.
HEALTH DEPT.
TOM SAYERS, I PRESUME?
IT'S WONDERFUL TO MEET A PUGILIST OF SUCH REPUTE.
UH-HUH, I'VE SEEN YOU ON THE CIRCUS POSTERS.
E.L. BARTLETT AT YOUR SERVICE.
I'VE BEEN WATCHING YOUR PROGRESS, TOM.
THAT RIGHT?
YOU'LL EXCUSE ME SAYING, BUT YOU DON'T SEEM THE TYPE TO TAKE AN INTEREST IN US CAMP FOLK.
I HAVE A NUMBER OF FRIENDS THAT USED TO ATTEND YOUR BOUTS.
I'M TOLD YOU PUT ON QUITE A SHOW.

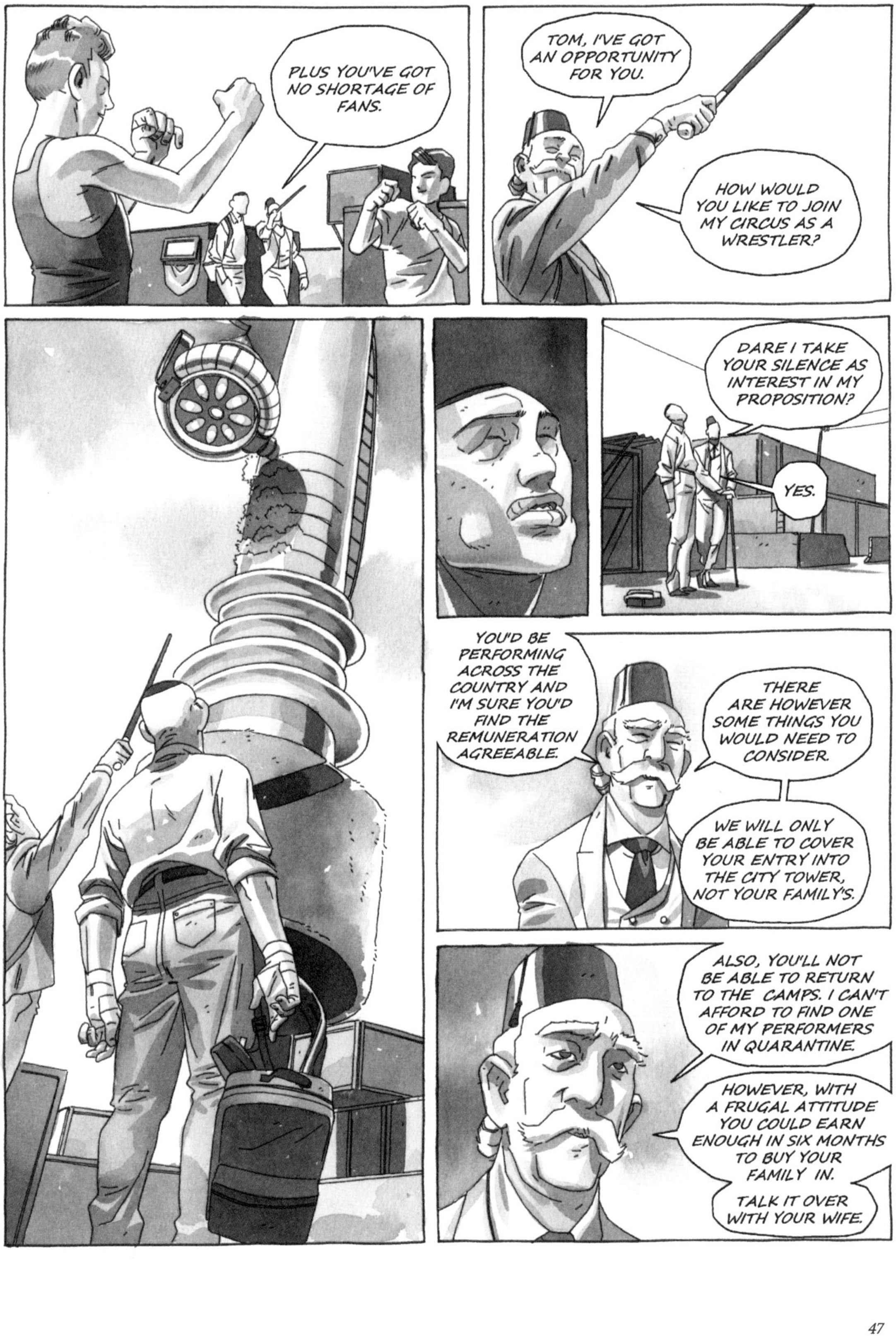
PLUS YOU'VE GOT NO SHORTAGE OF FANS.
TOM, I'VE GOT AN OPPORTUNITY FOR YOU.
HOW WOULD YOU LIKE TO JOIN MY CIRCUS AS A WRESTLER?
DARE I TAKE YOUR SILENCE AS INTEREST IN MY PROPOSITION?
YES.
YOU'D BE PERFORMING ACROSS THE COUNTRY AND I'M SURE YOU'D FIND THE REMUNERATION AGREEABLE.
THERE ARE HOWEVER SOME THINGS YOU WOULD NEED TO CONSIDER.
WE WILL ONLY BE ABLE TO COVER YOUR ENTRY INTO THE CITY TOWER, NOT YOUR FAMILY'S.
ALSO, YOU'LL NOT BE ABLE TO RETURN TO THE CAMPS. I CAN'T AFFORD TO FIND ONE OF MY PERFORMERS IN QUARANTINE.
HOWEVER, WITH A FRUGAL ATTITUDE YOU COULD EARN ENOUGH IN SIX MONTHS TO BUY YOUR FAMILY IN.
TALK IT OVER WITH YOUR WIFE.

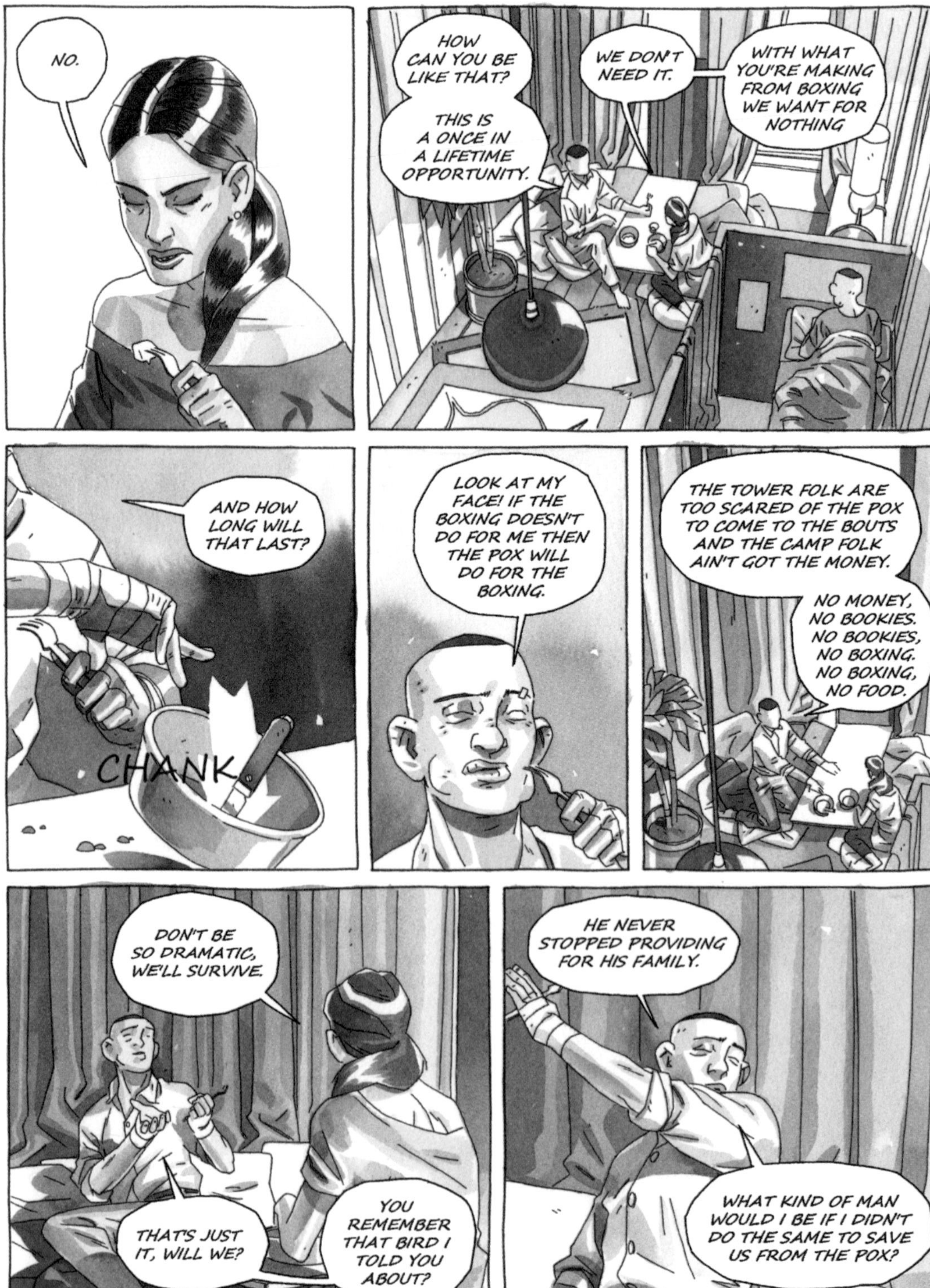
NO.
HOW CAN YOU BE LIKE THAT?
THIS IS A ONCE IN A LIFETIME OPPORTUNITY.
WE DON'T NEED IT.
WITH WHAT YOU'RE MAKING FROM BOXING WE WANT FOR NOTHING
AND HOW LONG WILL THAT LAST?
CHANK
LOOK AT MY FACE! IF THE BOXING DOESN'T DO FOR ME THEN THE POX WILL DO FOR THE BOXING.
THE TOWER FOLK ARE TOO SCARED OF THE POX TO COME TO THE BOUTS AND THE CAMP FOLK AIN'T GOT THE MONEY.
NO MONEY, NO BOOKIES. NO BOOKIES, NO BOXING. NO BOXING, NO FOOD.
DON'T BE SO DRAMATIC, WE'LL SURVIVE.
THAT'S JUST IT, WILL WE?
YOU REMEMBER THAT BIRD I TOLD YOU ABOUT?
HE NEVER STOPPED PROVIDING FOR HIS FAMILY.
WHAT KIND OF MAN WOULD I BE IF I DIDN'T DO THE SAME TO SAVE US FROM THE POX?

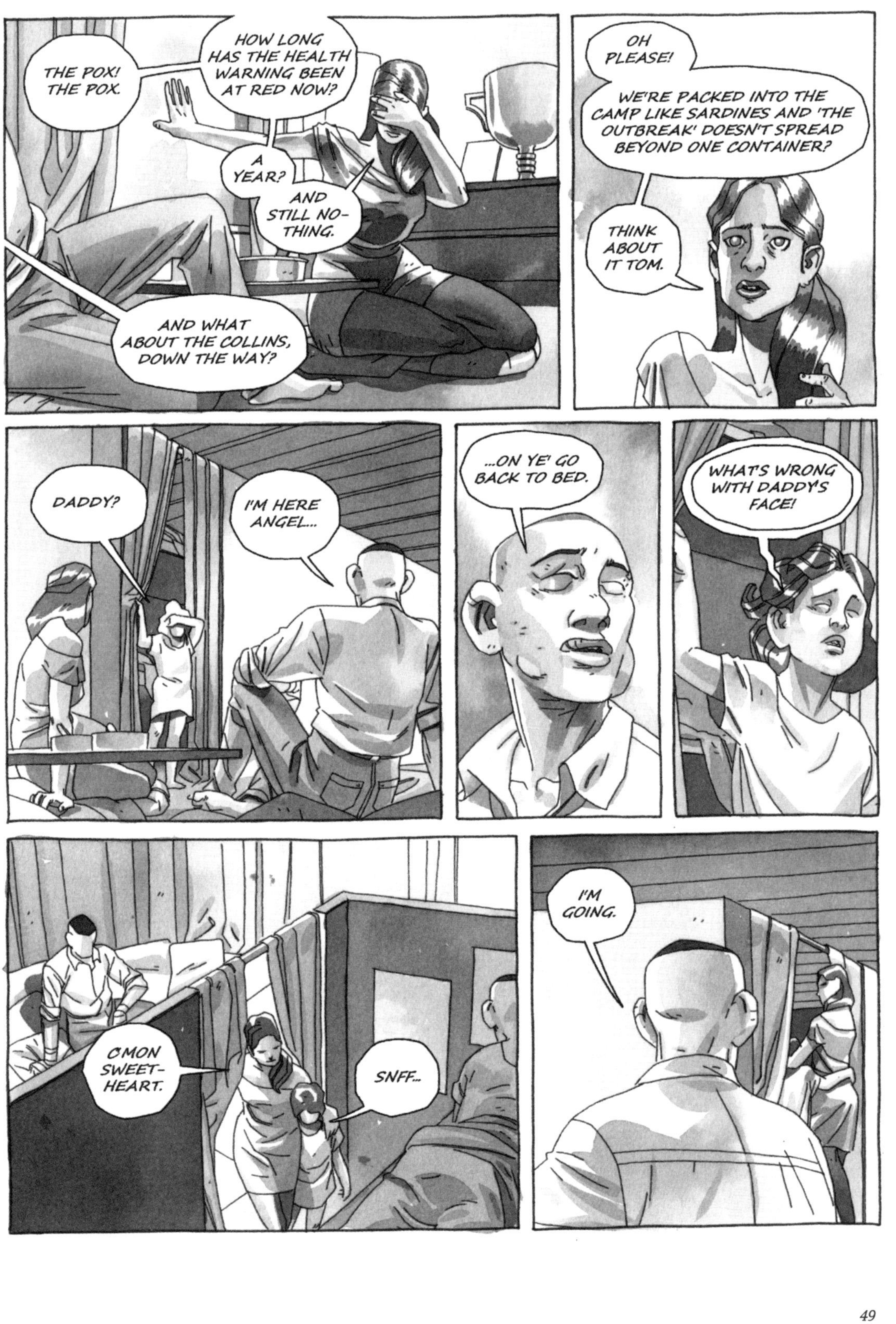
THE POX! THE POX.
HOW LONG HAS THE HEALTH WARNING BEEN AT RED NOW?
A YEAR?
AND STILL NO-THING.
AND WHAT ABOUT THE COLLINS, DOWN THE WAY?
OH PLEASE!
WE'RE PACKED INTO THE CAMP LIKE SARDINES AND 'THE OUTBREAK' DOESN'T SPREAD BEYOND ONE CONTAINER?
THINK ABOUT IT TOM.
DADDY?
I'M HERE ANGEL...
...ON YE' GO BACK TO BED.
WHAT'S WRONG WITH DADDY'S FACE!
C'MON SWEET-HEART.
SNFF...
I'M GOING.

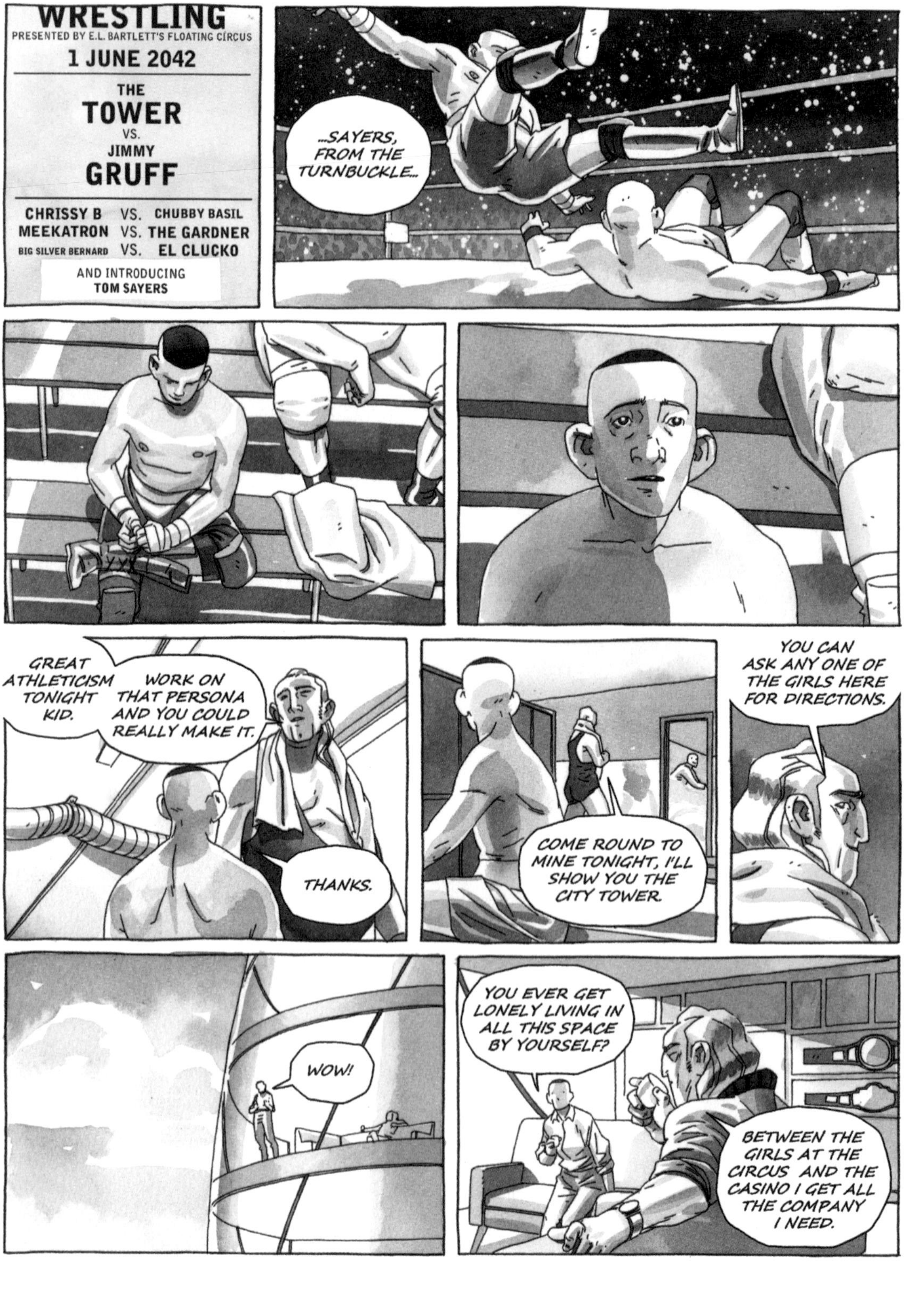
WRESTLING
PRESENTED BY E.L. BARTLETT'S FLOATING CIRCUS
1 JUNE 2042
THE TOWER VS. JIMMY GRUFF
CHRISSY B VS. CHUBBY BASIL
MEEKATRON VS. THE GARDNER
BIG SILVER BERNARD VS. EL CLUCKO
AND INTRODUCING TOM SAYERS
...SAYERS, FROM THE TURNBUCKLE...
GREAT ATHLETICISM TONIGHT KID.
WORK ON THAT PERSONA AND YOU COULD REALLY MAKE IT.
THANKS.
COME ROUND TO MINE TONIGHT, I'LL SHOW YOU THE CITY TOWER.
YOU CAN ASK ANY ONE OF THE GIRLS HERE FOR DIRECTIONS.
WOW!
YOU EVER GET LONELY LIVING IN ALL THIS SPACE BY YOURSELF?
BETWEEN THE GIRLS AT THE CIRCUS AND THE CASINO I GET ALL THE COMPANY I NEED.

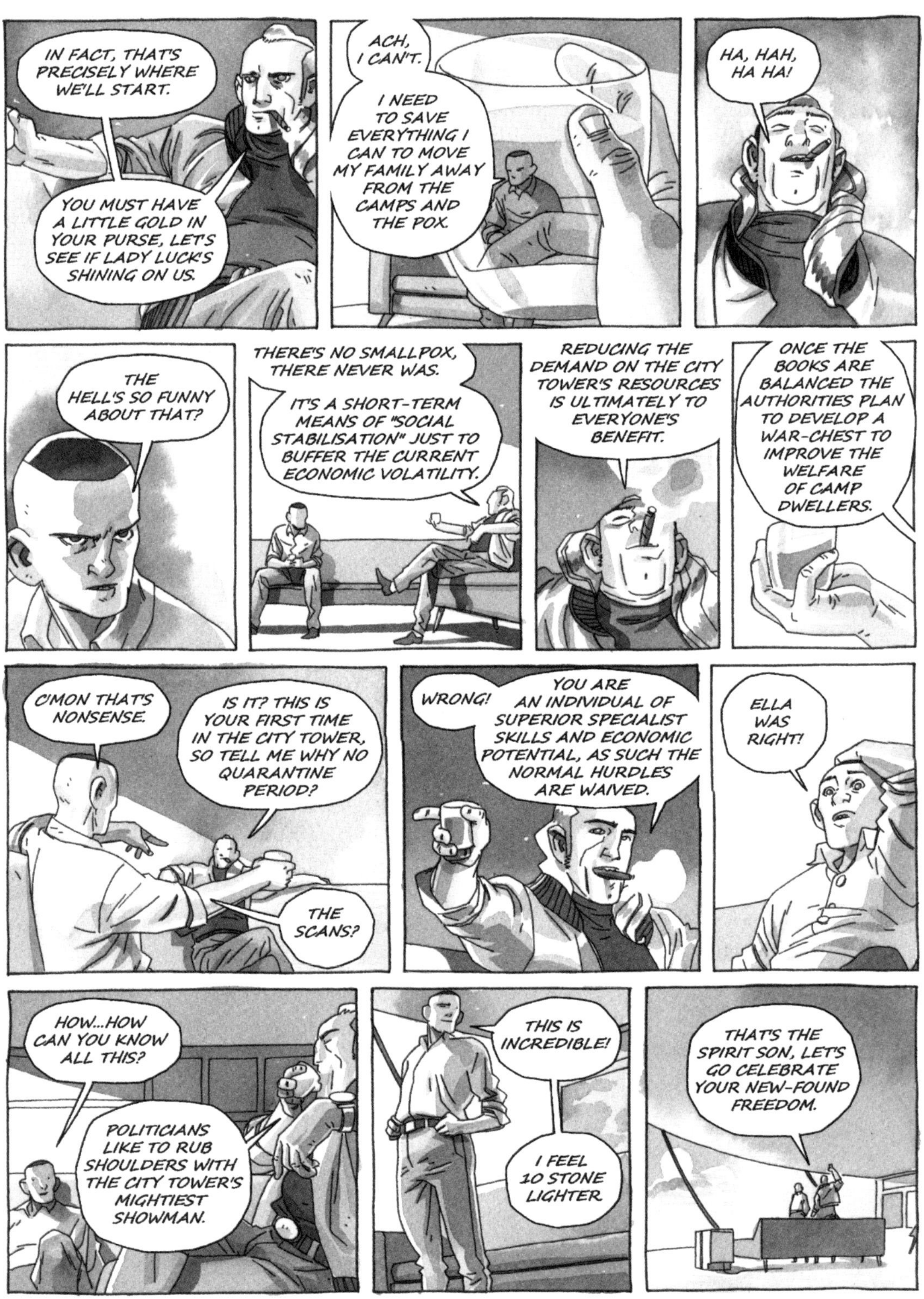
IN FACT, THAT'S PRECISELY WHERE WE'LL START.
YOU MUST HAVE A LITTLE GOLD IN YOUR PURSE, LET'S SEE IF LADY LUCK'S SHINING ON US.
ACH, I CAN'T.
I NEED TO SAVE EVERYTHING I CAN TO MOVE MY FAMILY AWAY FROM THE CAMPS AND THE POX.
HA, HAH, HA HA!
THE HELL'S SO FUNNY ABOUT THAT?
THERE'S NO SMALLPOX, THERE NEVER WAS.
IT'S A SHORT-TERM MEANS OF "SOCIAL STABILISATION" JUST TO BUFFER THE CURRENT ECONOMIC VOLATILITY.
REDUCING THE DEMAND ON THE CITY TOWER'S RESOURCES IS ULTIMATELY TO EVERYONE'S BENEFIT.
ONCE THE BOOKS ARE BALANCED THE AUTHORITIES PLAN TO DEVELOP A WAR-CHEST TO IMPROVE THE WELFARE OF CAMP DWELLERS.
C'MON THAT'S NONSENSE.
IS IT? THIS IS YOUR FIRST TIME IN THE CITY TOWER, SO TELL ME WHY NO QUARANTINE PERIOD?
THE SCANS?
WRONG!
YOU ARE AN INDIVIDUAL OF SUPERIOR SPECIALIST SKILLS AND ECONOMIC POTENTIAL, AS SUCH THE NORMAL HURDLES ARE WAIVED.
ELLA WAS RIGHT!
HOW...HOW CAN YOU KNOW ALL THIS?
POLITICIANS LIKE TO RUB SHOULDERS WITH THE CITY TOWER'S MIGHTIEST SHOWMAN.
THIS IS INCREDIBLE!
I FEEL 10 STONE LIGHTER
THAT'S THE SPIRIT SON, LET'S GO CELEBRATE YOUR NEW-FOUND FREEDOM.

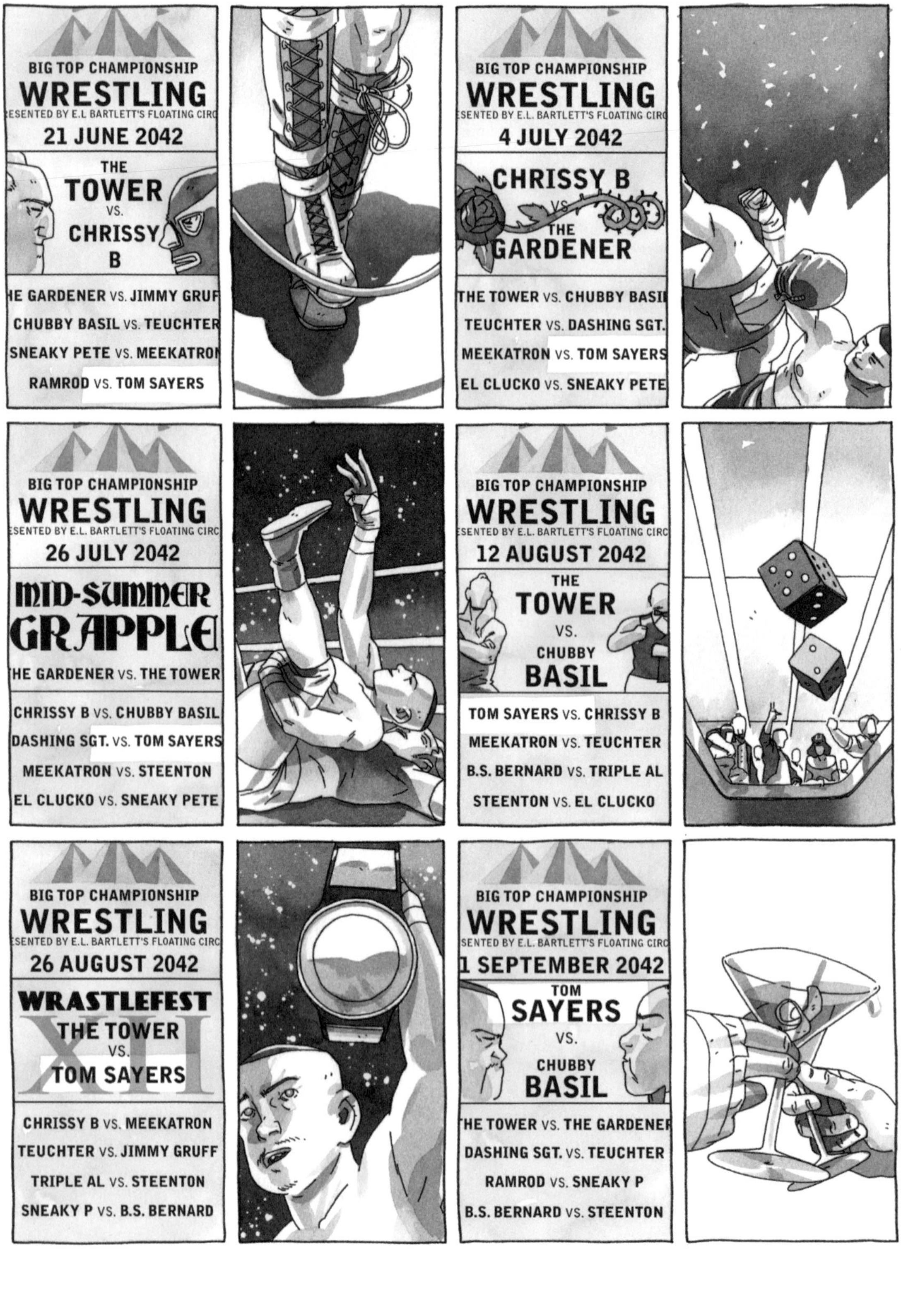
BIG TOP CHAMPIONSHIP
WRESTLING
ESENTED BY E.L. BARTLETT'S FLOATING CIRC
21 JUNE 2042
THE TOWER VS. CHRISSY B
HE GARDENER VS. JIMMY GRUF
CHUBBY BASIL VS. TEUCHTER
SNEAKY PETE VS. MEEKATRON
RAMROD VS. TOM SAYERS
BIG TOP CHAMPIONSHIP
WRESTLING
ESENTED BY E.L. BARTLETT'S FLOATING CIRC
4 JULY 2042
CHRISSY B VS THE GARDENER
THE TOWER VS. CHUBBY BASI
TEUCHTER VS. DASHING SGT.
MEEKATRON VS. TOM SAYERS
EL CLUCKO VS. SNEAKY PETE
BIG TOP CHAMPIONSHIP
WRESTLING
ESENTED BY E.L. BARTLETT'S FLOATING CIRC
26 JULY 2042
MID-SUMMER GRAPPLE
THE GARDENER VS. THE TOWER
CHRISSY B VS. CHUBBY BASIL
DASHING SGT. VS. TOM SAYERS
MEEKATRON VS. STEENTON
EL CLUCKO VS. SNEAKY PETE
BIG TOP CHAMPIONSHIP
WRESTLING
ESENTED BY E.L. BARTLETT'S FLOATING CIRC
12 AUGUST 2042
THE TOWER VS. CHUBBY BASIL
TOM SAYERS VS. CHRISSY B
MEEKATRON VS. TEUCHTER
B.S. BERNARD VS. TRIPLE AL
STEENTON VS. EL CLUCKO
BIG TOP CHAMPIONSHIP
WRESTLING
ESENTED BY E.L. BARTLETT'S FLOATING CIRC
26 AUGUST 2042
WRASTLEFEST XII
THE TOWER VS. TOM SAYERS
CHRISSY B VS. MEEKATRON
TEUCHTER VS. JIMMY GRUFF
TRIPLE AL VS. STEENTON
SNEAKY P VS. B.S. BERNARD
BIG TOP CHAMPIONSHIP
WRESTLING
ESENTED BY E.L. BARTLETT'S FLOATING CIRC
1 SEPTEMBER 2042
TOM SAYERS VS. CHUBBY BASIL
THE TOWER VS. THE GARDENER
DASHING SGT. VS. TEUCHTER
RAMROD VS. SNEAKY P
B.S. BERNARD VS. STEENTON

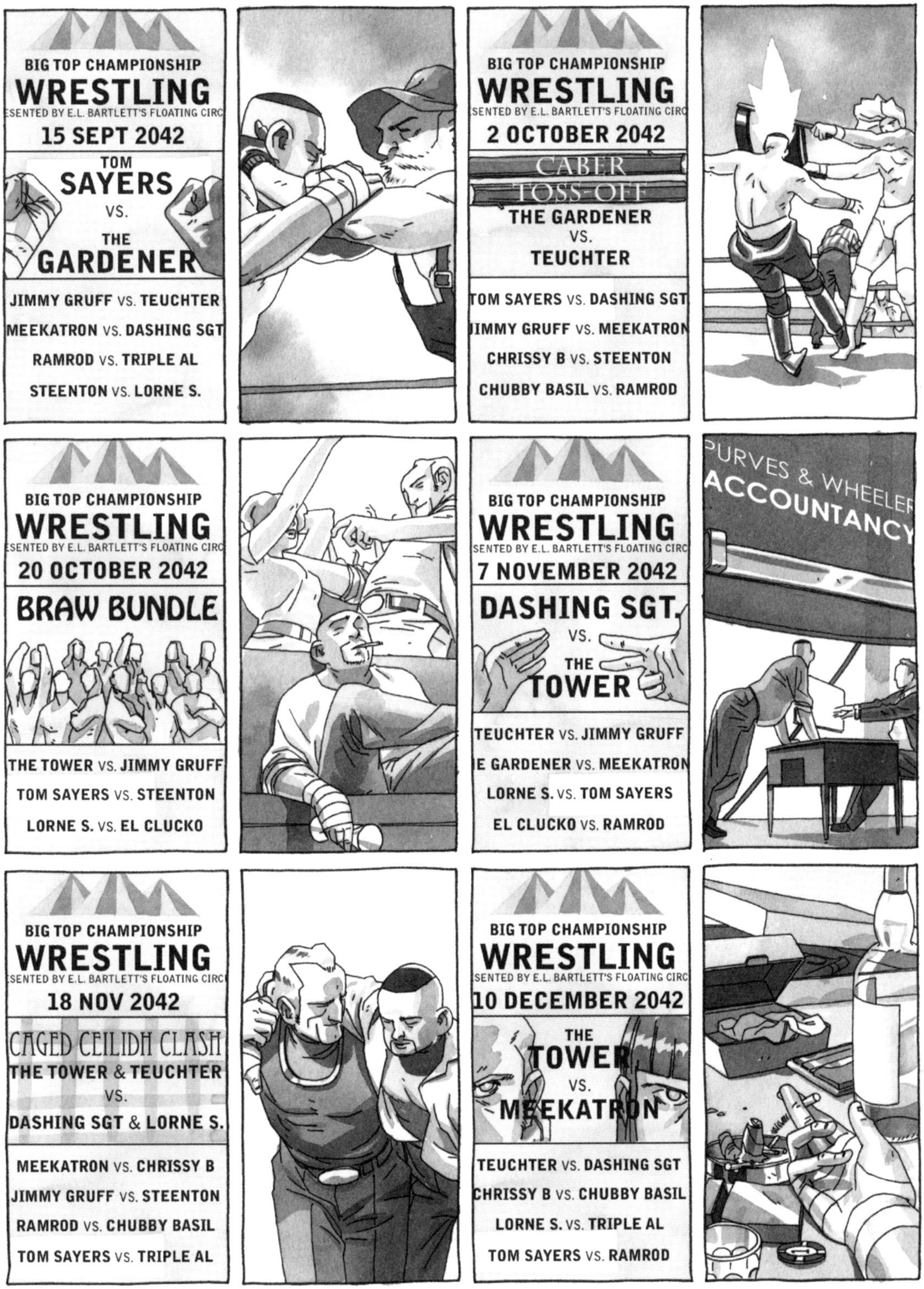
BIG TOP CHAMPIONSHIP
WRESTLING
SENTED BY E.L. BARTLETT'S FLOATING CIRC
15 SEPT 2042
TOM SAYERS VS. THE GARDENER
JIMMY GRUFF VS. TEUCHTER
MEEKATRON VS. DASHING SGT
RAMROD VS. TRIPLE AL
STEENTON VS. LORNE S.
BIG TOP CHAMPIONSHIP
WRESTLING
SENTED BY E.L. BARTLETT'S FLOATING CIRC
2 OCTOBER 2042
CABER TOSS-OFF
THE GARDENER VS. TEUCHTER
TOM SAYERS VS. DASHING SGT
JIMMY GRUFF VS. MEEKATRON
CHRISSY B VS. STEENTON
CHUBBY BASIL VS. RAMROD
BIG TOP CHAMPIONSHIP
WRESTLING
SENTED BY E.L. BARTLETT'S FLOATING CIRC
20 OCTOBER 2042
BRAW BUNDLE
THE TOWER VS. JIMMY GRUFF
TOM SAYERS VS. STEENTON
LORNE S. VS. EL CLUCKO
BIG TOP CHAMPIONSHIP
WRESTLING
SENTED BY E.L. BARTLETT'S FLOATING CIRC
7 NOVEMBER 2042
DASHING SGT. VS. THE TOWER
TEUCHTER VS. JIMMY GRUFF
E GARDENER VS. MEEKATRON
LORNE S. VS. TOM SAYERS
EL CLUCKO VS. RAMROD
URVES & WHEELER
ACCOUNTANCY
BIG TOP CHAMPIONSHIP
WRESTLING
SENTED BY E.L. BARTLETT'S FLOATING CIRC
18 NOV 2042
CAGED CEILIDH CLASH
THE TOWER & TEUCHTER VS. DASHING SGT & LORNE S.
MEEKATRON VS. CHRISSY B
JIMMY GRUFF VS. STEENTON
RAMROD VS. CHUBBY BASIL
TOM SAYERS VS. TRIPLE AL
BIG TOP CHAMPIONSHIP
WRESTLING
SENTED BY E.L. BARTLETT'S FLOATING CIRC
10 DECEMBER 2042
THE TOWER VS. MEEKATRON
TEUCHTER VS. DASHING SGT
CHRISSY B VS. CHUBBY BASIL
LORNE S. VS. TRIPLE AL
TOM SAYERS VS. RAMROD

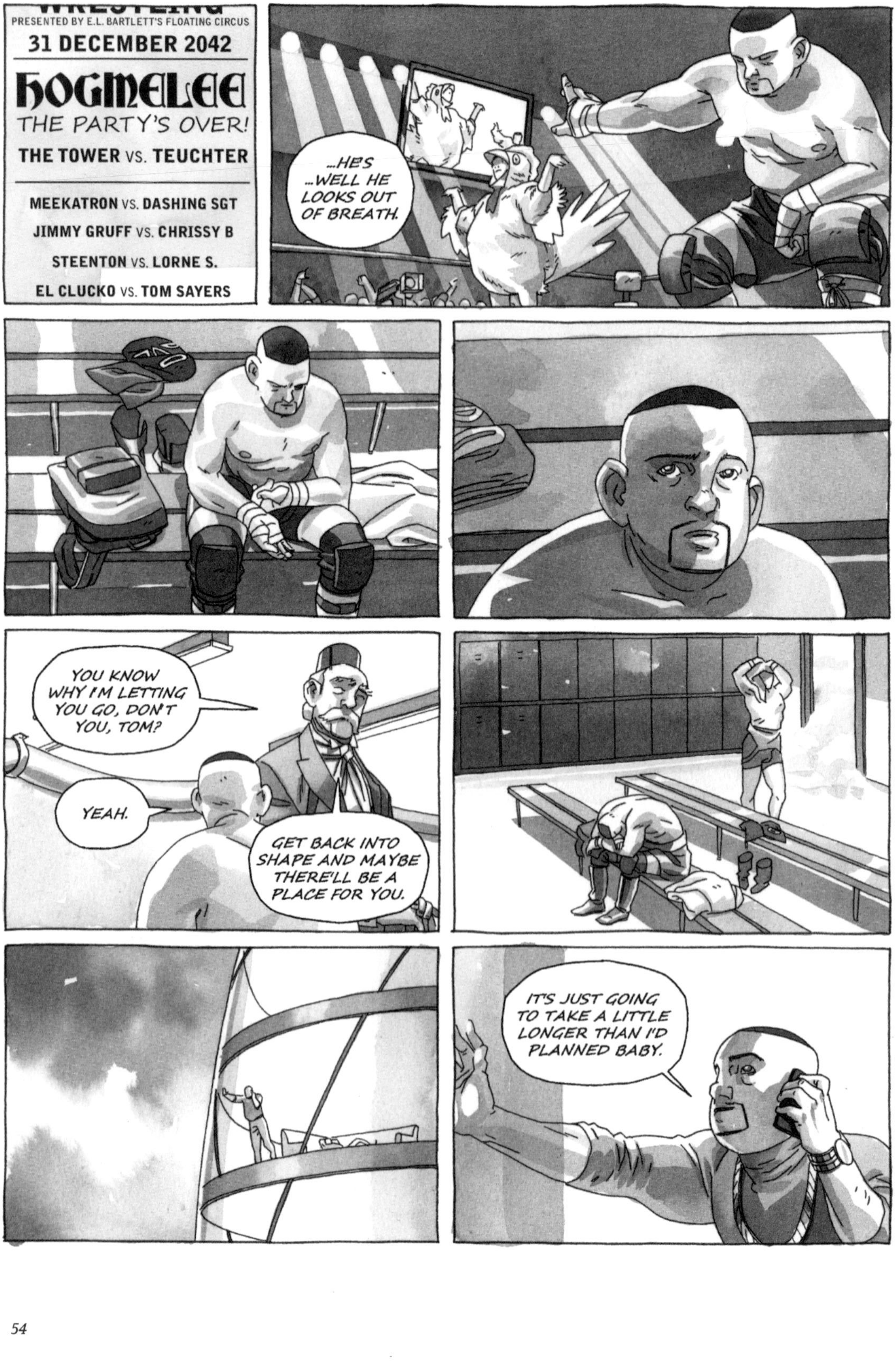
PRESENTED BY E.L. BARTLETT'S FLOATING CIRCUS
31 DECEMBER 2042
HOGMELEE
THE PARTY'S OVER!
THE TOWER VS. TEUCHTER
MEEKATRON VS. DASHING SGT
JIMMY GRUFF VS. CHRISSY B
STEENTON VS. LORNE S.
EL CLUCKO VS. TOM SAYERS
...HE'S ...WELL HE LOOKS OUT OF BREATH.
YOU KNOW WHY I'M LETTING YOU GO, DON'T YOU, TOM?
YEAH.
GET BACK INTO SHAPE AND MAYBE THERE'LL BE A PLACE FOR YOU.
IT'S JUST GOING TO TAKE A LITTLE LONGER THAN I'D PLANNED BABY.

COME HOME, TOM.

HA! THAT'S CRAZY. YOU GUYS WILL LOVE IT HERE, YOU WON'T BELIEVE WHAT YOU'VE BEEN MISSING...

ELLA?

ELLA? HONEY?

WHAT AM I GONNA' DO?

I CAN'T AFFORD MY APARTMENT, LET ALONE GET MY FAMILY IN.

YOU CAN ALWAYS BUNK DOWN HERE, BUDDY.

THANKS, BUT MY FAMILY STILL NEED TO EAT.

FIRST THING YOU NEED TO DO IS RELAX.

NOW, WHAT ABOUT THAT SHADY CHARACTER YOU MENTIONED, SAID HE COULD HELP YOU OUT?

FINGERS...

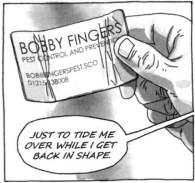

BOBBY FINGERS
PEST CONTROL AND PREVENTION
BOB@FINGERSPEST.SCO
0121538008

JUST TO TIDE ME OVER WHILE I GET BACK IN SHAPE.

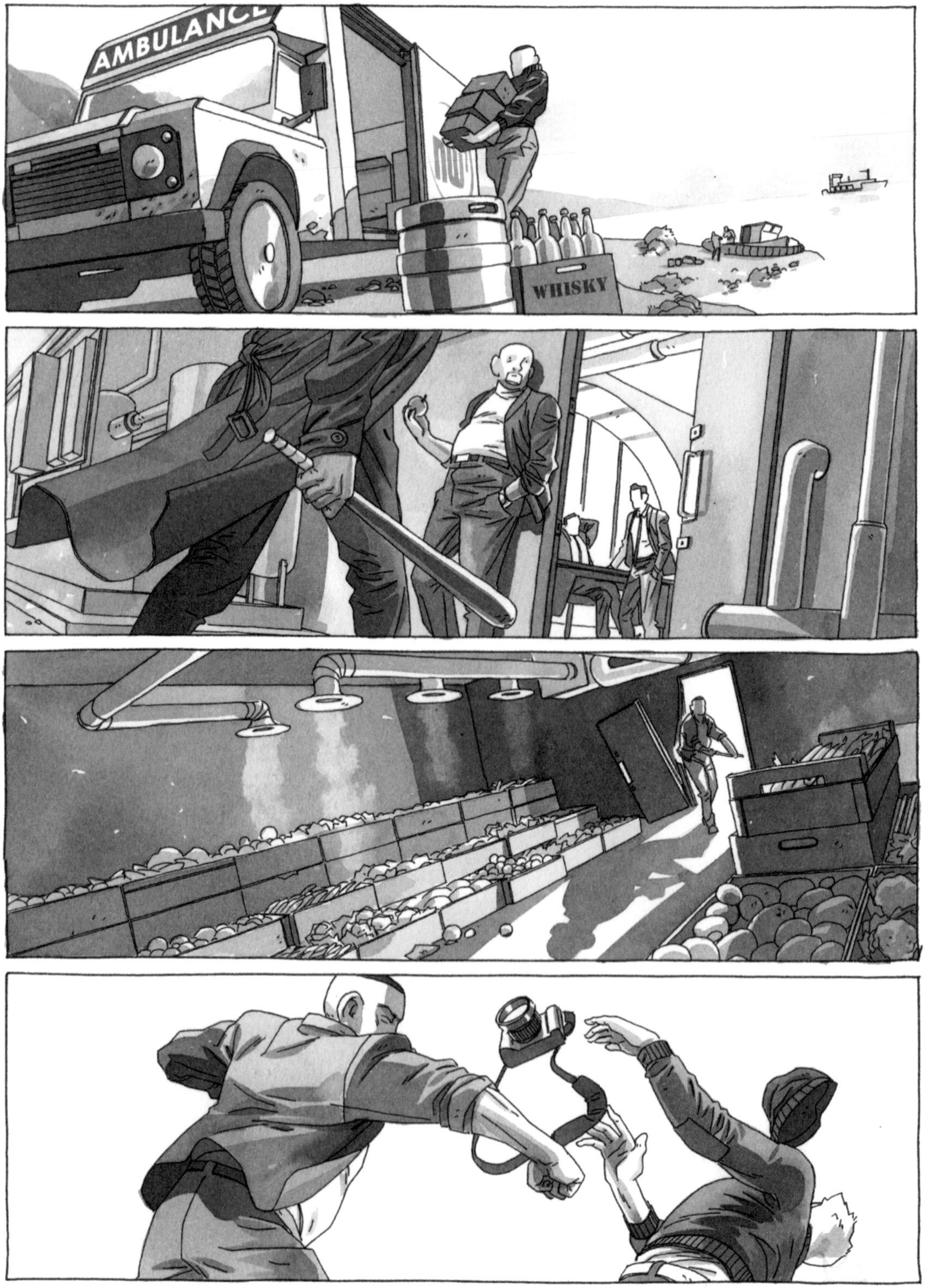
AMBULANCE
WHISKY

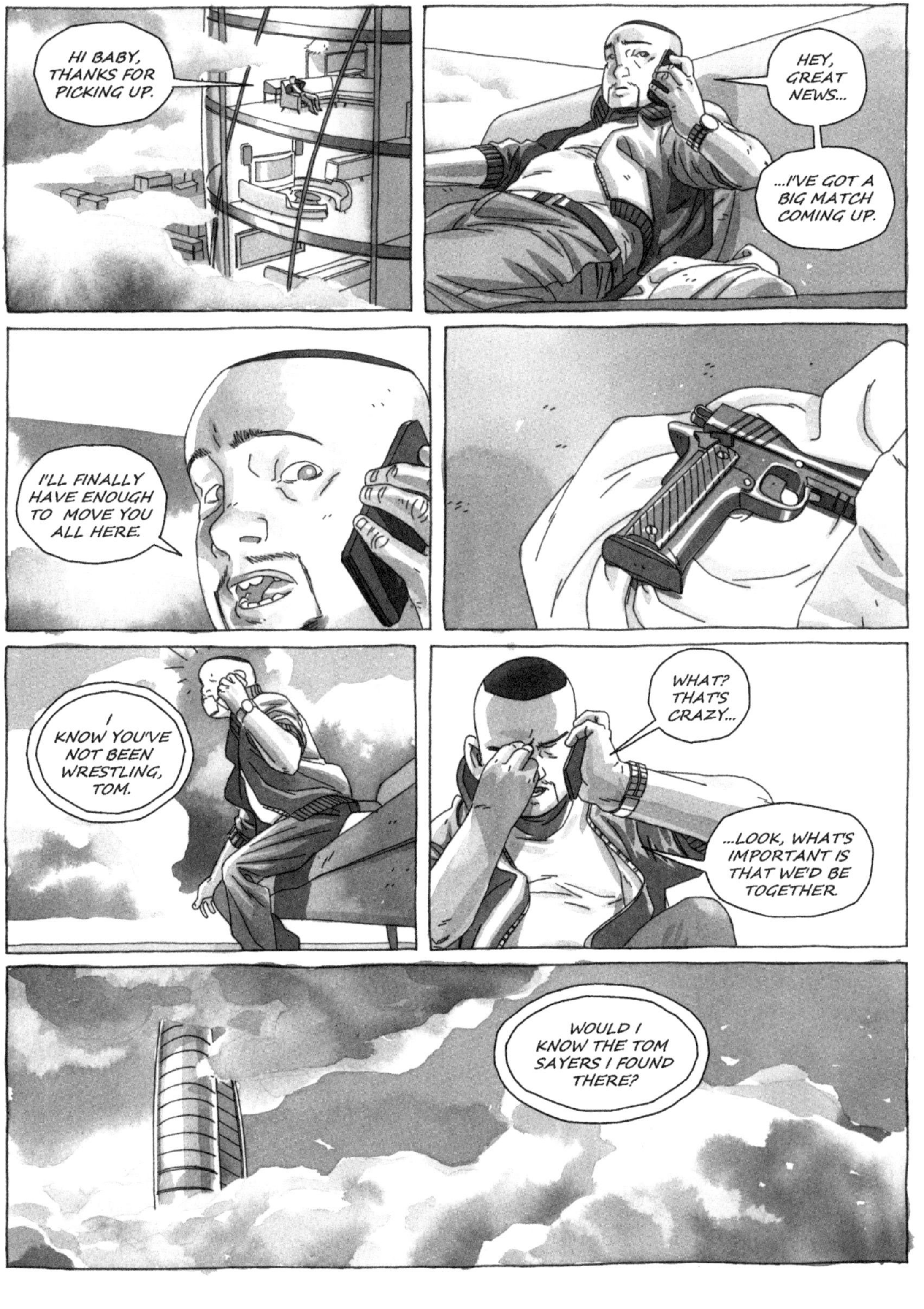
HI BABY, THANKS FOR PICKING UP.
HEY, GREAT NEWS...
...I'VE GOT A BIG MATCH COMING UP.
I'LL FINALLY HAVE ENOUGH TO MOVE YOU ALL HERE.
I KNOW YOU'VE NOT BEEN WRESTLING, TOM.
WHAT? THAT'S CRAZY...
...LOOK, WHAT'S IMPORTANT IS THAT WE'D BE TOGETHER.
WOULD I KNOW THE TOM SAYERS I FOUND THERE?

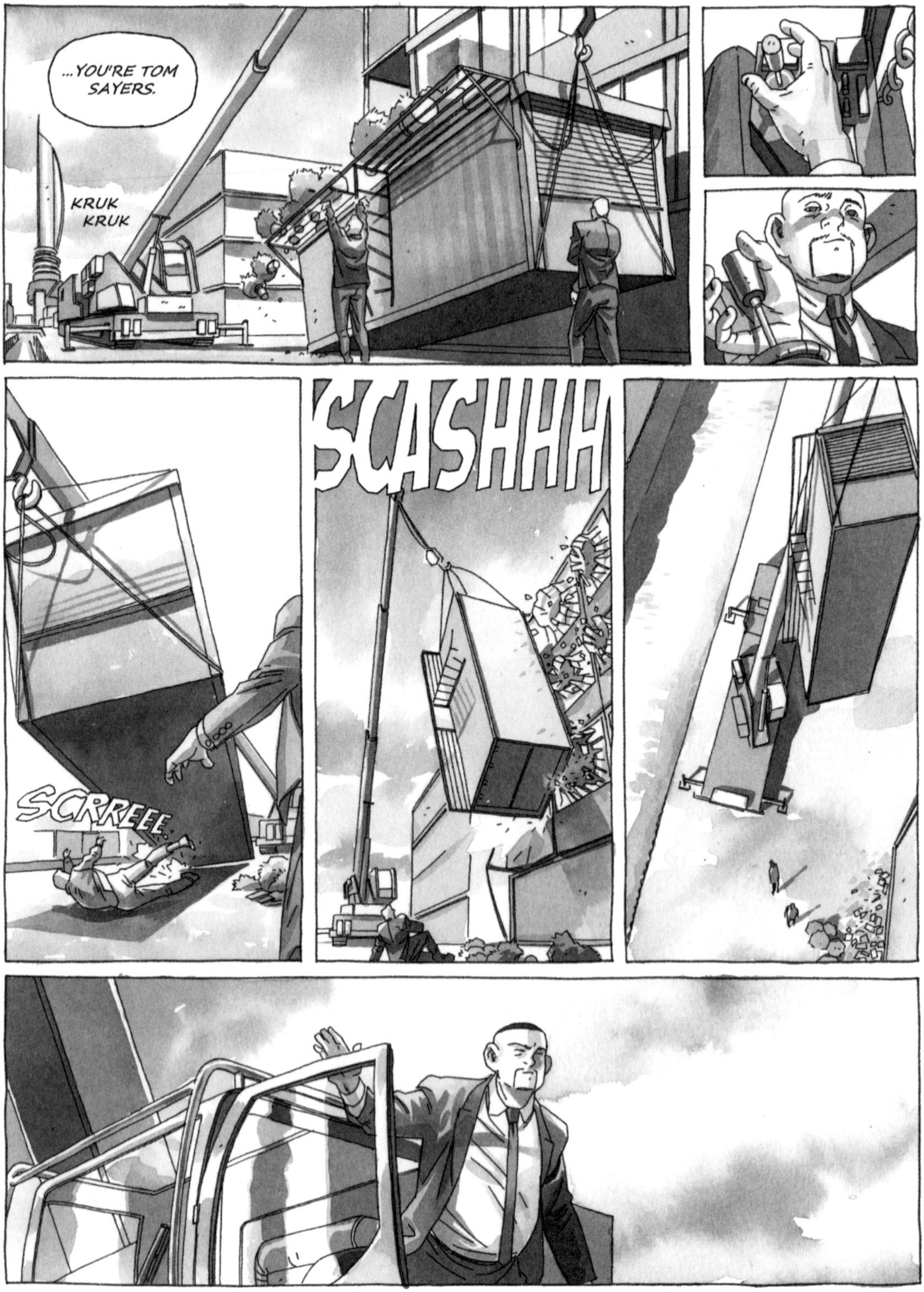
...YOU'RE TOM SAYERS.
KRUK KRUK
SCRREEE
SCASHHH

THE HELL, ARE YOU DOING?

I'M TOM SAYERS, BOXER, AND YOU'RE NOT GOING ANYWHERE NEAR THAT GIRL.

WHUUMP

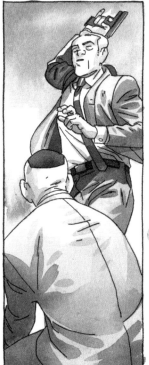

DUNCK

BLAM

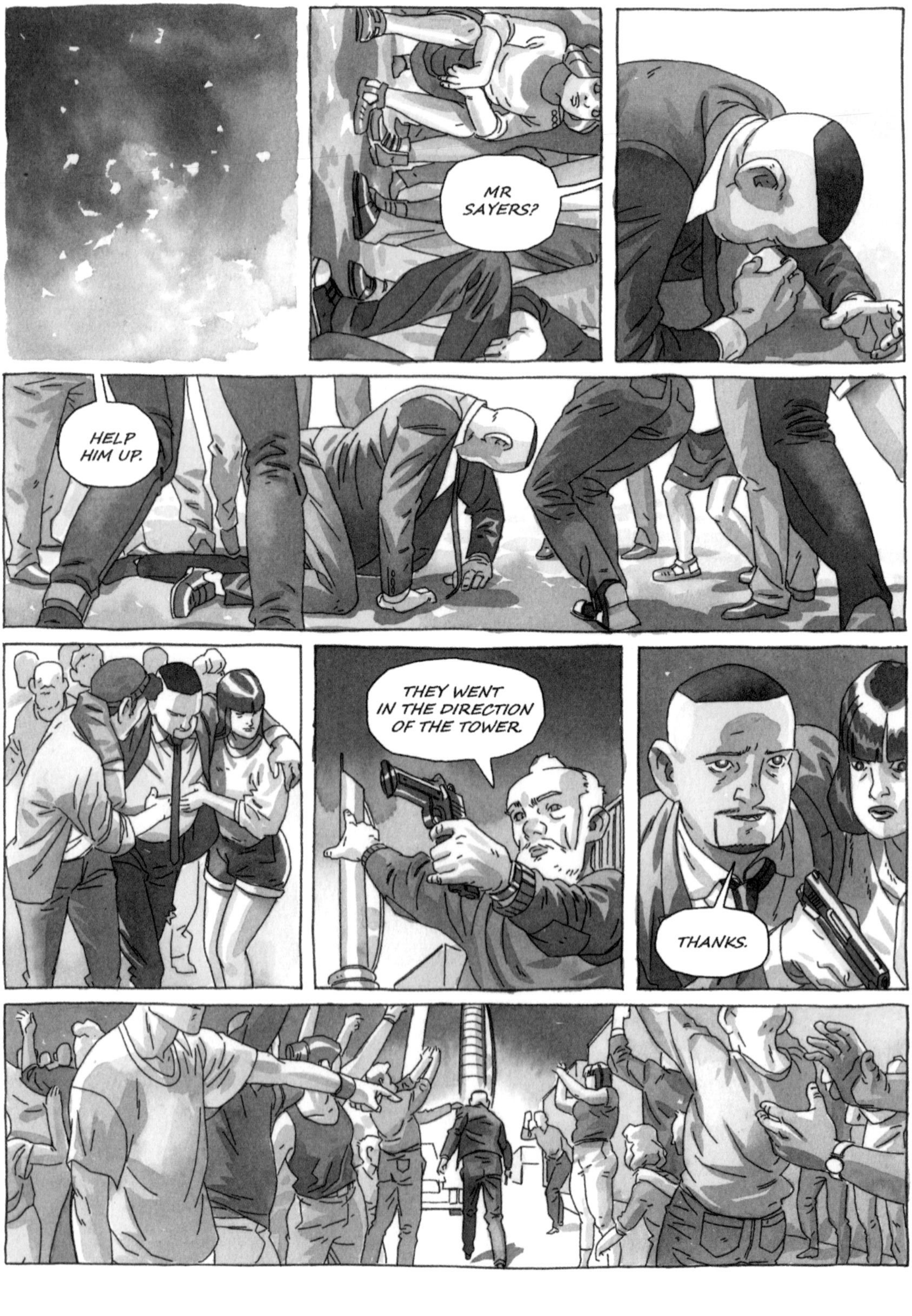
MR SAYERS?
HELP HIM UP.
THEY WENT IN THE DIRECTION OF THE TOWER.
THANKS.

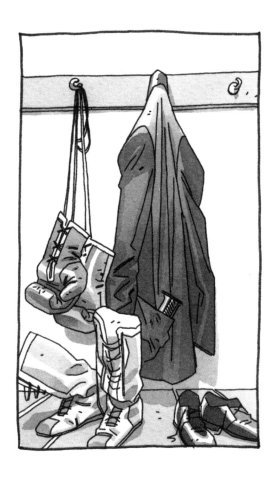

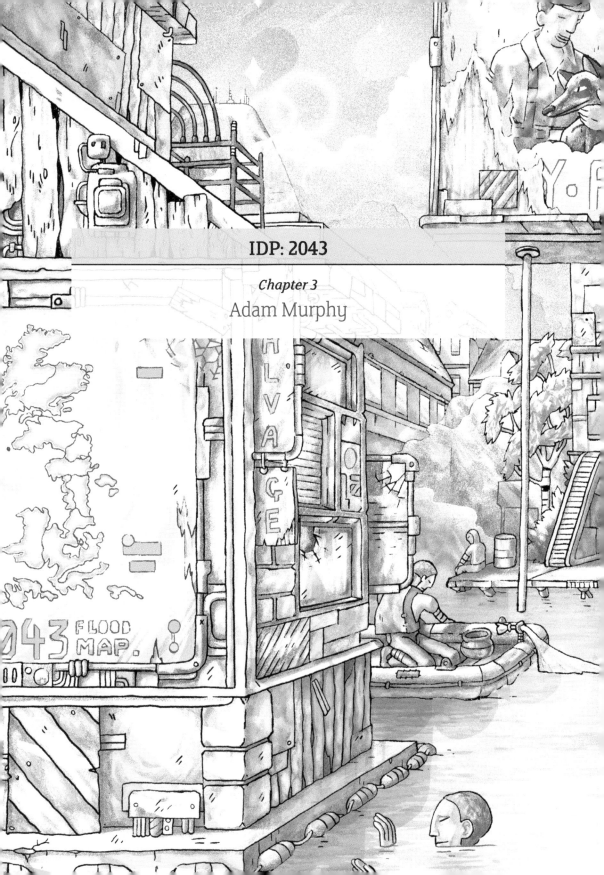

IDP: 2043

Chapter 3

Adam Murphy

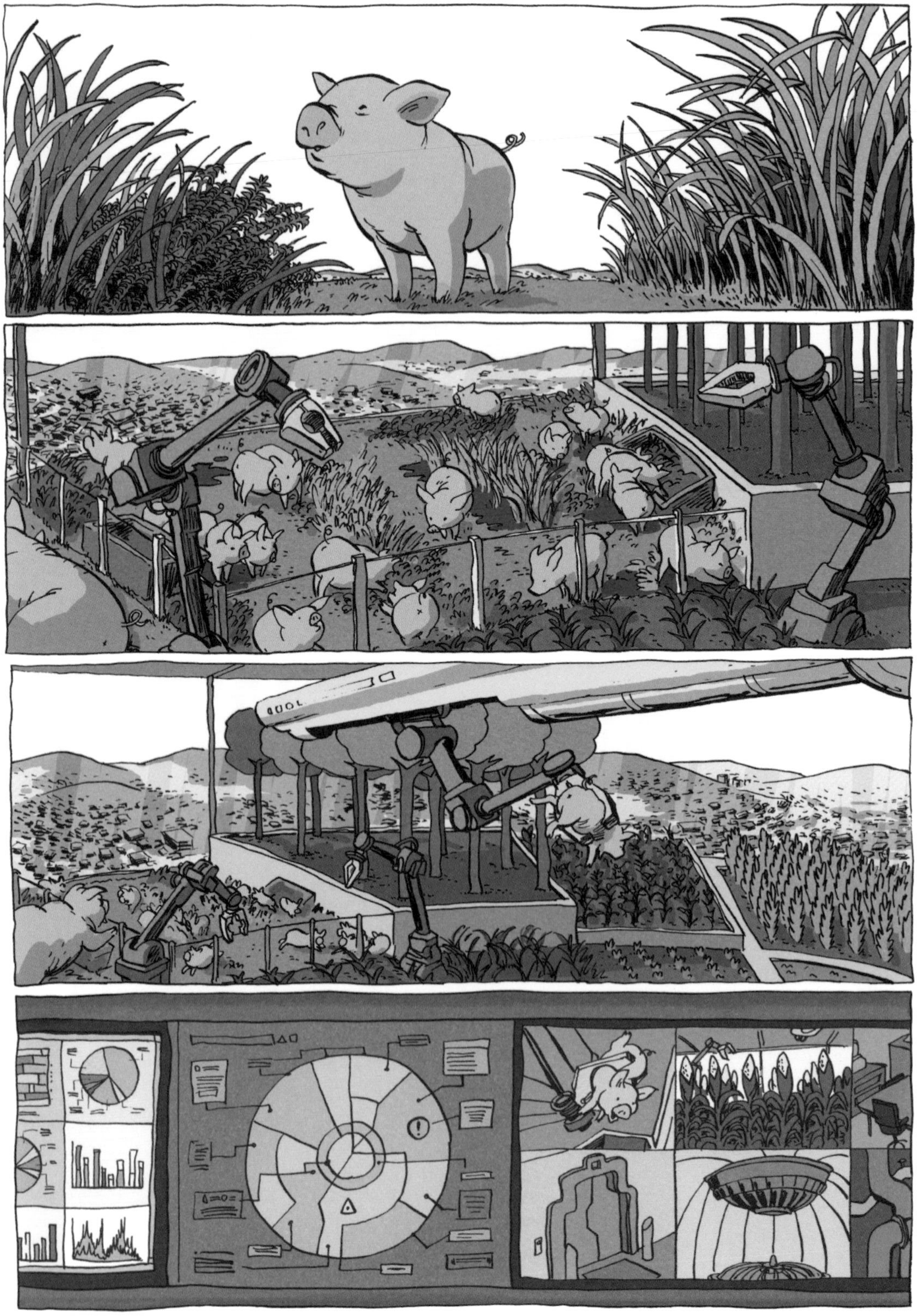

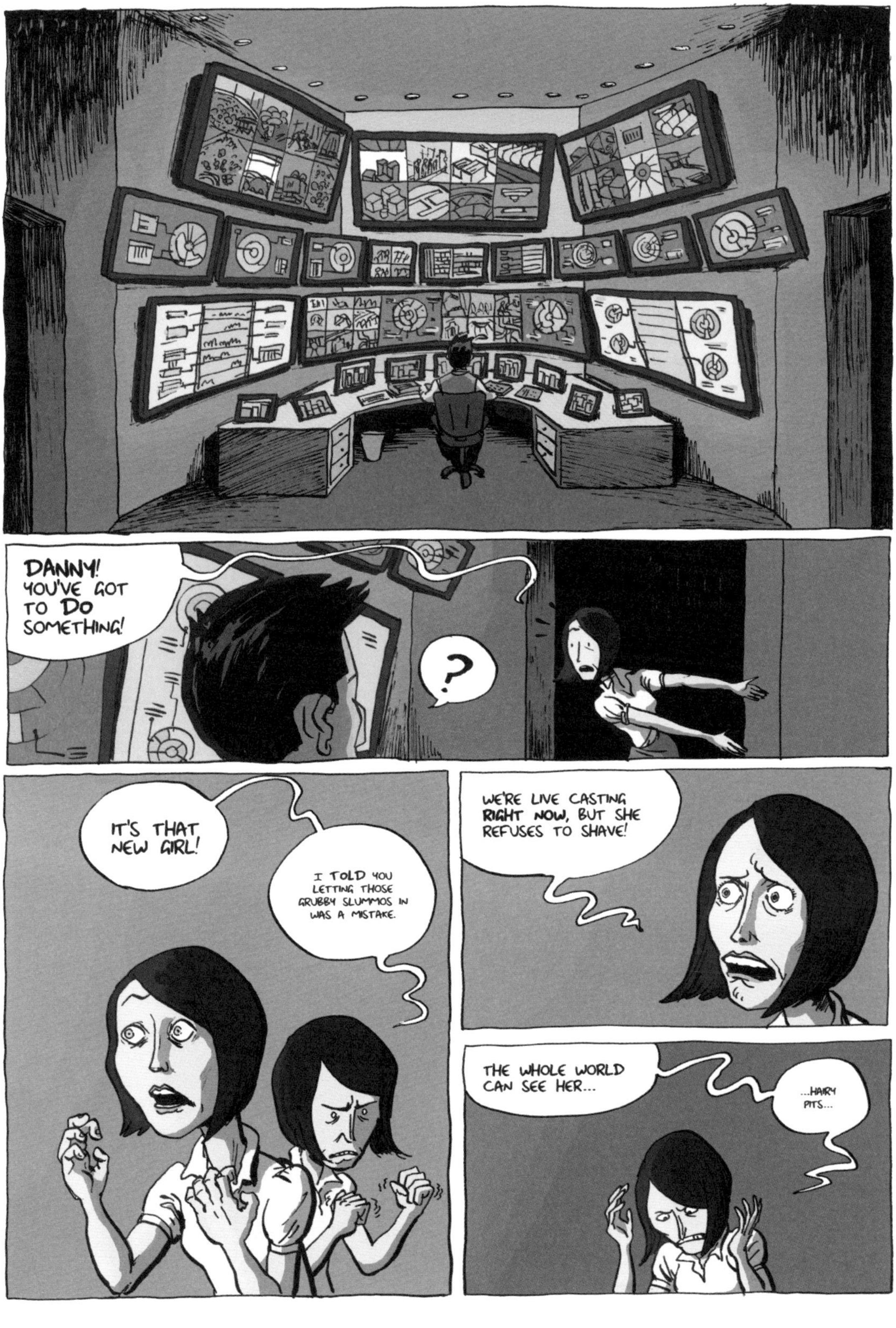
DANNY! YOU'VE GOT TO DO SOMETHING!
?
IT'S THAT NEW GIRL!
I TOLD YOU LETTING THOSE GRUBBY SLUMMOS IN WAS A MISTAKE.
WE'RE LIVE CASTING RIGHT NOW, BUT SHE REFUSES TO SHAVE!
THE WHOLE WORLD CAN SEE HER...
...HAIRY PITS...

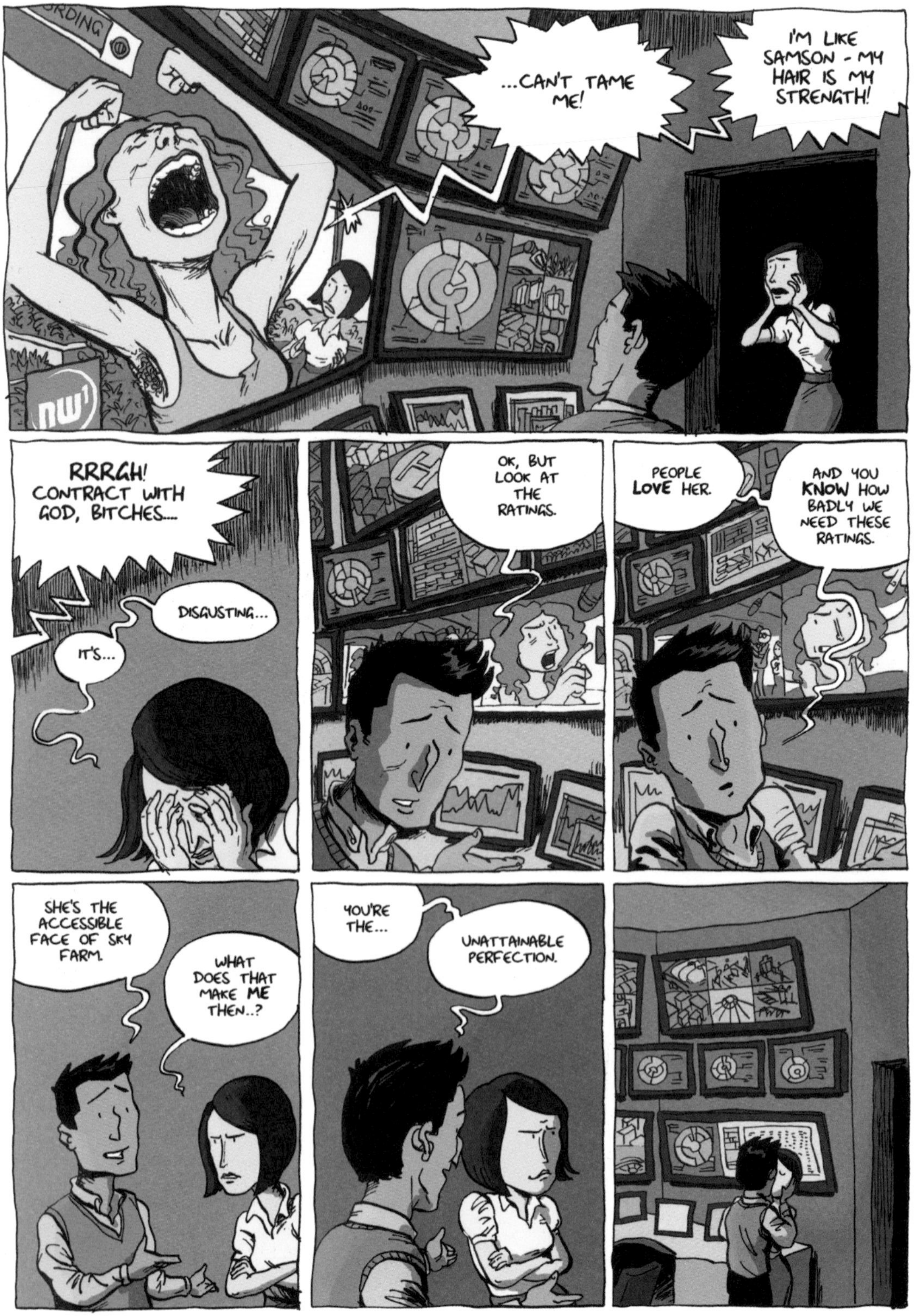
RDING
NW1
...CAN'T TAME ME!
I'M LIKE SAMSON - MY HAIR IS MY STRENGTH!
RRRGH! CONTRACT WITH GOD, BITCHES....
IT'S...
DISGUSTING...
OK, BUT LOOK AT THE RATINGS.
PEOPLE **LOVE** HER.
AND YOU **KNOW** HOW BADLY WE NEED THESE RATINGS.
SHE'S THE ACCESSIBLE FACE OF SKY FARM.
WHAT DOES THAT MAKE **ME** THEN..?
YOU'RE THE...
UNATTAINABLE PERFECTION.

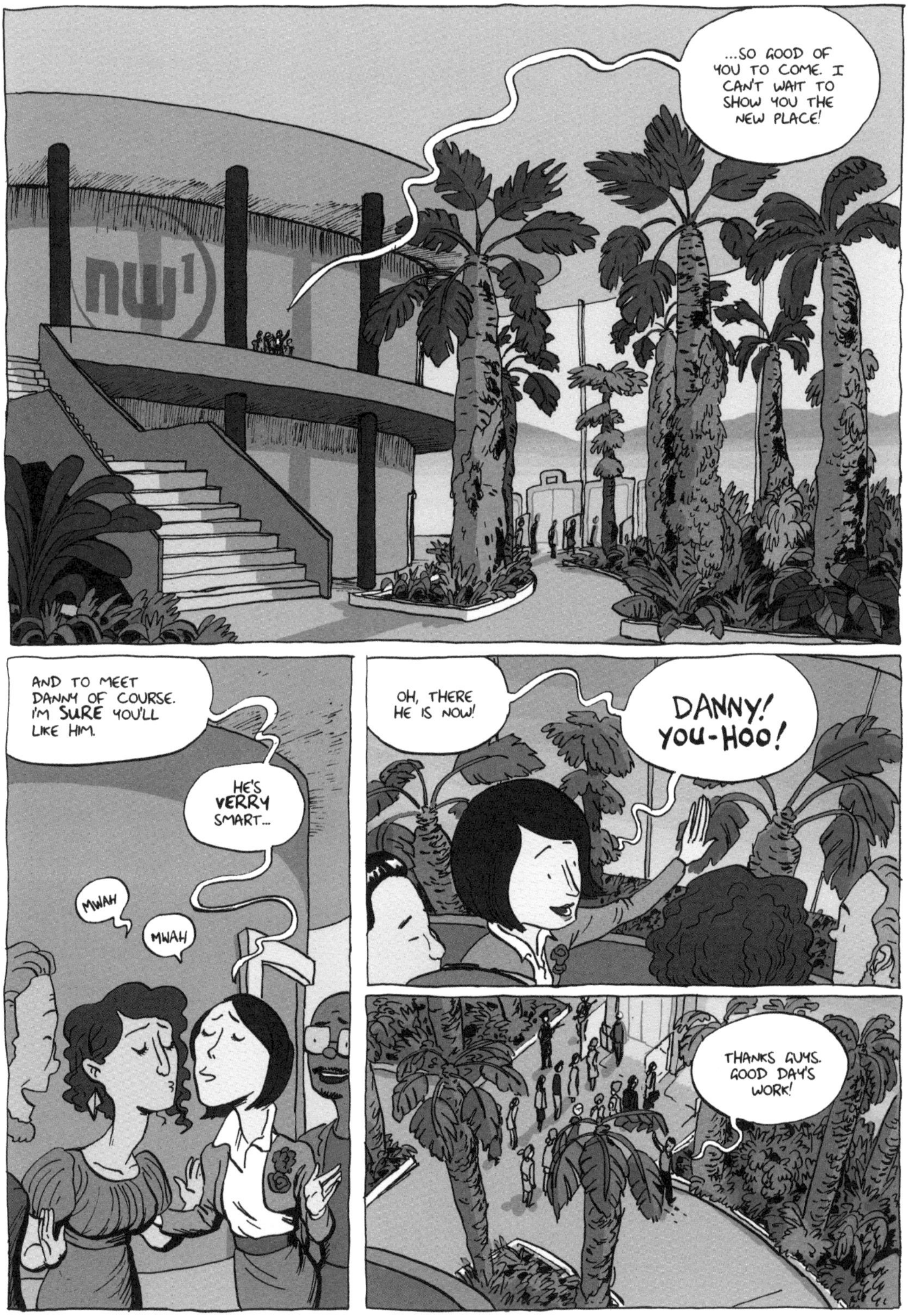
...SO GOOD OF YOU TO COME. I CAN'T WAIT TO SHOW YOU THE NEW PLACE!
nw1
AND TO MEET DANNY OF COURSE. I'M SURE YOU'LL LIKE HIM.
HE'S VERRY SMART...
MWAH
MWAH
OH, THERE HE IS NOW!
DANNY! YOU-HOO!
THANKS GUYS. GOOD DAY'S WORK!

HEY - CONGRATULATIONS, MAN!

?

ON THE **VOGUE** THING...

DIDN'T YOU SEE IT?

BEEP BOOP

VOGUE

THE LA BEOUF FOUNDATION 25 YEARS ON

GET THIS SEASON'S HOT NEW LOOK!

THE NEW MODERN BRUT

DUDE - THAT'S A BIG DEAL.

WAS THAT THE NEW iHAND 2.0?

OH HEY, LOOK! THERE SHE IS!

CONGRATS! OH WOU SO COOL YOU GO GIRL! SWEET RIGHT ON. A REAL CELEBRITY! WOAH.

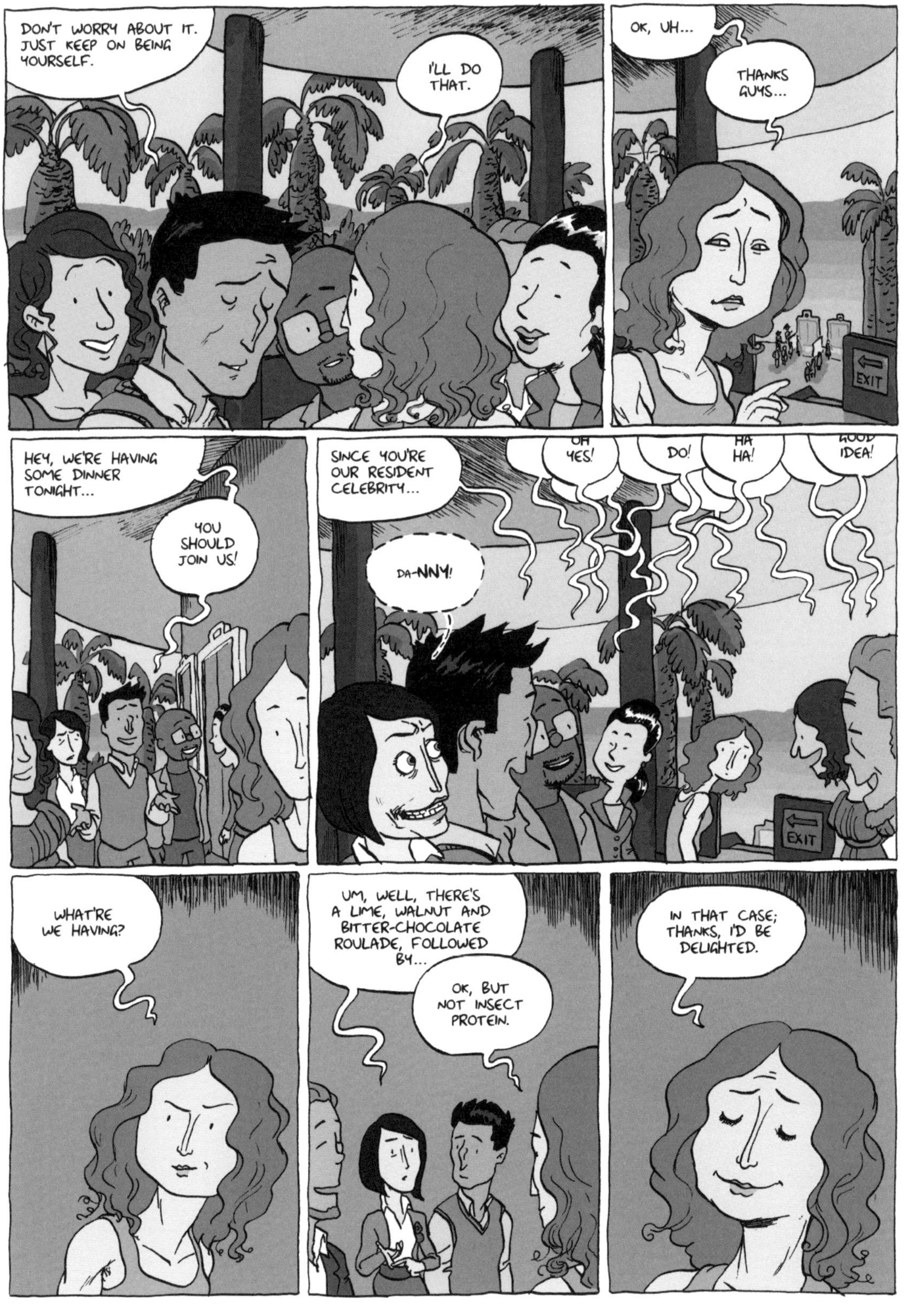
DON'T WORRY ABOUT IT. JUST KEEP ON BEING YOURSELF.
I'LL DO THAT.
OK, UH...
THANKS GUYS...
EXIT
HEY, WE'RE HAVING SOME DINNER TONIGHT...
YOU SHOULD JOIN US!
SINCE YOU'RE OUR RESIDENT CELEBRITY...
DA-NNY!
YES!
DO!
HA!
IDEA!
EXIT
WHAT'RE WE HAVING?
UM, WELL, THERE'S A LIME, WALNUT AND BITTER-CHOCOLATE ROULADE, FOLLOWED BY...
OK, BUT NOT INSECT PROTEIN.
IN THAT CASE; THANKS, I'D BE DELIGHTED.

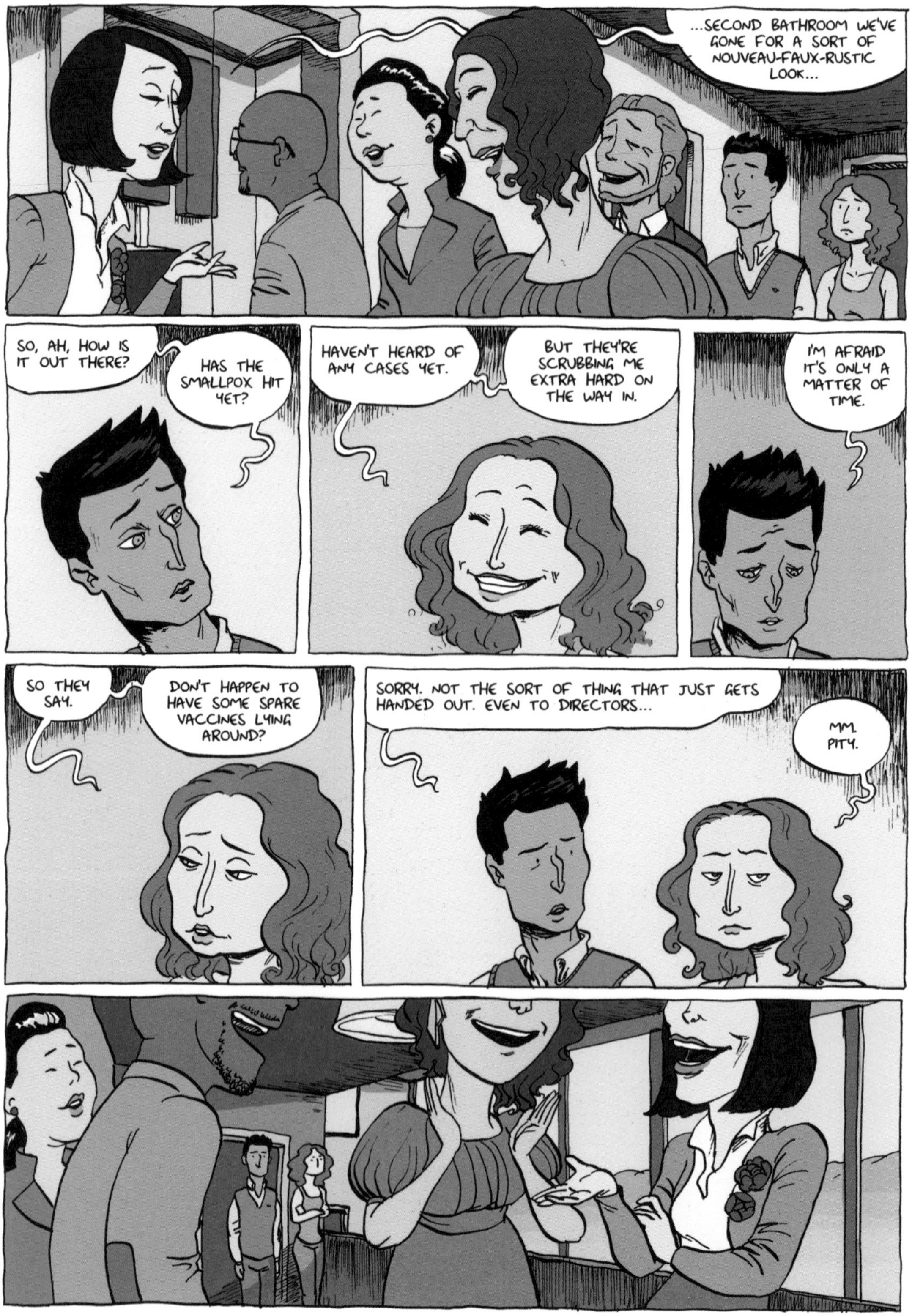
...SECOND BATHROOM WE'VE GONE FOR A SORT OF NOUVEAU-FAUX-RUSTIC LOOK...
SO, AH, HOW IS IT OUT THERE?
HAS THE SMALLPOX HIT YET?
HAVEN'T HEARD OF ANY CASES YET.
BUT THEY'RE SCRUBBING ME EXTRA HARD ON THE WAY IN.
I'M AFRAID IT'S ONLY A MATTER OF TIME.
SO THEY SAY.
DON'T HAPPEN TO HAVE SOME SPARE VACCINES LYING AROUND?
SORRY. NOT THE SORT OF THING THAT JUST GETS HANDED OUT. EVEN TO DIRECTORS...
MM. PITY.

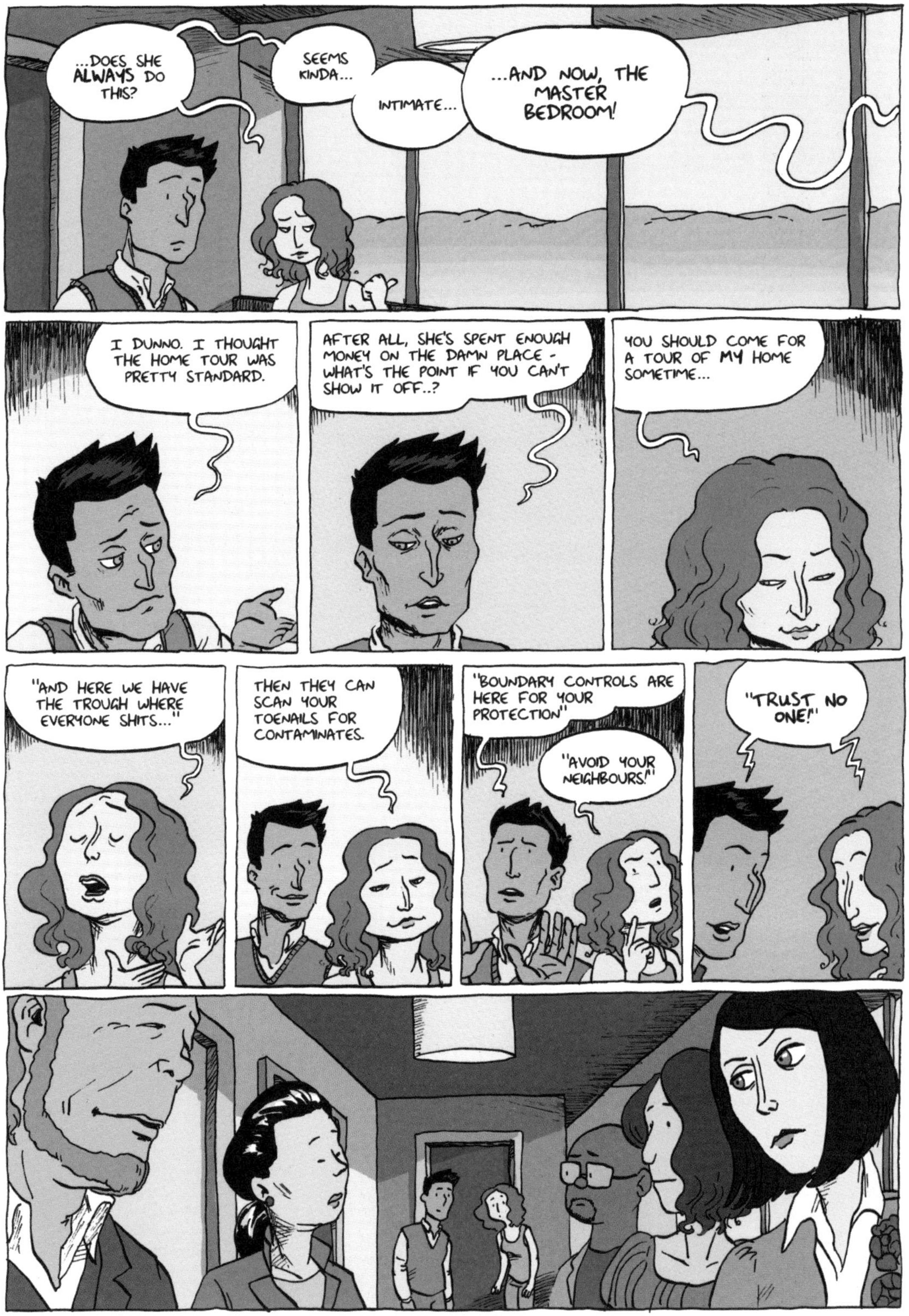
...DOES SHE ALWAYS DO THIS?
SEEMS KINDA...
INTIMATE...
...AND NOW, THE MASTER BEDROOM!
I DUNNO. I THOUGHT THE HOME TOUR WAS PRETTY STANDARD.
AFTER ALL, SHE'S SPENT ENOUGH MONEY ON THE DAMN PLACE - WHAT'S THE POINT IF YOU CAN'T SHOW IT OFF..?
YOU SHOULD COME FOR A TOUR OF MY HOME SOMETIME...
"AND HERE WE HAVE THE TROUGH WHERE EVERYONE SHITS..."
THEN THEY CAN SCAN YOUR TOENAILS FOR CONTAMINATES.
"BOUNDARY CONTROLS ARE HERE FOR YOUR PROTECTION"
"AVOID YOUR NEIGHBOURS!"
"TRUST NO ONE!"

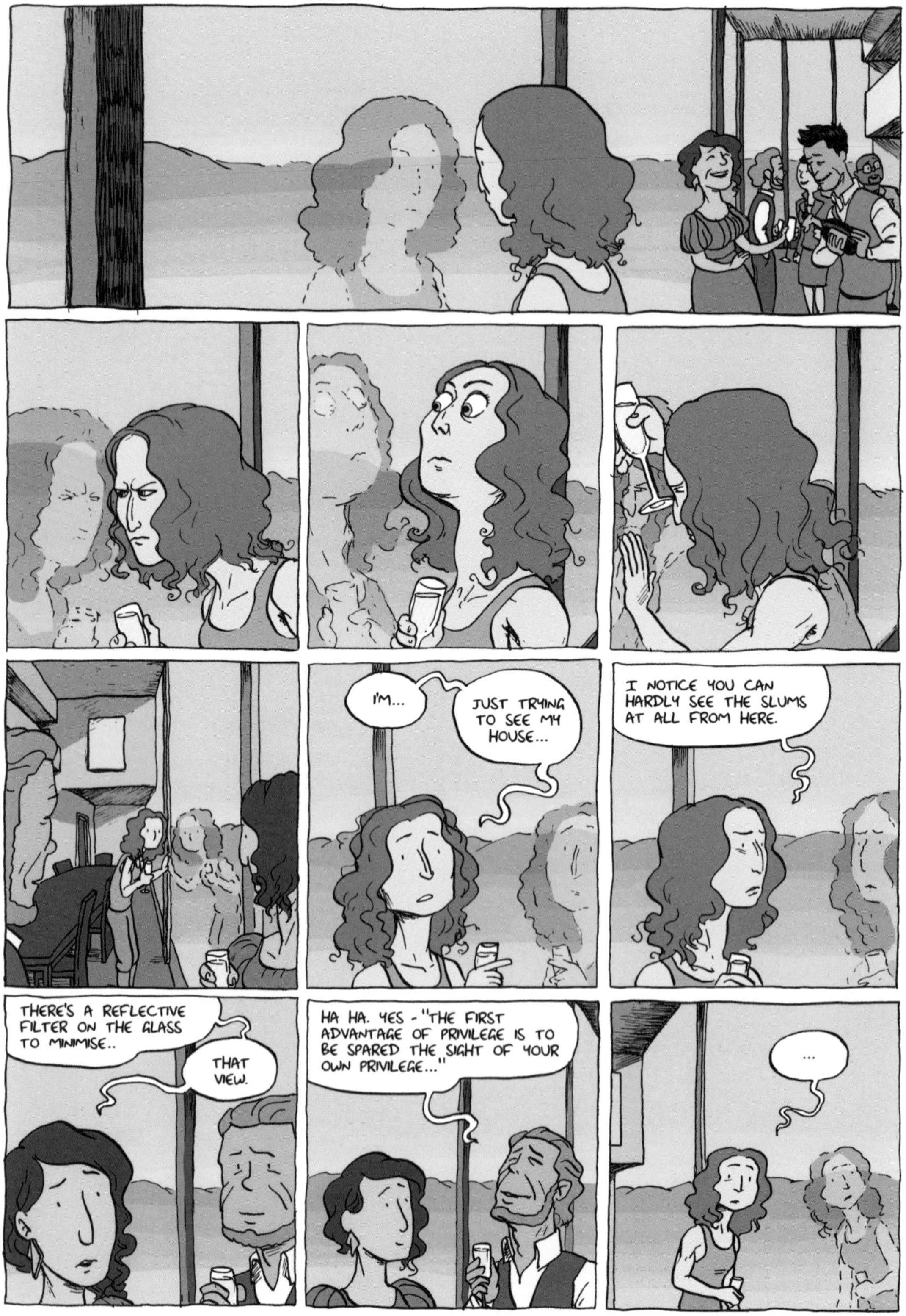
I'M...
JUST TRYING TO SEE MY HOUSE...
I NOTICE YOU CAN HARDLY SEE THE SLUMS AT ALL FROM HERE.
THERE'S A REFLECTIVE FILTER ON THE GLASS TO MINIMISE..
THAT VIEW.
HA HA. YES - "THE FIRST ADVANTAGE OF PRIVILEGE IS TO BE SPARED THE SIGHT OF YOUR OWN PRIVILEGE..."
...

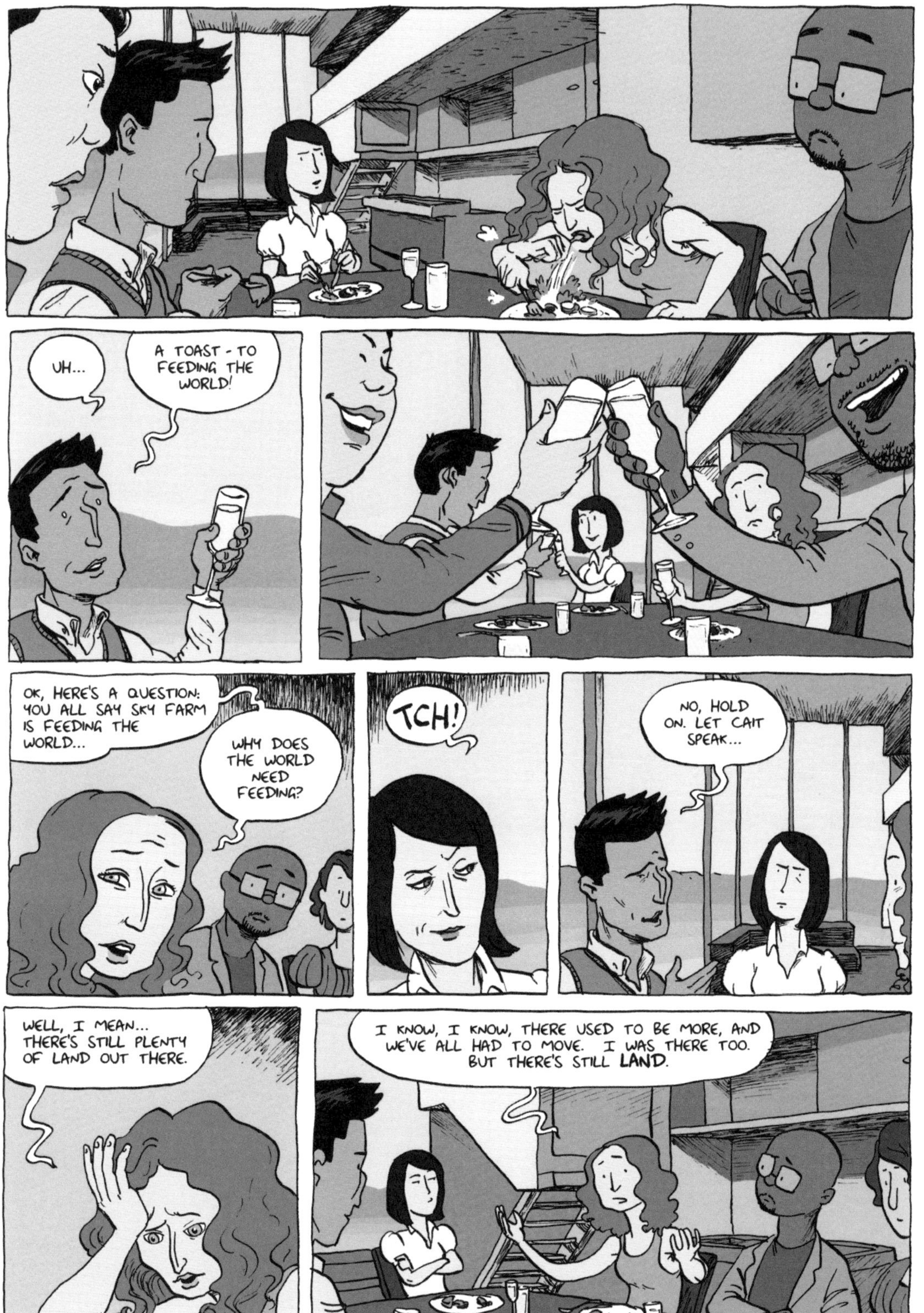
UH...
A TOAST - TO FEEDING THE WORLD!
OK, HERE'S A QUESTION: YOU ALL SAY SKY FARM IS FEEDING THE WORLD...
WHY DOES THE WORLD NEED FEEDING?
TCH!
NO, HOLD ON. LET CAIT SPEAK...
WELL, I MEAN... THERE'S STILL PLENTY OF LAND OUT THERE.
I KNOW, I KNOW, THERE USED TO BE MORE, AND WE'VE ALL HAD TO MOVE. I WAS THERE TOO. BUT THERE'S STILL **LAND**.

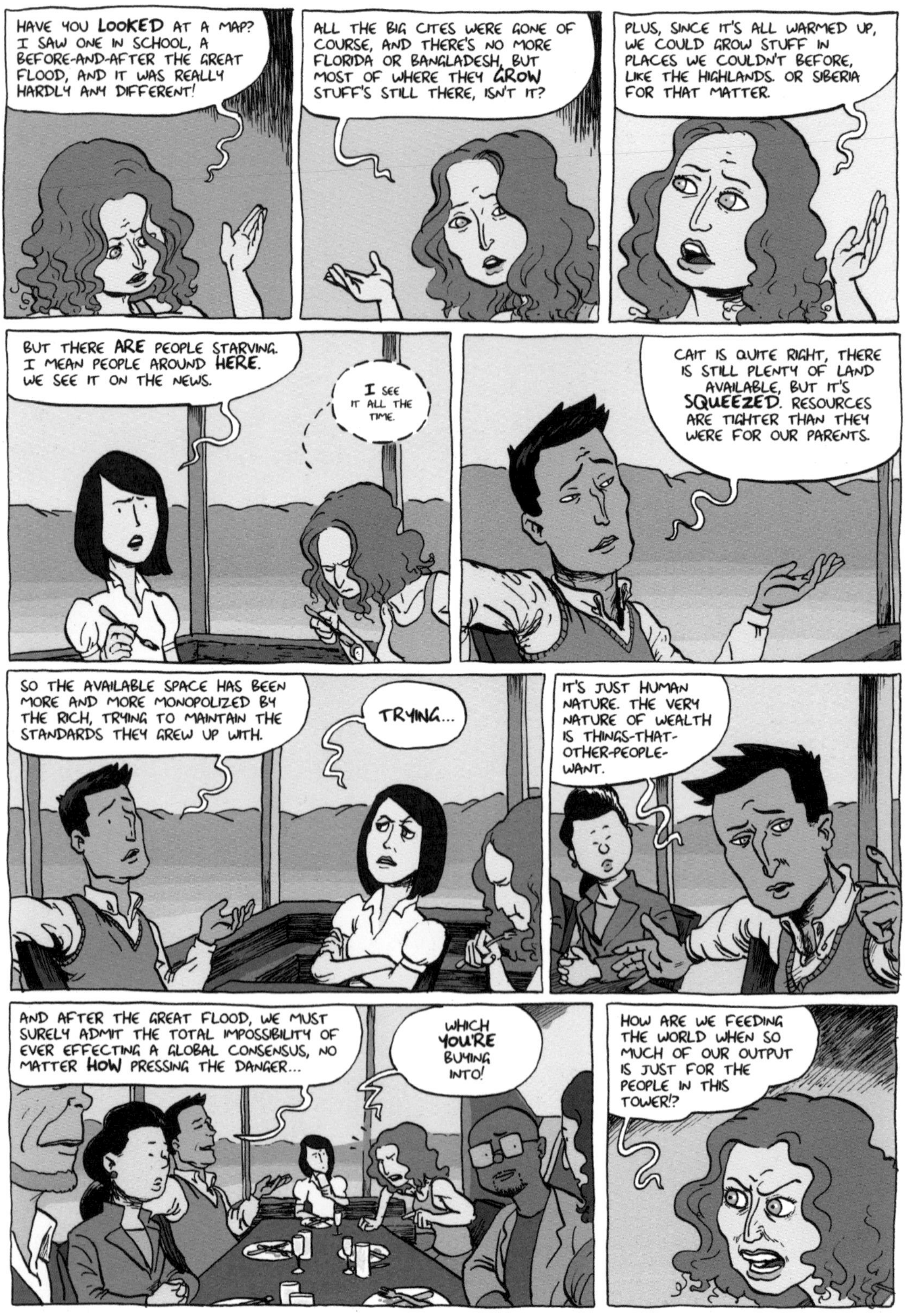
HAVE YOU **LOOKED** AT A MAP? I SAW ONE IN SCHOOL, A BEFORE-AND-AFTER THE GREAT FLOOD, AND IT WAS REALLY HARDLY ANY DIFFERENT!
ALL THE BIG CITES WERE GONE OF COURSE, AND THERE'S NO MORE FLORIDA OR BANGLADESH, BUT MOST OF WHERE THEY **GROW** STUFF'S STILL THERE, ISN'T IT?
PLUS, SINCE IT'S ALL WARMED UP, WE COULD GROW STUFF IN PLACES WE COULDN'T BEFORE, LIKE THE HIGHLANDS. OR SIBERIA FOR THAT MATTER.
BUT THERE **ARE** PEOPLE STARVING. I MEAN PEOPLE AROUND **HERE**. WE SEE IT ON THE NEWS.
I SEE IT ALL THE TIME.
CAIT IS QUITE RIGHT, THERE IS STILL PLENTY OF LAND AVAILABLE, BUT IT'S **SQUEEZED**. RESOURCES ARE TIGHTER THAN THEY WERE FOR OUR PARENTS.
SO THE AVAILABLE SPACE HAS BEEN MORE AND MORE MONOPOLIZED BY THE RICH, TRYING TO MAINTAIN THE STANDARDS THEY GREW UP WITH.
TRYING...
IT'S JUST HUMAN NATURE. THE VERY NATURE OF WEALTH IS THINGS-THAT-OTHER-PEOPLE-WANT.
AND AFTER THE GREAT FLOOD, WE MUST SURELY ADMIT THE TOTAL IMPOSSIBILITY OF EVER EFFECTING A GLOBAL CONSENSUS, NO MATTER **HOW** PRESSING THE DANGER...
WHICH **YOU'RE** BUYING INTO!
HOW ARE WE FEEDING THE WORLD WHEN SO MUCH OF OUR OUTPUT IS JUST FOR THE PEOPLE IN THIS TOWER!?

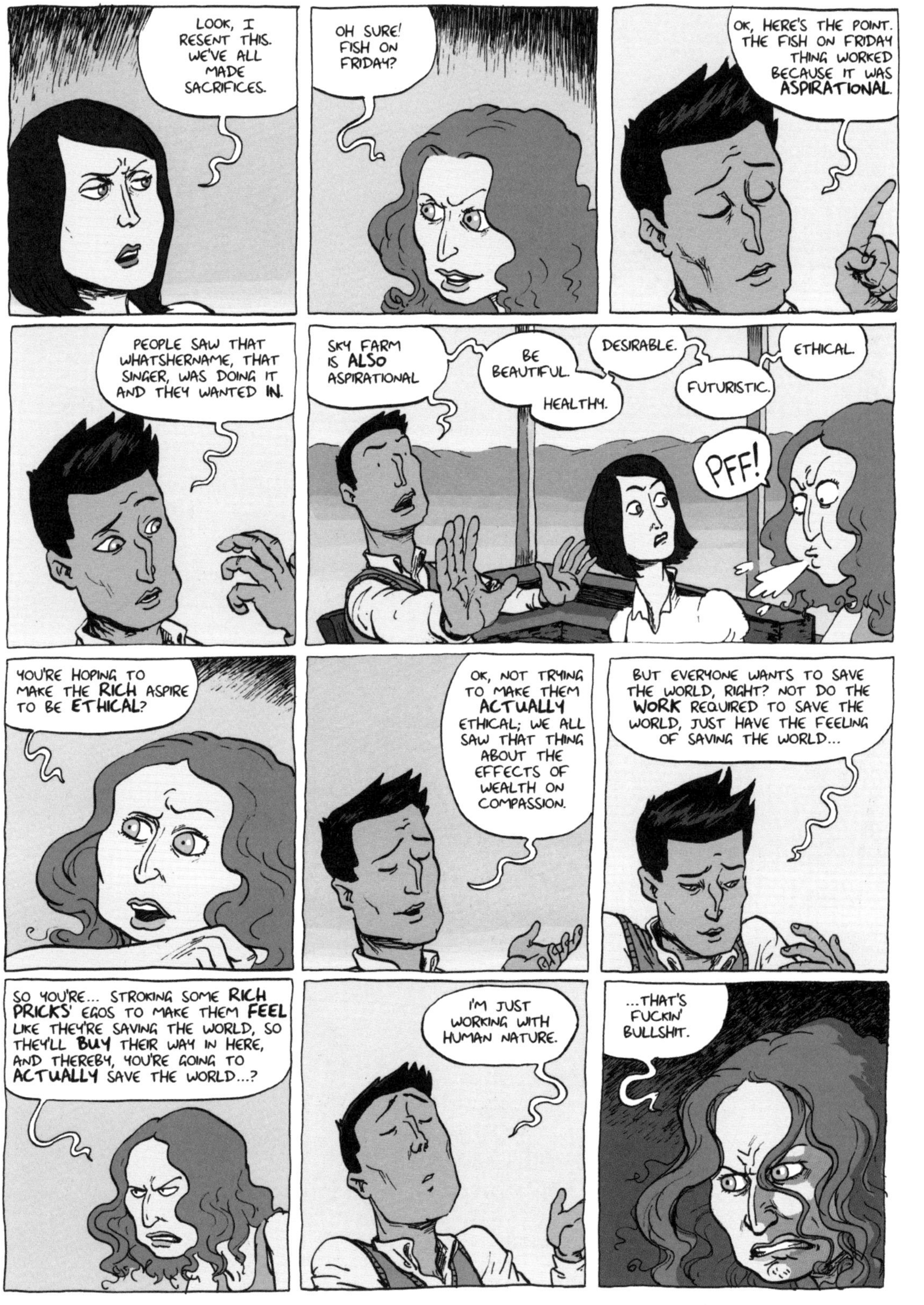
LOOK, I RESENT THIS. WE'VE ALL MADE SACRIFICES.
OH SURE! FISH ON FRIDAY?
OK, HERE'S THE POINT. THE FISH ON FRIDAY THING WORKED BECAUSE IT WAS ASPIRATIONAL.
PEOPLE SAW THAT WHATSHERNAME, THAT SINGER, WAS DOING IT AND THEY WANTED IN.
SKY FARM IS ALSO ASPIRATIONAL
BE BEAUTIFUL.
HEALTHY.
DESIRABLE.
FUTURISTIC.
ETHICAL.
PFF!
YOU'RE HOPING TO MAKE THE RICH ASPIRE TO BE ETHICAL?
OK, NOT TRYING TO MAKE THEM ACTUALLY ETHICAL; WE ALL SAW THAT THING ABOUT THE EFFECTS OF WEALTH ON COMPASSION.
BUT EVERYONE WANTS TO SAVE THE WORLD, RIGHT? NOT DO THE WORK REQUIRED TO SAVE THE WORLD, JUST HAVE THE FEELING OF SAVING THE WORLD...
SO YOU'RE... STROKING SOME RICH PRICKS' EGOS TO MAKE THEM FEEL LIKE THEY'RE SAVING THE WORLD, SO THEY'LL BUY THEIR WAY IN HERE, AND THEREBY, YOU'RE GOING TO ACTUALLY SAVE THE WORLD...?
I'M JUST WORKING WITH HUMAN NATURE.
...THAT'S FUCKIN' BULLSHIT.

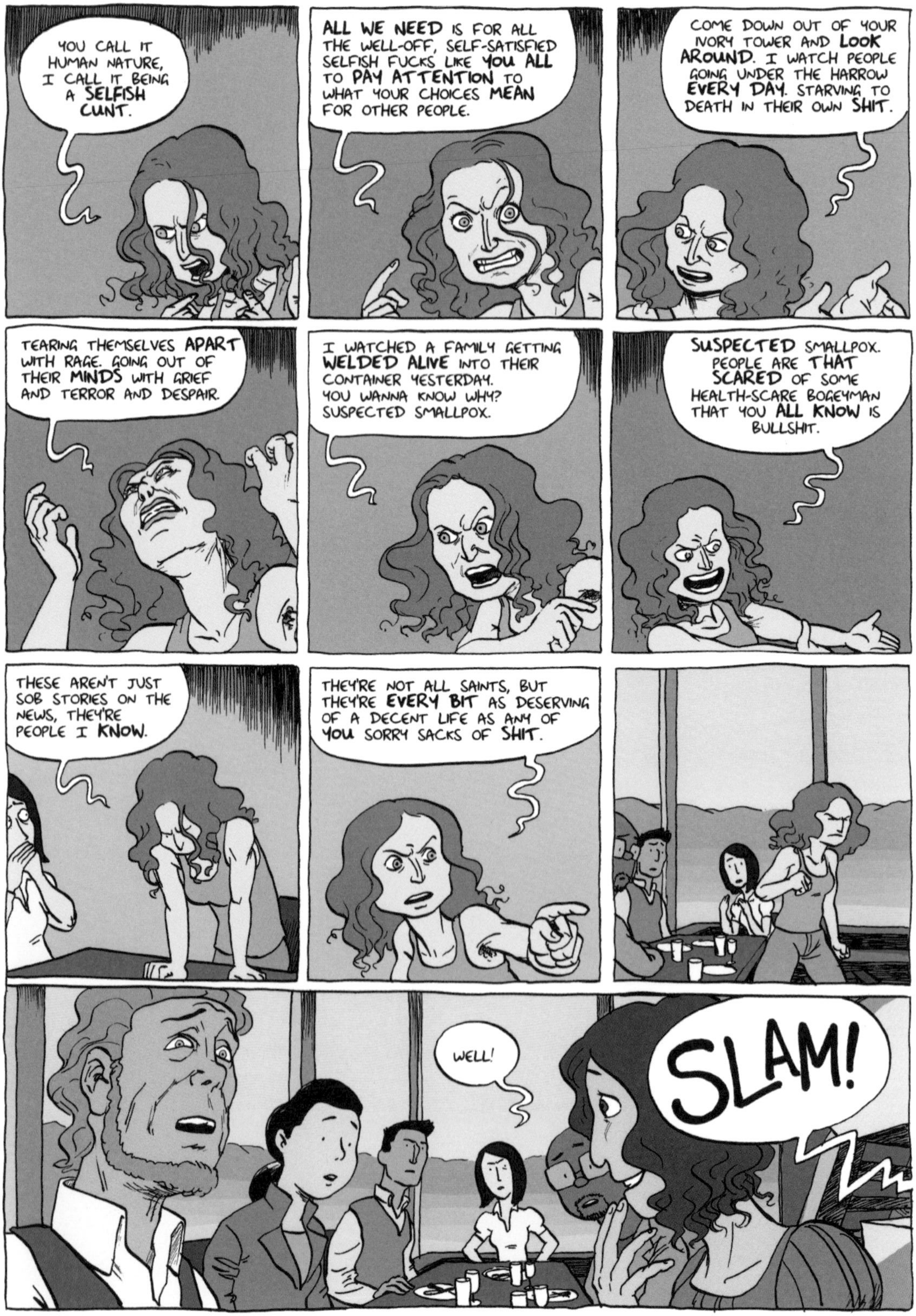
YOU CALL IT HUMAN NATURE, I CALL IT BEING A SELFISH CUNT.
ALL WE NEED IS FOR ALL THE WELL-OFF, SELF-SATISFIED SELFISH FUCKS LIKE YOU ALL TO PAY ATTENTION TO WHAT YOUR CHOICES MEAN FOR OTHER PEOPLE.
COME DOWN OUT OF YOUR IVORY TOWER AND LOOK AROUND. I WATCH PEOPLE GOING UNDER THE HARROW EVERY DAY. STARVING TO DEATH IN THEIR OWN SHIT.
TEARING THEMSELVES APART WITH RAGE. GOING OUT OF THEIR MINDS WITH GRIEF AND TERROR AND DESPAIR.
I WATCHED A FAMILY GETTING WELDED ALIVE INTO THEIR CONTAINER YESTERDAY. YOU WANNA KNOW WHY? SUSPECTED SMALLPOX.
SUSPECTED SMALLPOX. PEOPLE ARE THAT SCARED OF SOME HEALTH-SCARE BOGEYMAN THAT YOU ALL KNOW IS BULLSHIT.
THESE AREN'T JUST SOB STORIES ON THE NEWS, THEY'RE PEOPLE I KNOW.
THEY'RE NOT ALL SAINTS, BUT THEY'RE EVERY BIT AS DESERVING OF A DECENT LIFE AS ANY OF YOU SORRY SACKS OF SHIT.
WELL!
SLAM!

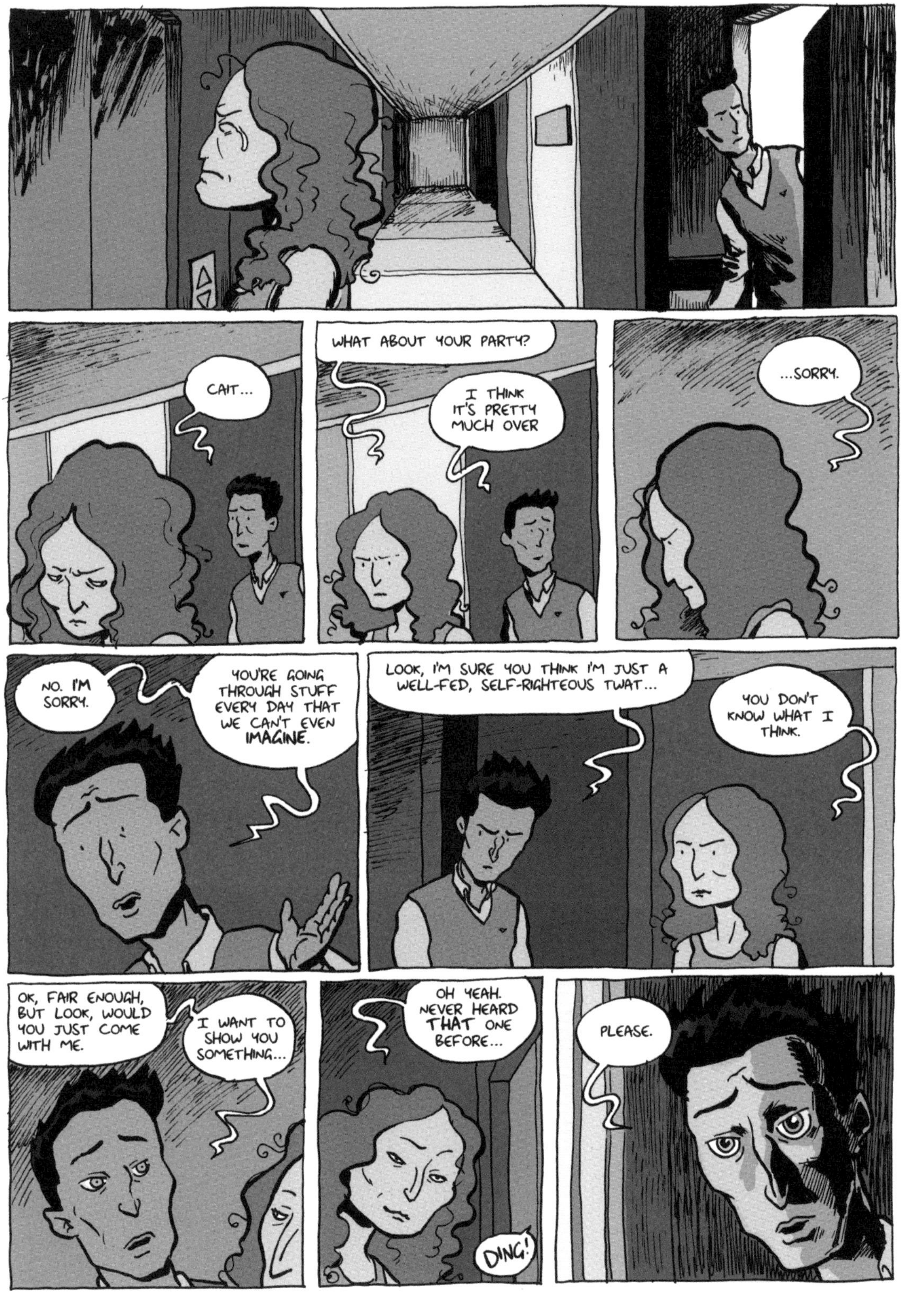
CAIT...
WHAT ABOUT YOUR PARTY?
I THINK IT'S PRETTY MUCH OVER
...SORRY.
NO. I'M SORRY.
YOU'RE GOING THROUGH STUFF EVERY DAY THAT WE CAN'T EVEN IMAGINE.
LOOK, I'M SURE YOU THINK I'M JUST A WELL-FED, SELF-RIGHTEOUS TWAT...
YOU DON'T KNOW WHAT I THINK.
OK, FAIR ENOUGH, BUT LOOK, WOULD YOU JUST COME WITH ME.
I WANT TO SHOW YOU SOMETHING...
OH YEAH. NEVER HEARD THAT ONE BEFORE...
DING!
PLEASE.

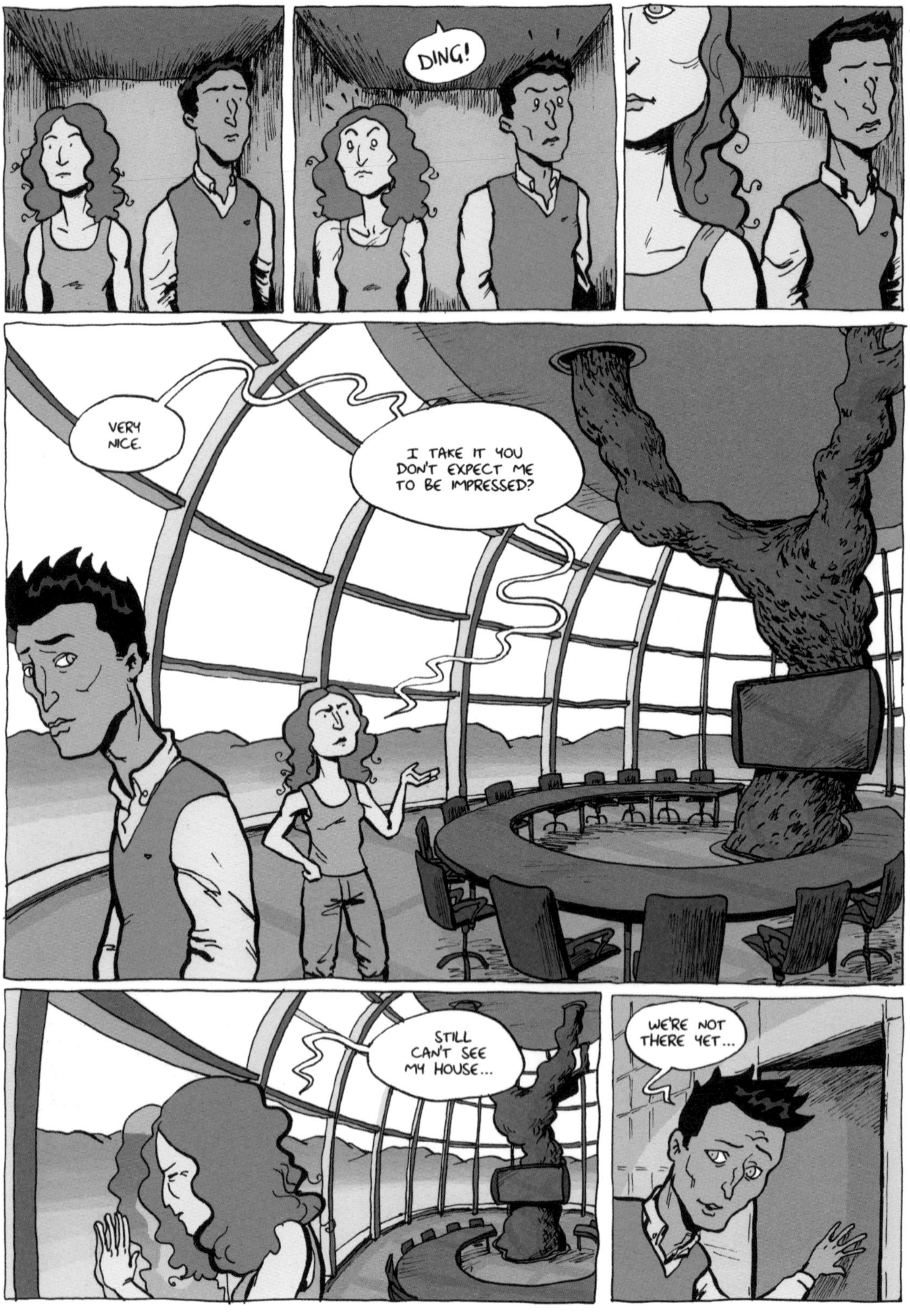
DING!
VERY NICE.
I TAKE IT YOU DON'T EXPECT ME TO BE IMPRESSED?
STILL CAN'T SEE MY HOUSE...
WE'RE NOT THERE YET...

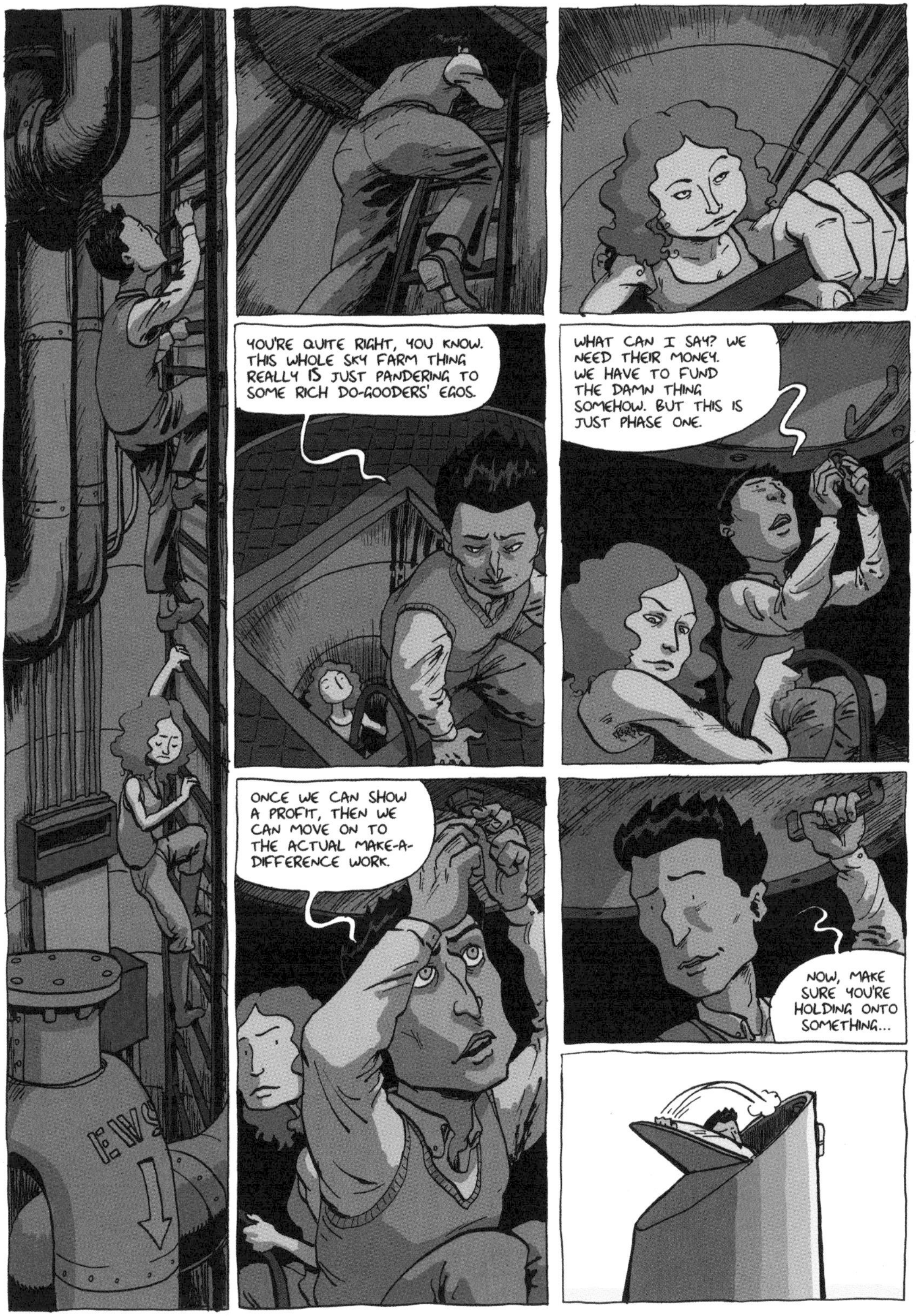
E.V.S
YOU'RE QUITE RIGHT, YOU KNOW. THIS WHOLE SKY FARM THING REALLY IS JUST PANDERING TO SOME RICH DO-GOODERS' EGOS.
WHAT CAN I SAY? WE NEED THEIR MONEY. WE HAVE TO FUND THE DAMN THING SOMEHOW. BUT THIS IS JUST PHASE ONE.
ONCE WE CAN SHOW A PROFIT, THEN WE CAN MOVE ON TO THE ACTUAL MAKE-A-DIFFERENCE WORK.
NOW, MAKE SURE YOU'RE HOLDING ONTO SOMETHING...

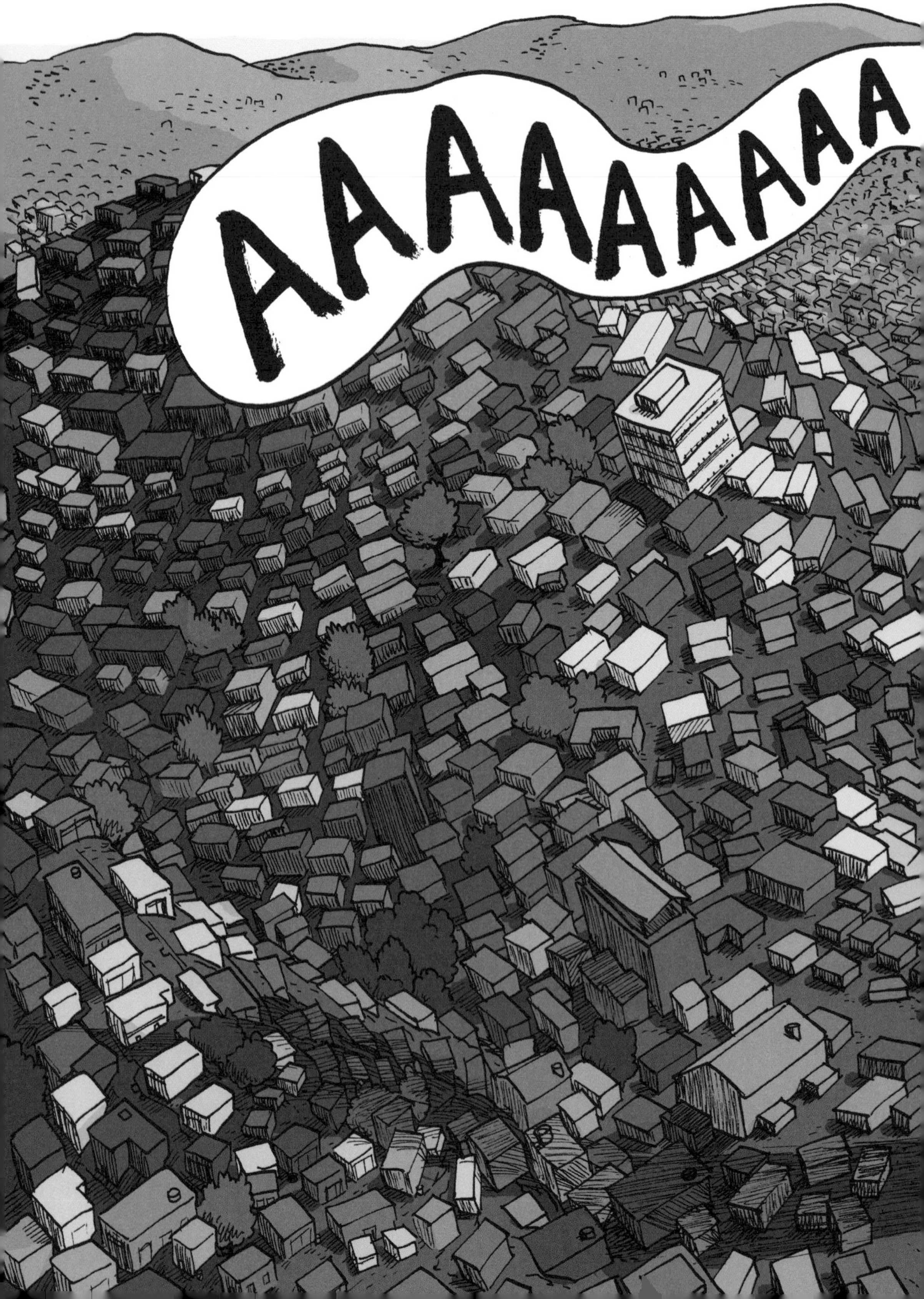
AAAAAAAAA

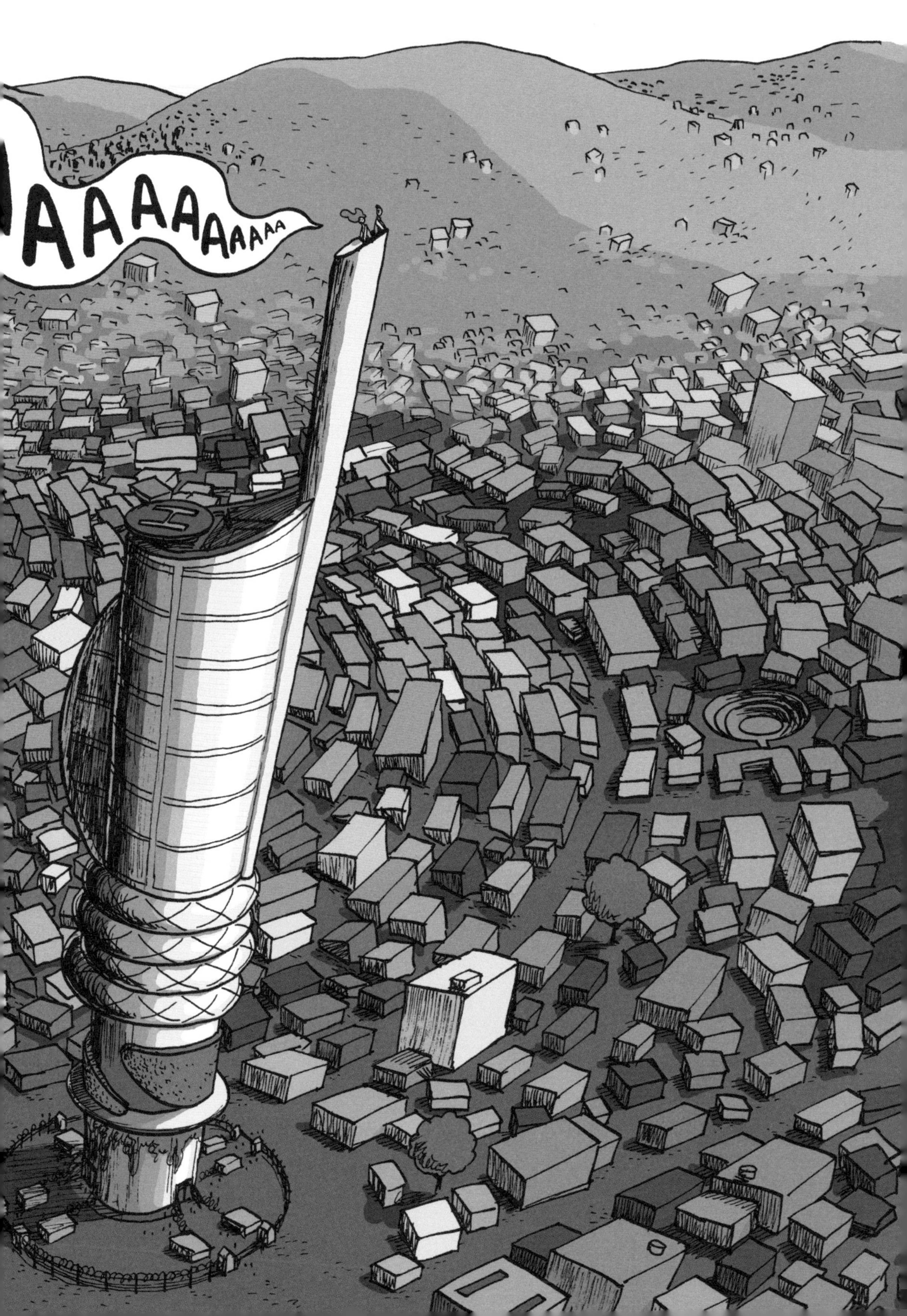
AAAAAAAAAAA

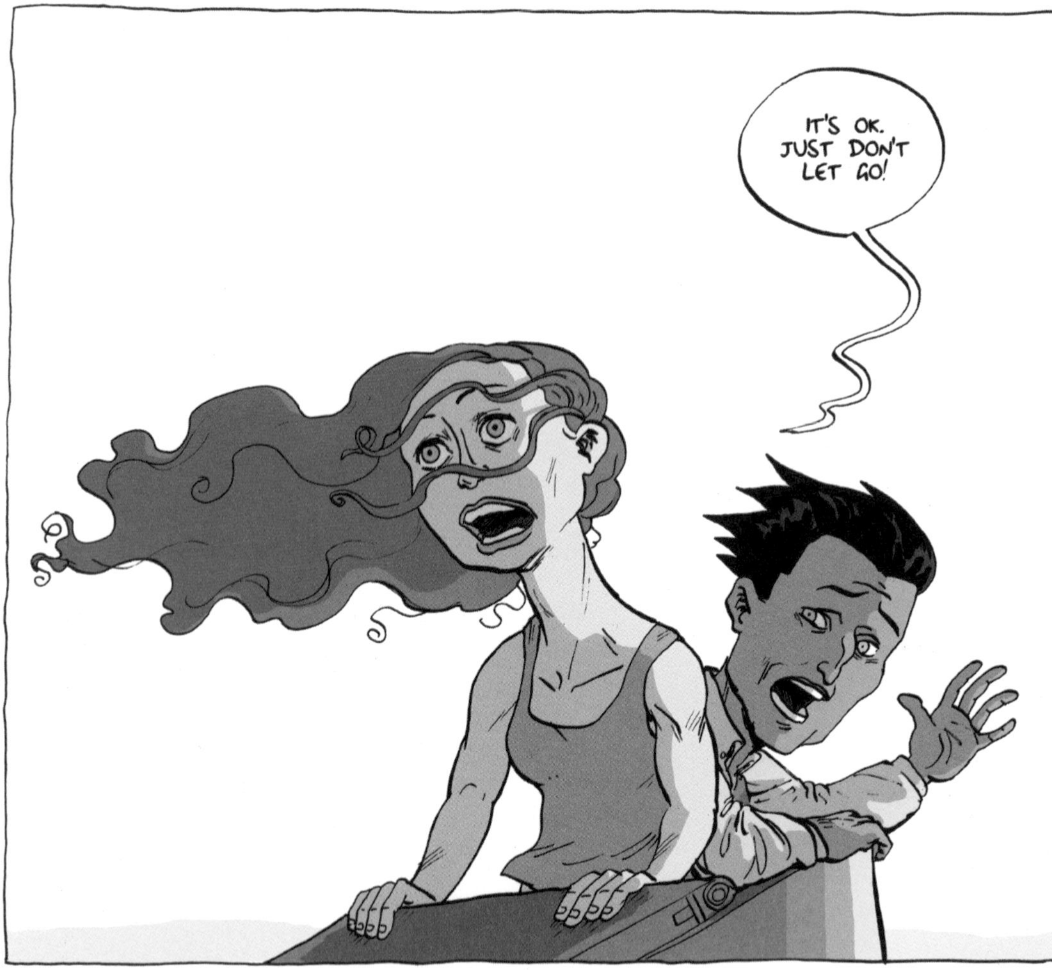
IT'S OK. JUST DON'T LET GO!

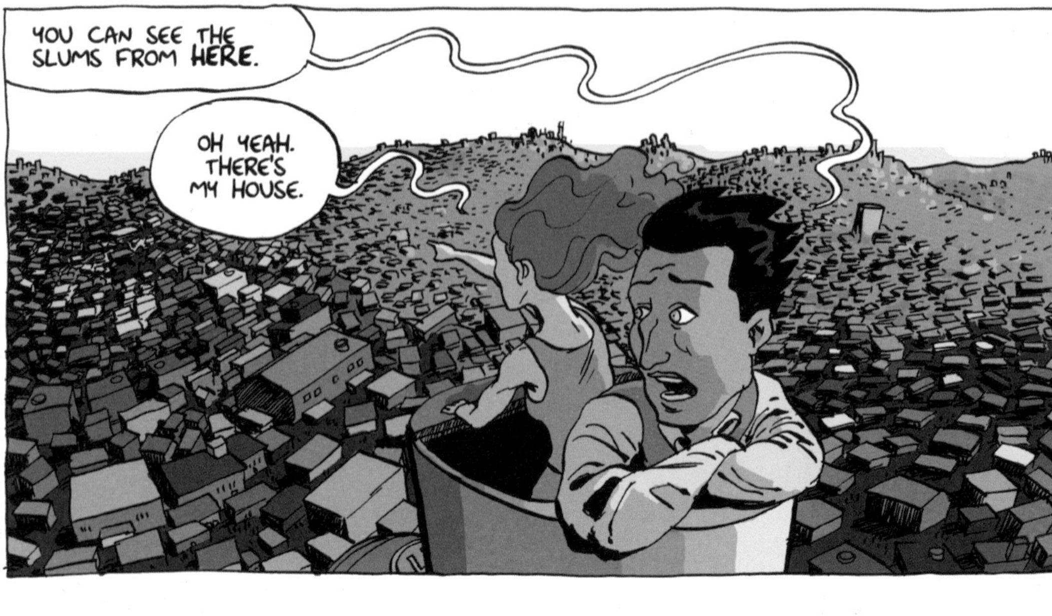
YOU CAN SEE THE SLUMS FROM HERE.
OH YEAH. THERE'S MY HOUSE.

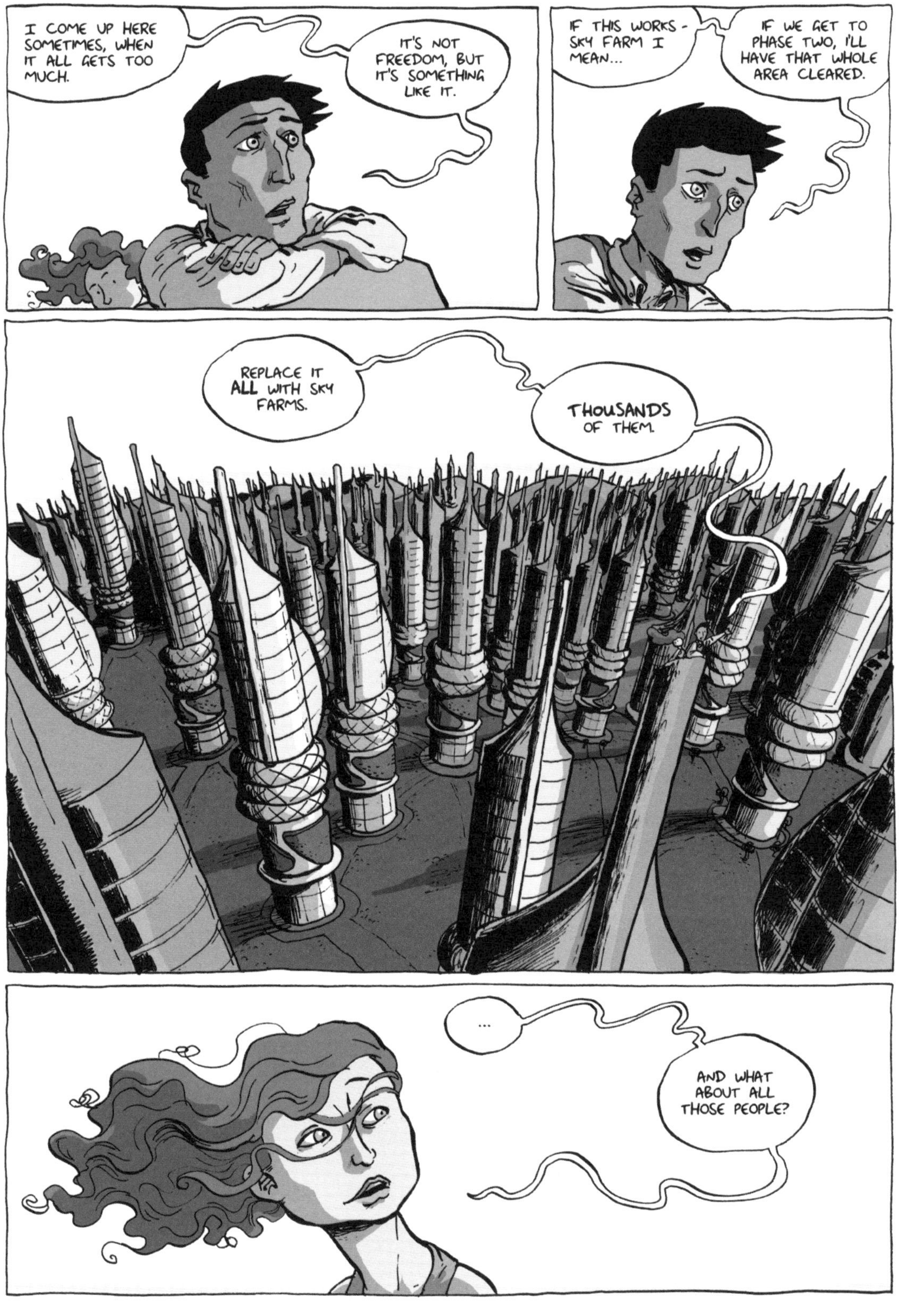
I COME UP HERE SOMETIMES, WHEN IT ALL GETS TOO MUCH.
IT'S NOT FREEDOM, BUT IT'S SOMETHING LIKE IT.
IF THIS WORKS - SKY FARM I MEAN...
IF WE GET TO PHASE TWO, I'LL HAVE THAT WHOLE AREA CLEARED.
REPLACE IT ALL WITH SKY FARMS.
THOUSANDS OF THEM.
...
AND WHAT ABOUT ALL THOSE PEOPLE?

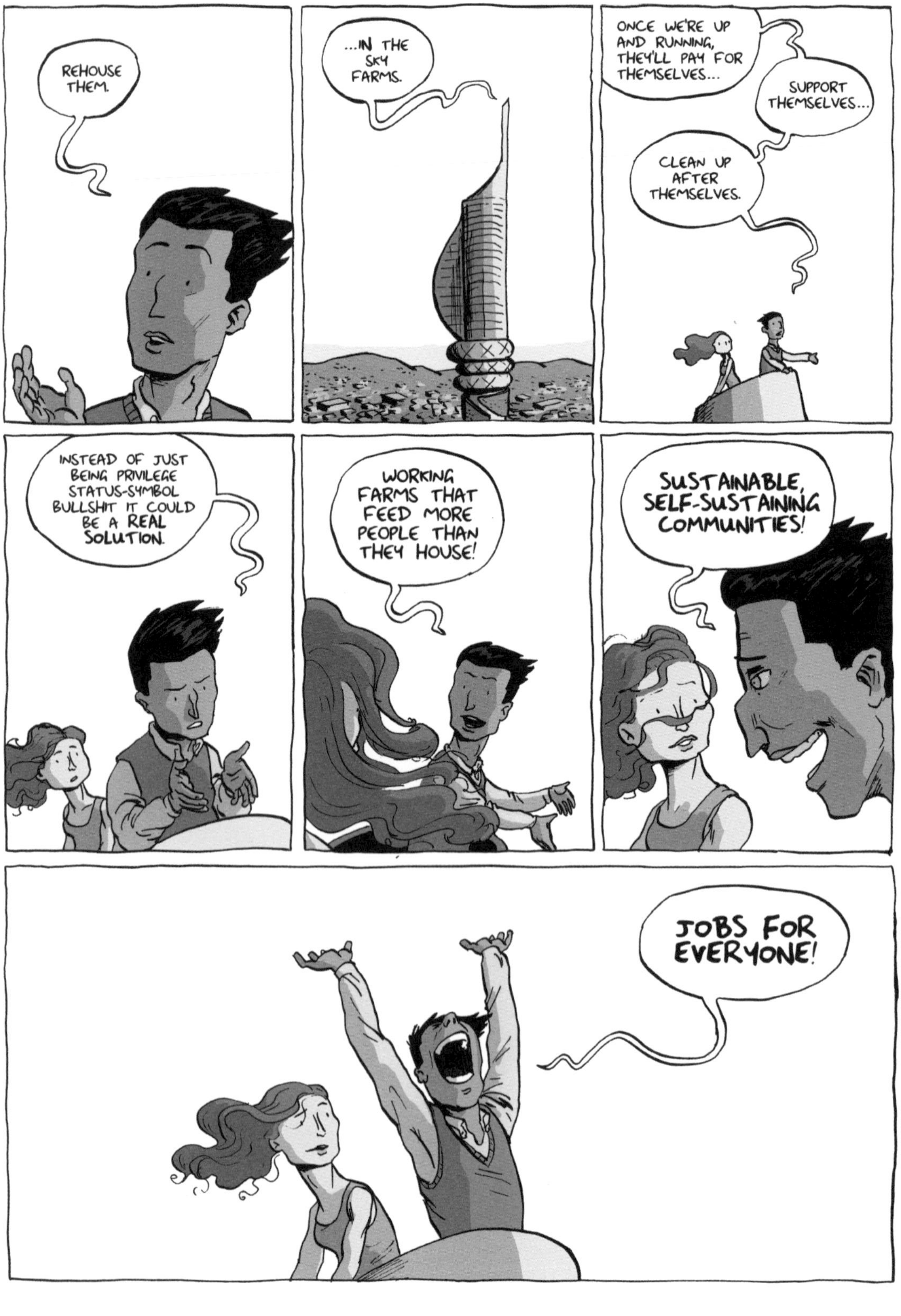
REHOUSE THEM.
...IN THE SKY FARMS.
ONCE WE'RE UP AND RUNNING, THEY'LL PAY FOR THEMSELVES...
SUPPORT THEMSELVES...
CLEAN UP AFTER THEMSELVES.
INSTEAD OF JUST BEING PRIVILEGE STATUS-SYMBOL BULLSHIT IT COULD BE A REAL SOLUTION.
WORKING FARMS THAT FEED MORE PEOPLE THAN THEY HOUSE!
SUSTAINABLE, SELF-SUSTAINING COMMUNITIES!
JOBS FOR EVERYONE!

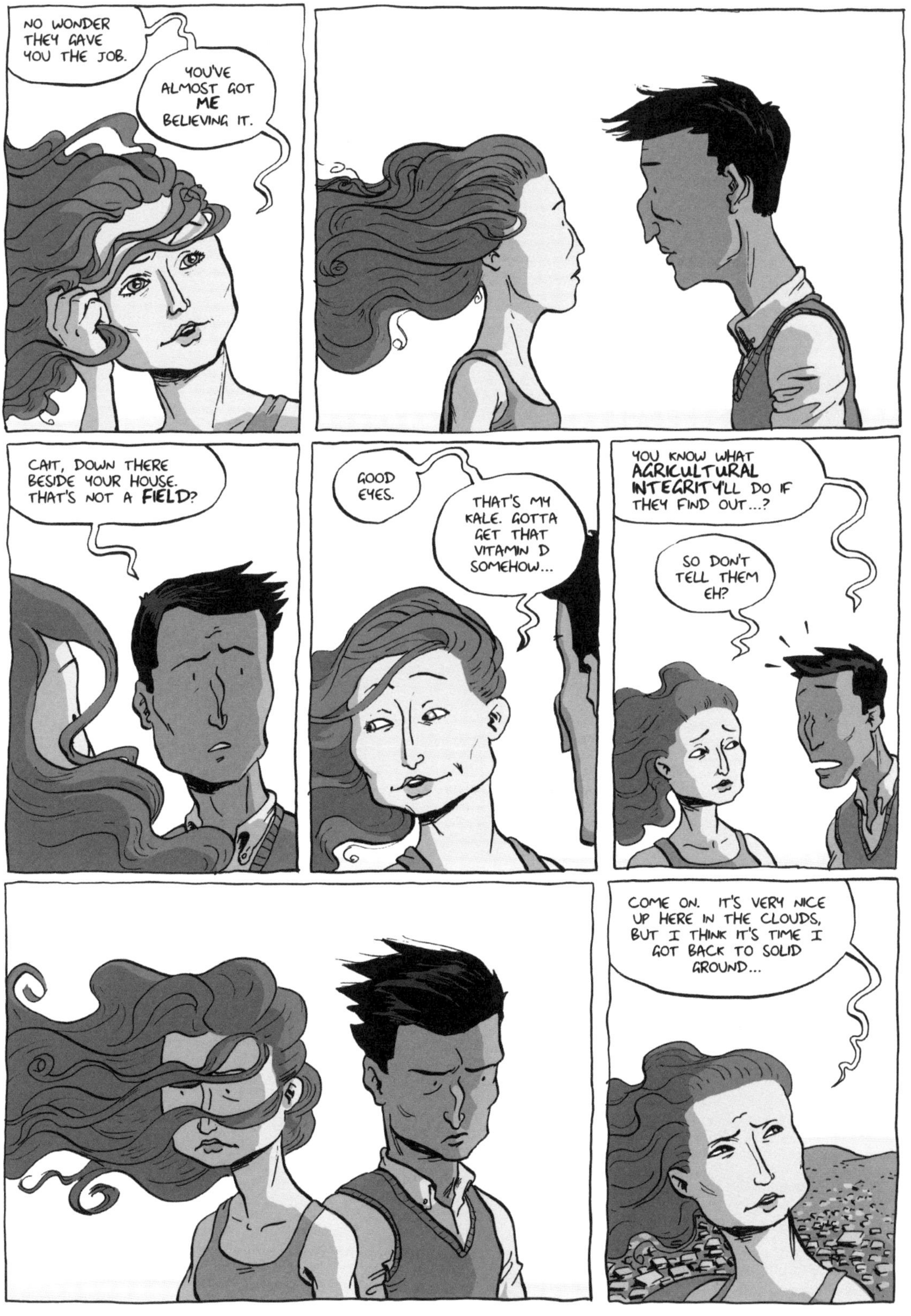
NO WONDER THEY GAVE YOU THE JOB.
YOU'VE ALMOST GOT **ME** BELIEVING IT.
CAIT, DOWN THERE BESIDE YOUR HOUSE. THAT'S NOT A **FIELD**?
GOOD EYES.
THAT'S MY KALE. GOTTA GET THAT VITAMIN D SOMEHOW...
YOU KNOW WHAT **AGRICULTURAL INTEGRITY**'LL DO IF THEY FIND OUT...?
SO DON'T TELL THEM EH?
COME ON. IT'S VERY NICE UP HERE IN THE CLOUDS, BUT I THINK IT'S TIME I GOT BACK TO SOLID GROUND...

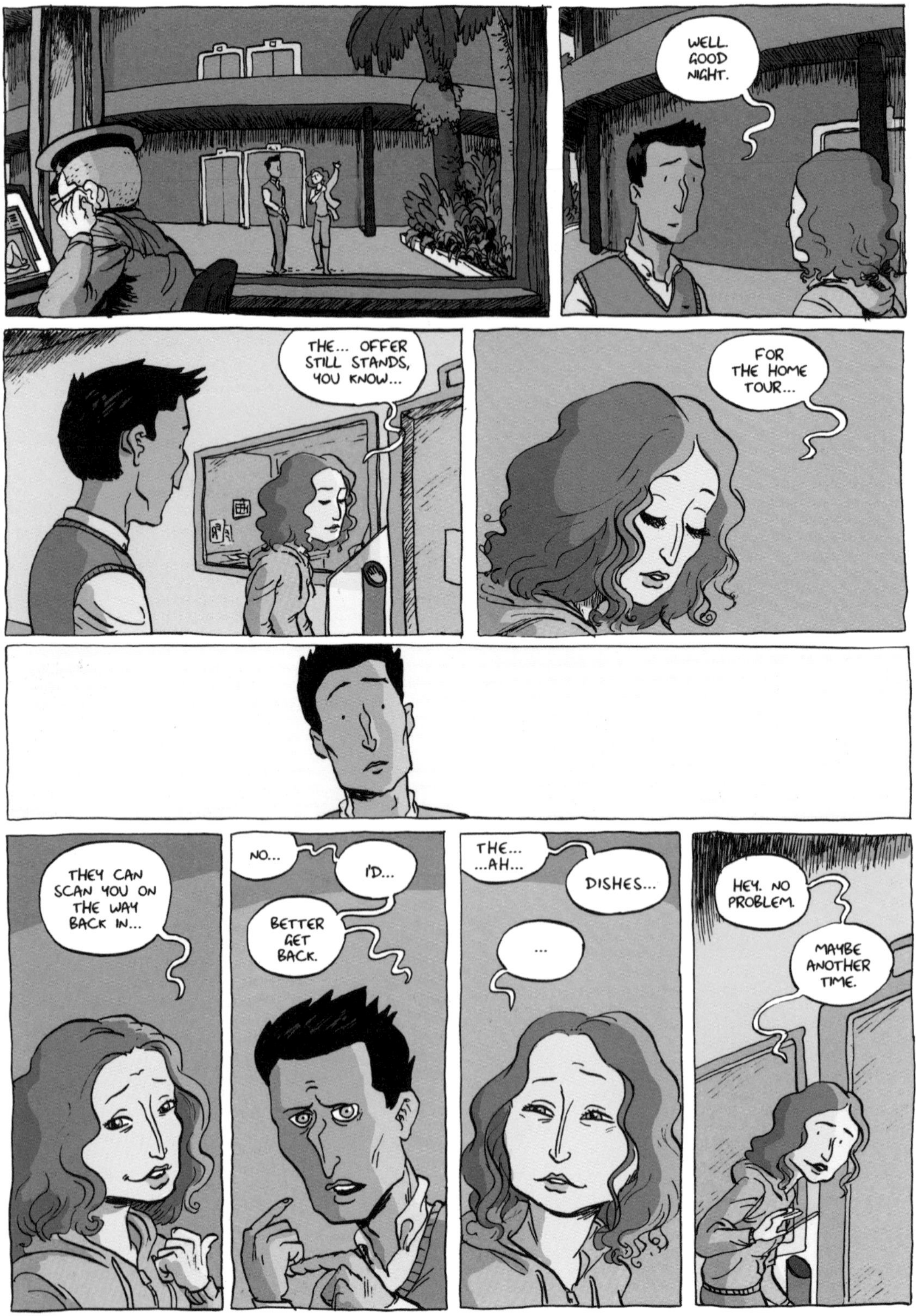
WELL. GOOD NIGHT.
THE... OFFER STILL STANDS, YOU KNOW...
FOR THE HOME TOUR...
THEY CAN SCAN YOU ON THE WAY BACK IN...
NO...
I'D...
BETTER GET BACK.
THE... ...AH...
DISHES...
...
HEY. NO PROBLEM.
MAYBE ANOTHER TIME.

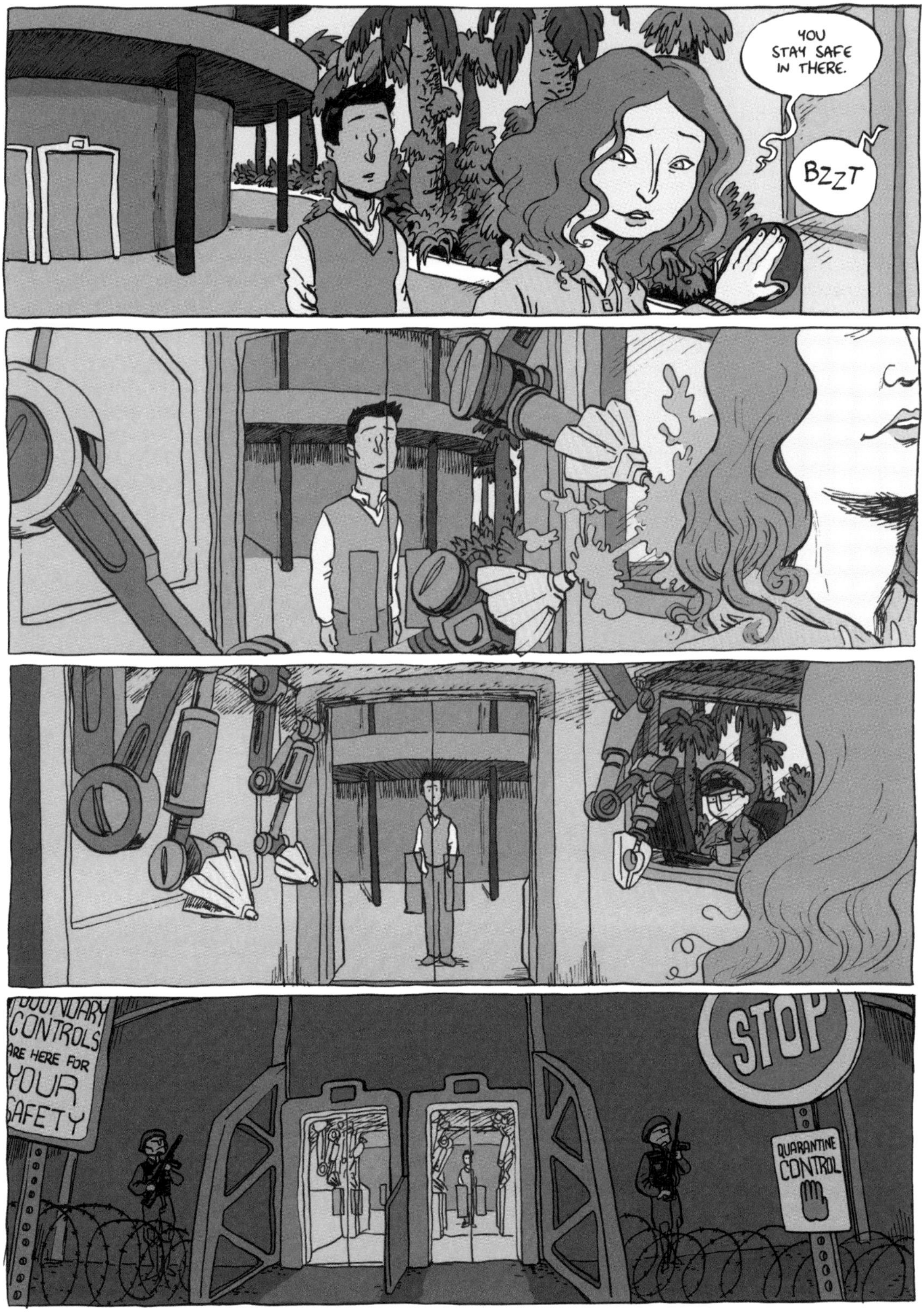
YOU STAY SAFE IN THERE.
BZZT
OUNDARY CONTROLS ARE HERE FOR YOUR AFETY
STOP
QUARANTINE CONTROL

IDP: 2043

Chapter 4

Irvine Welsh & Dan McDaid

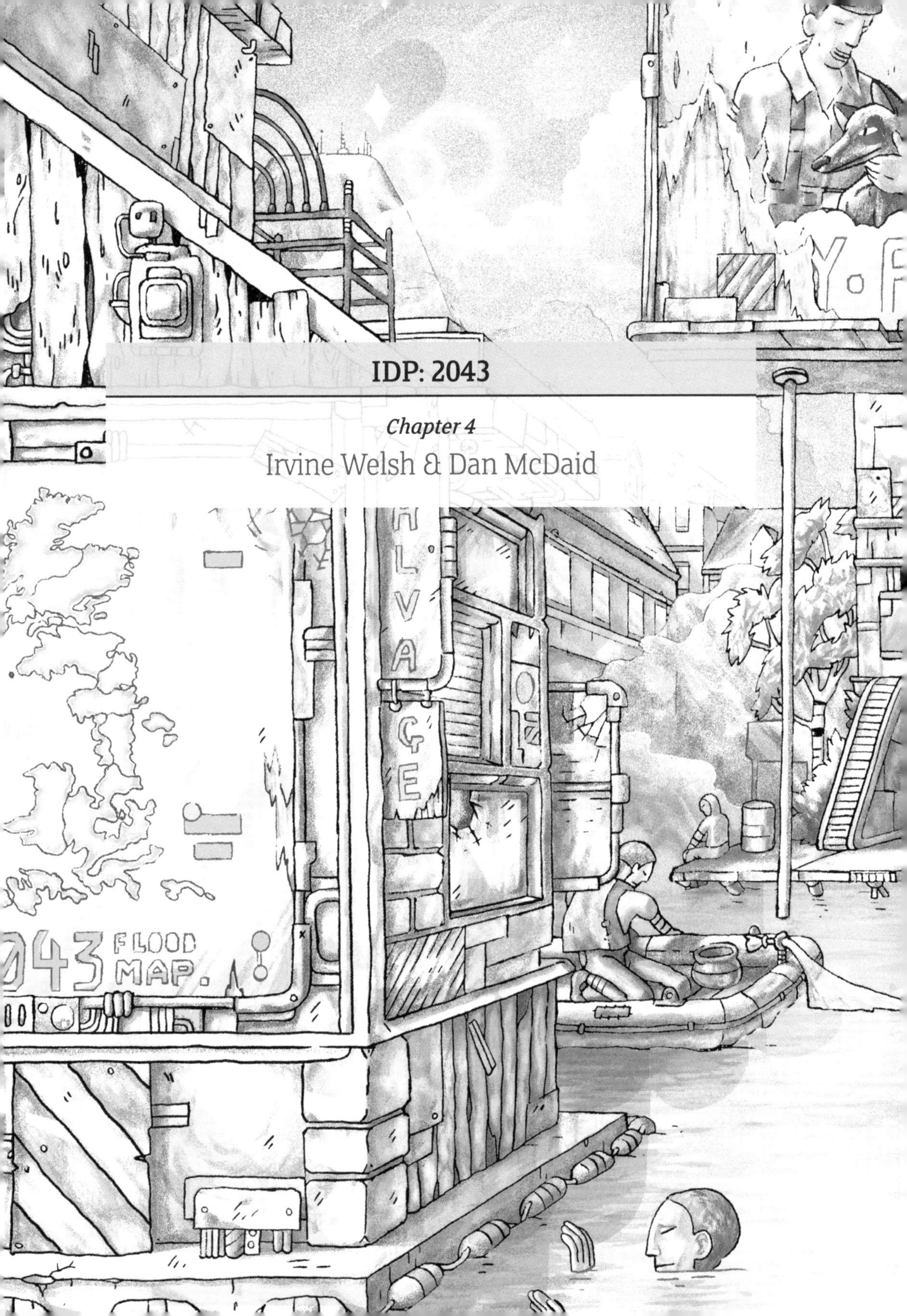
FLOOD MAP.

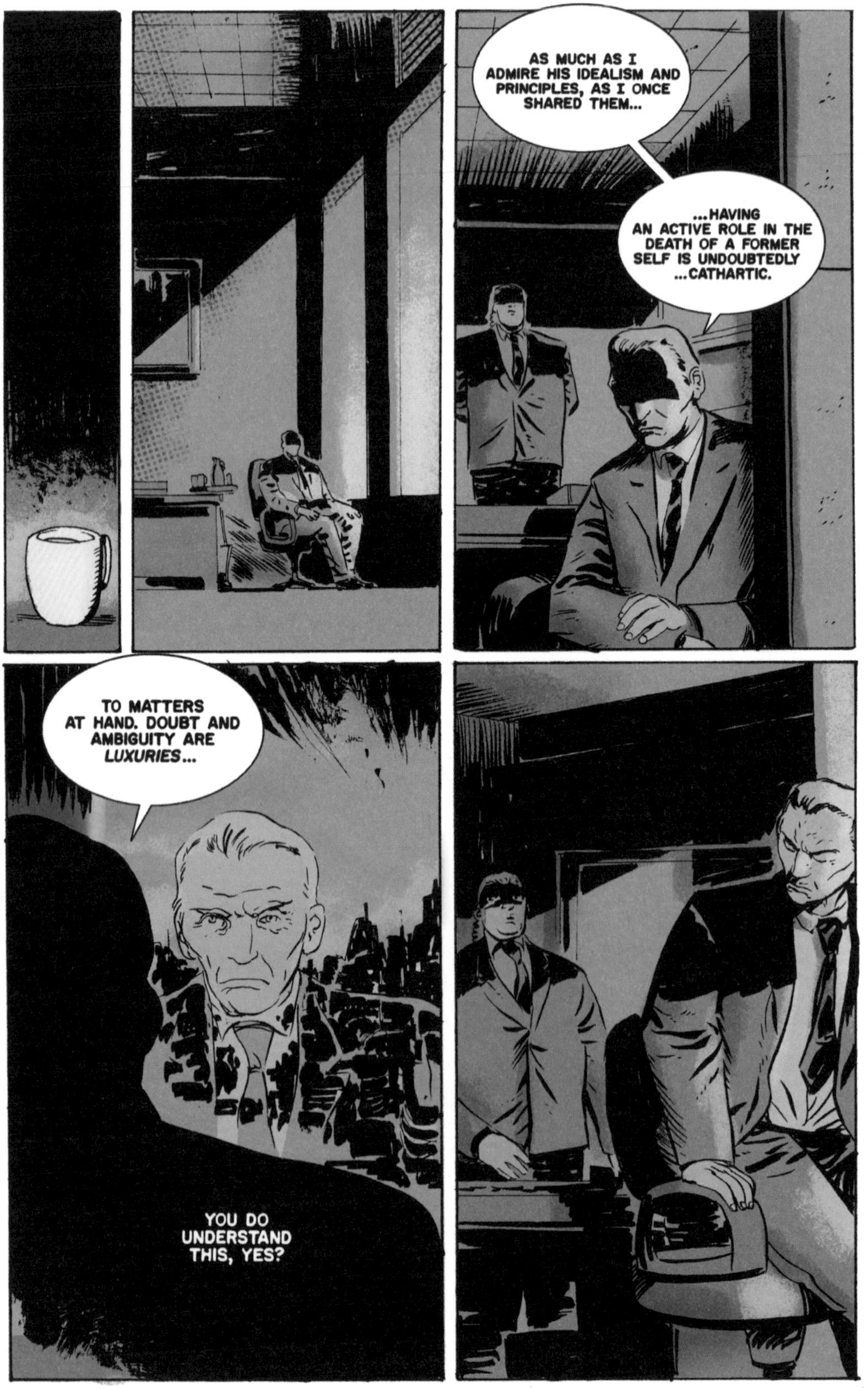
AS MUCH AS I ADMIRE HIS IDEALISM AND PRINCIPLES, AS I ONCE SHARED THEM...
...HAVING AN ACTIVE ROLE IN THE DEATH OF A FORMER SELF IS UNDOUBTEDLY ...CATHARTIC.
TO MATTERS AT HAND. DOUBT AND AMBIGUITY ARE *LUXURIES*...
YOU DO UNDERSTAND THIS, YES?

OF COURSE.

THE DOWNSIDE OF KILLING IS THAT IT BECOMES EASIER EACH TIME, AND SUCH A TEMPTING, LAZY WAY TO SOLVE ANY PERCEIVED PROBLEM.

AND THE DILEMMA IS THAT IF YOU ARE SEEN TO BE THAT SORT OF PERSON, THEN YOUR OWN DAYS BECOME NUMBERED.

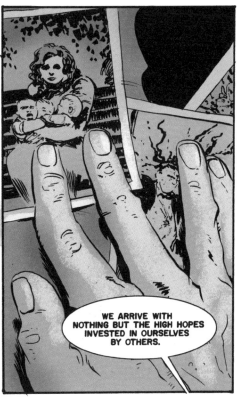

WE ARRIVE WITH NOTHING BUT THE HIGH HOPES INVESTED IN OURSELVES BY OTHERS.

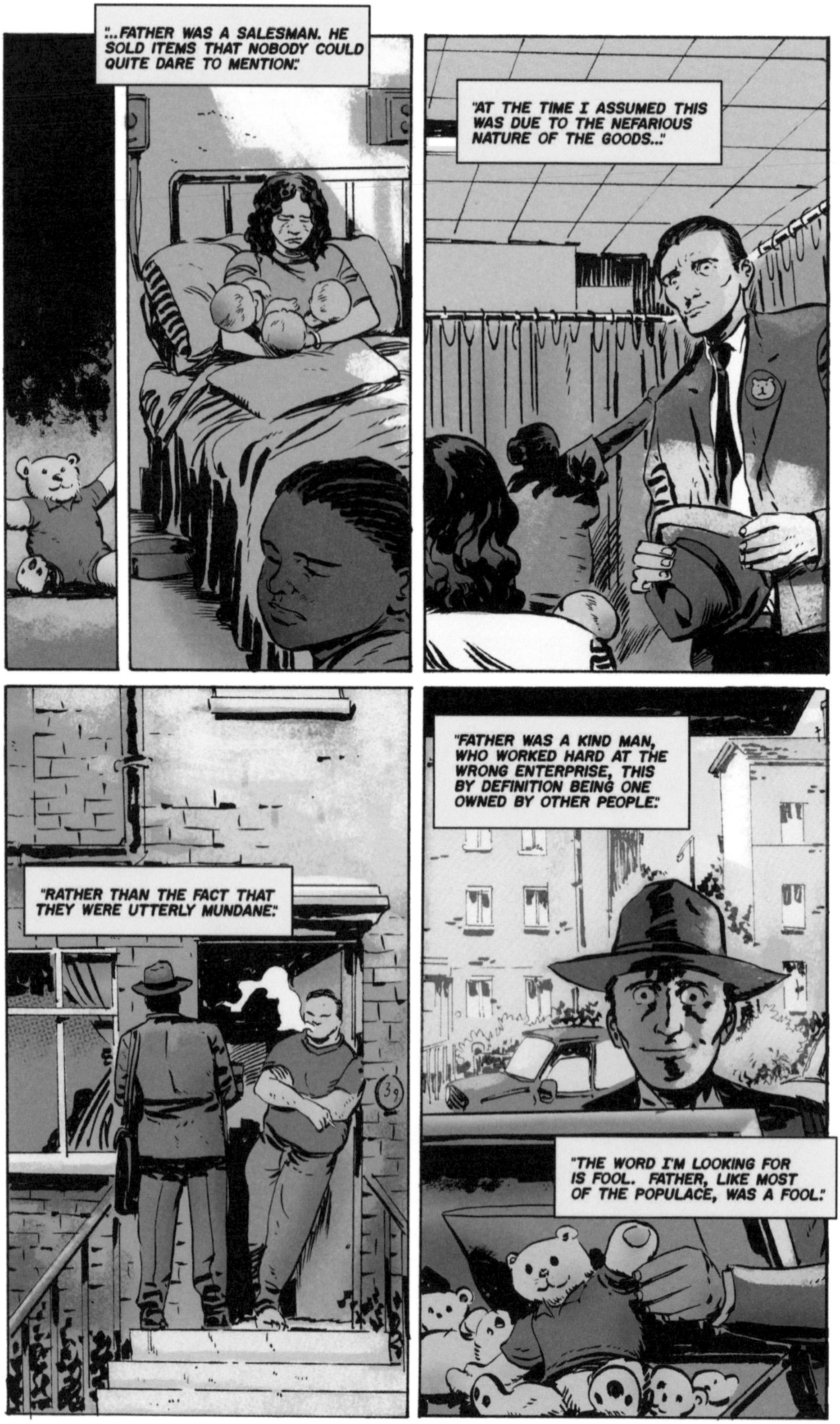
"...FATHER WAS A SALESMAN. HE SOLD ITEMS THAT NOBODY COULD QUITE DARE TO MENTION."
"AT THE TIME I ASSUMED THIS WAS DUE TO THE NEFARIOUS NATURE OF THE GOODS..."
"RATHER THAN THE FACT THAT THEY WERE UTTERLY MUNDANE."
39
"FATHER WAS A KIND MAN, WHO WORKED HARD AT THE WRONG ENTERPRISE, THIS BY DEFINITION BEING ONE OWNED BY OTHER PEOPLE."
"THE WORD I'M LOOKING FOR IS FOOL. FATHER, LIKE MOST OF THE POPULACE, WAS A FOOL."

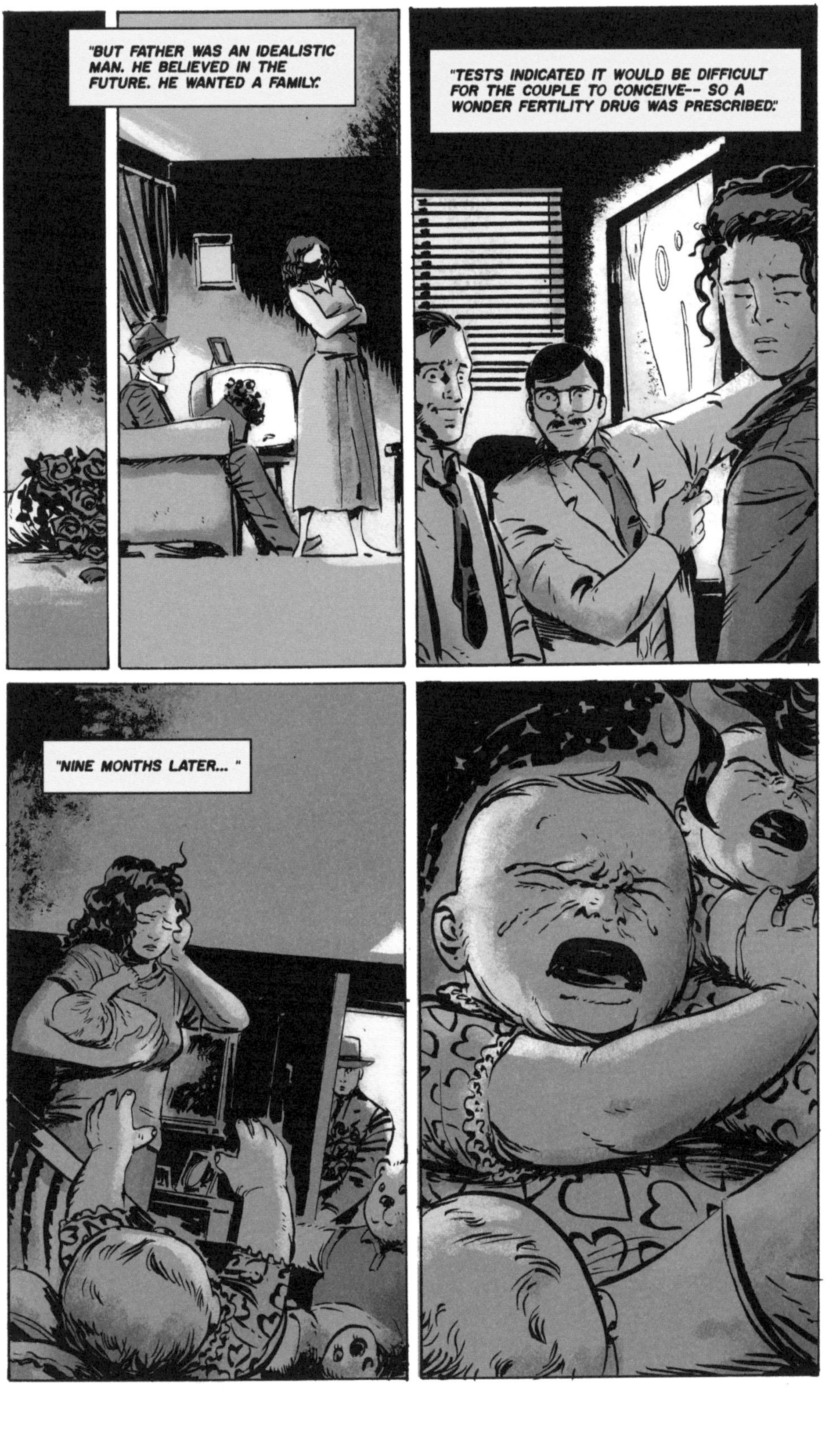
"BUT FATHER WAS AN IDEALISTIC MAN. HE BELIEVED IN THE FUTURE. HE WANTED A FAMILY."
"TESTS INDICATED IT WOULD BE DIFFICULT FOR THE COUPLE TO CONCEIVE-- SO A WONDER FERTILITY DRUG WAS PRESCRIBED."
"NINE MONTHS LATER... "

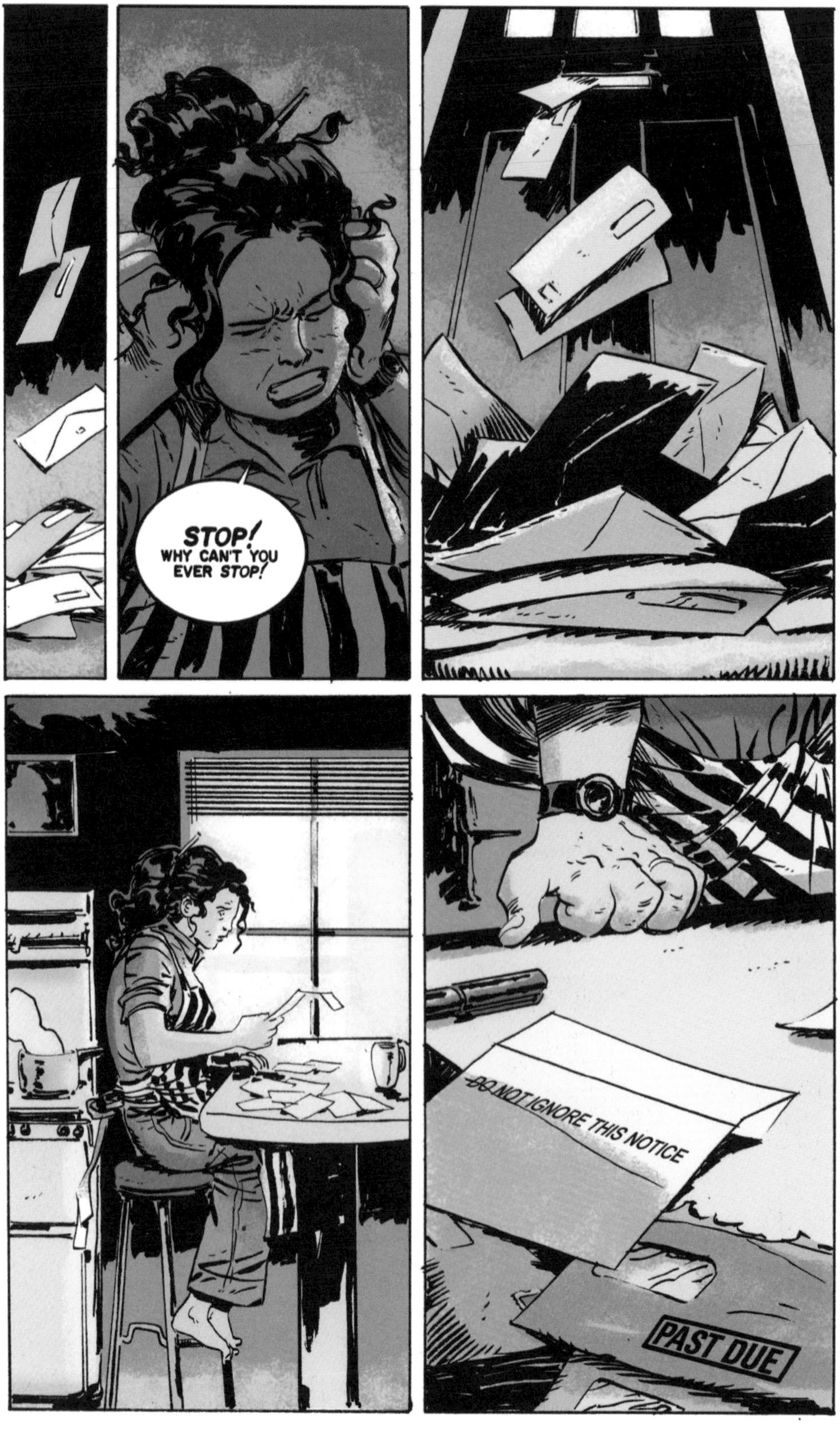
STOP! WHY CAN'T YOU EVER STOP!
DO NOT IGNORE THIS NOTICE
PAST DUE

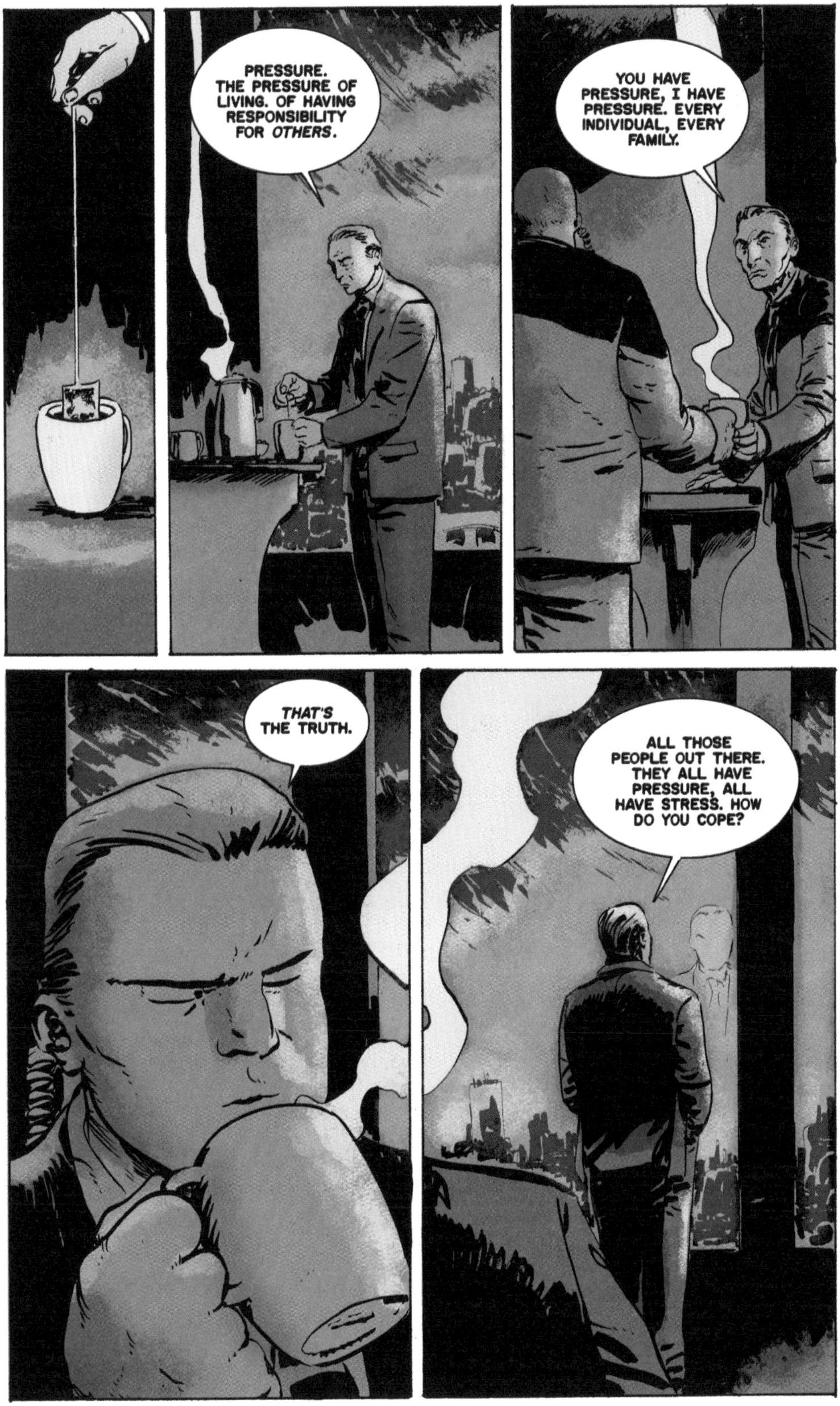
PRESSURE. THE PRESSURE OF LIVING. OF HAVING RESPONSIBILITY FOR *OTHERS*.
YOU HAVE PRESSURE, I HAVE PRESSURE. EVERY INDIVIDUAL, EVERY FAMILY.
THAT'S THE TRUTH.
ALL THOSE PEOPLE OUT THERE. THEY ALL HAVE PRESSURE, ALL HAVE STRESS. HOW DO YOU COPE?

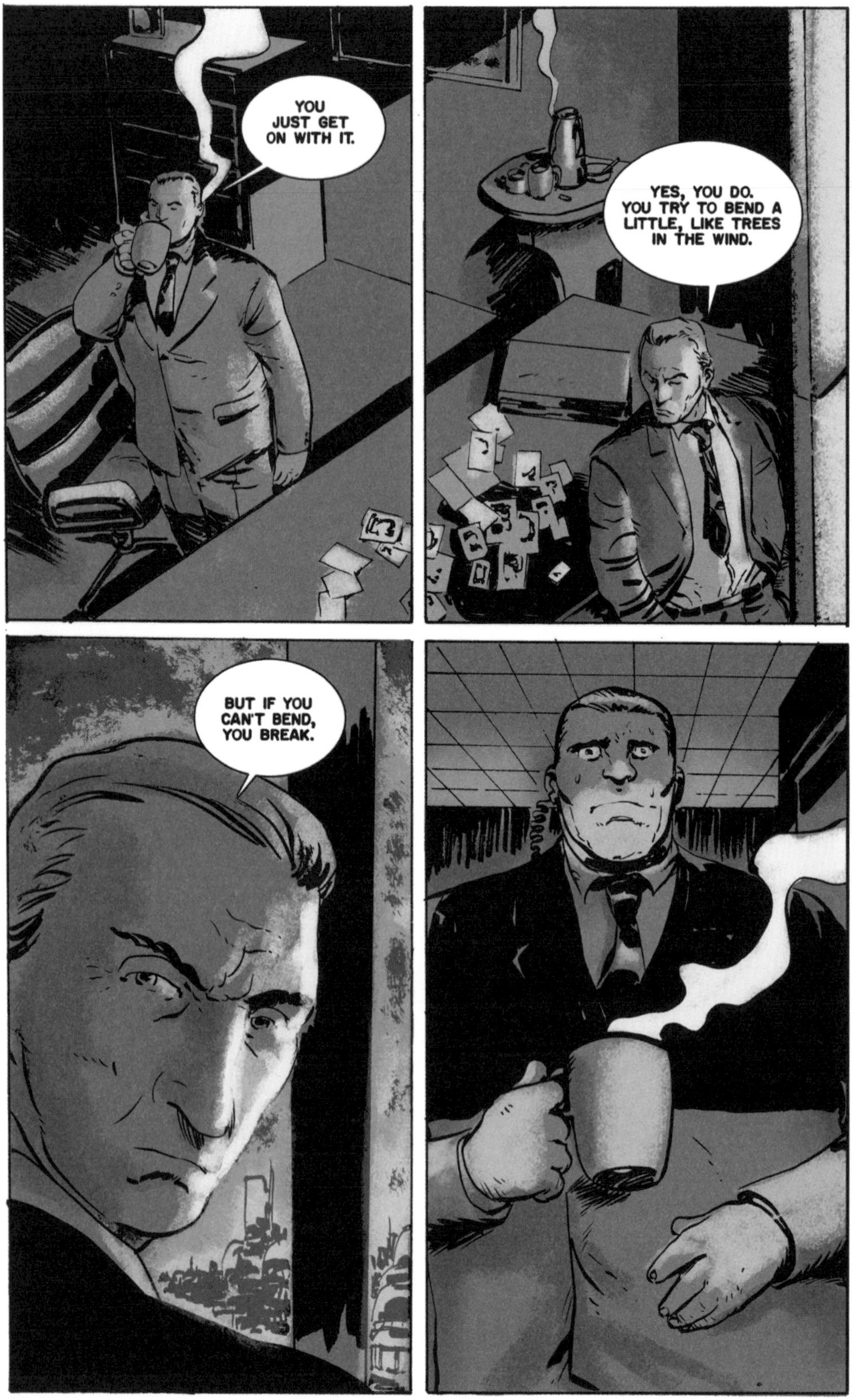
YOU JUST GET ON WITH IT.
YES, YOU DO. YOU TRY TO BEND A LITTLE, LIKE TREES IN THE WIND.
BUT IF YOU CAN'T BEND, YOU BREAK.

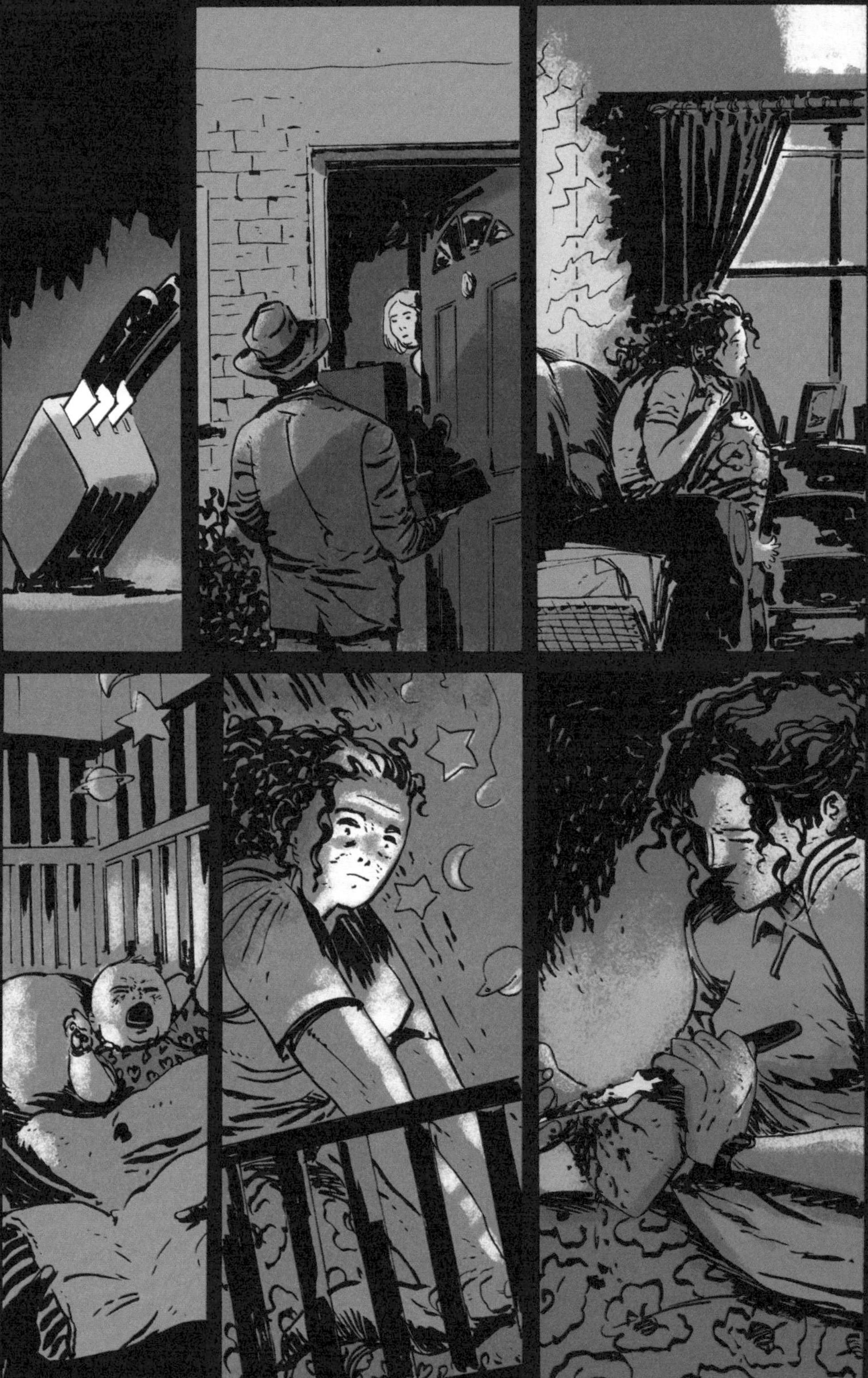

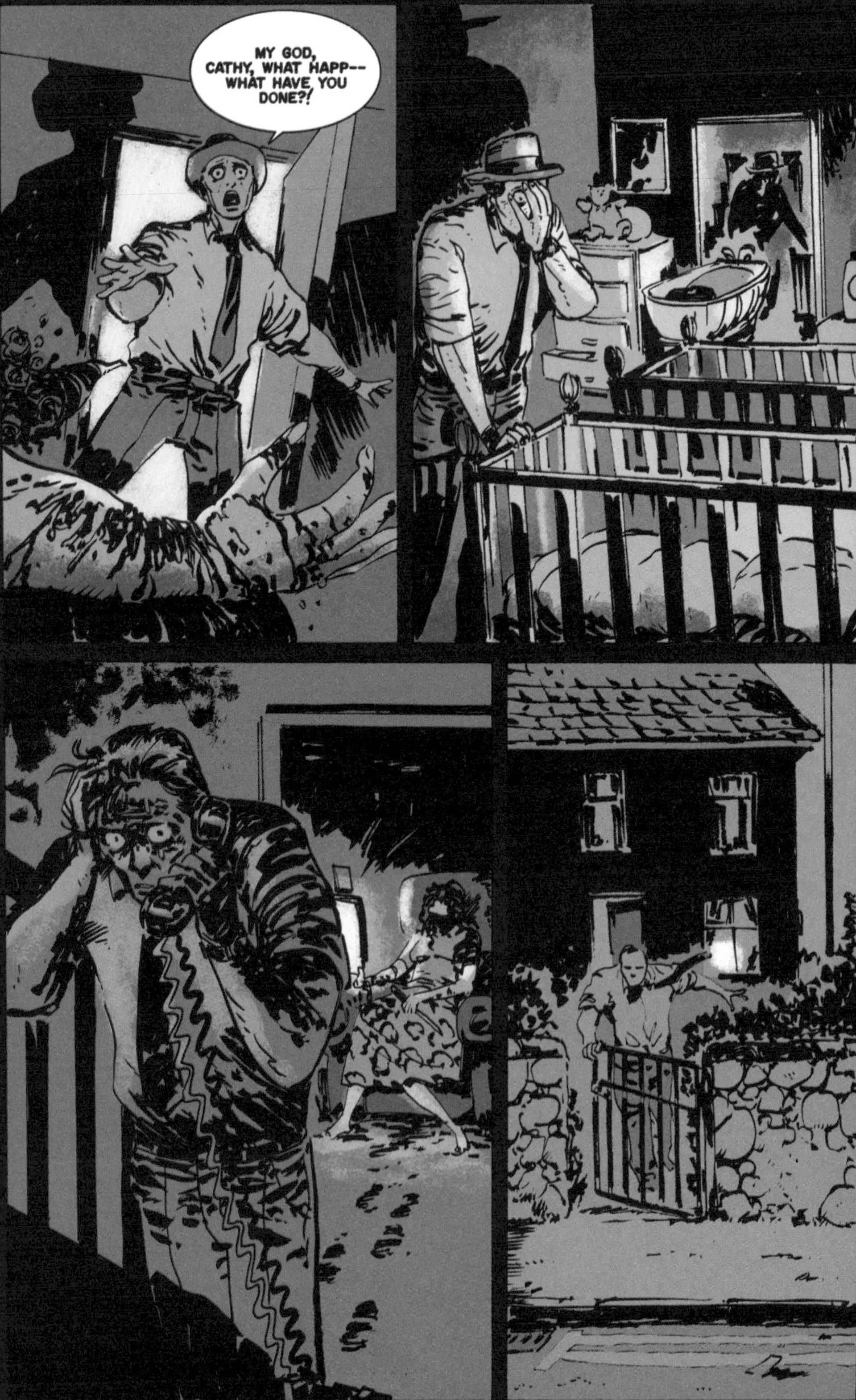
MY GOD, CATHY, WHAT HAPP-- WHAT HAVE YOU DONE?!

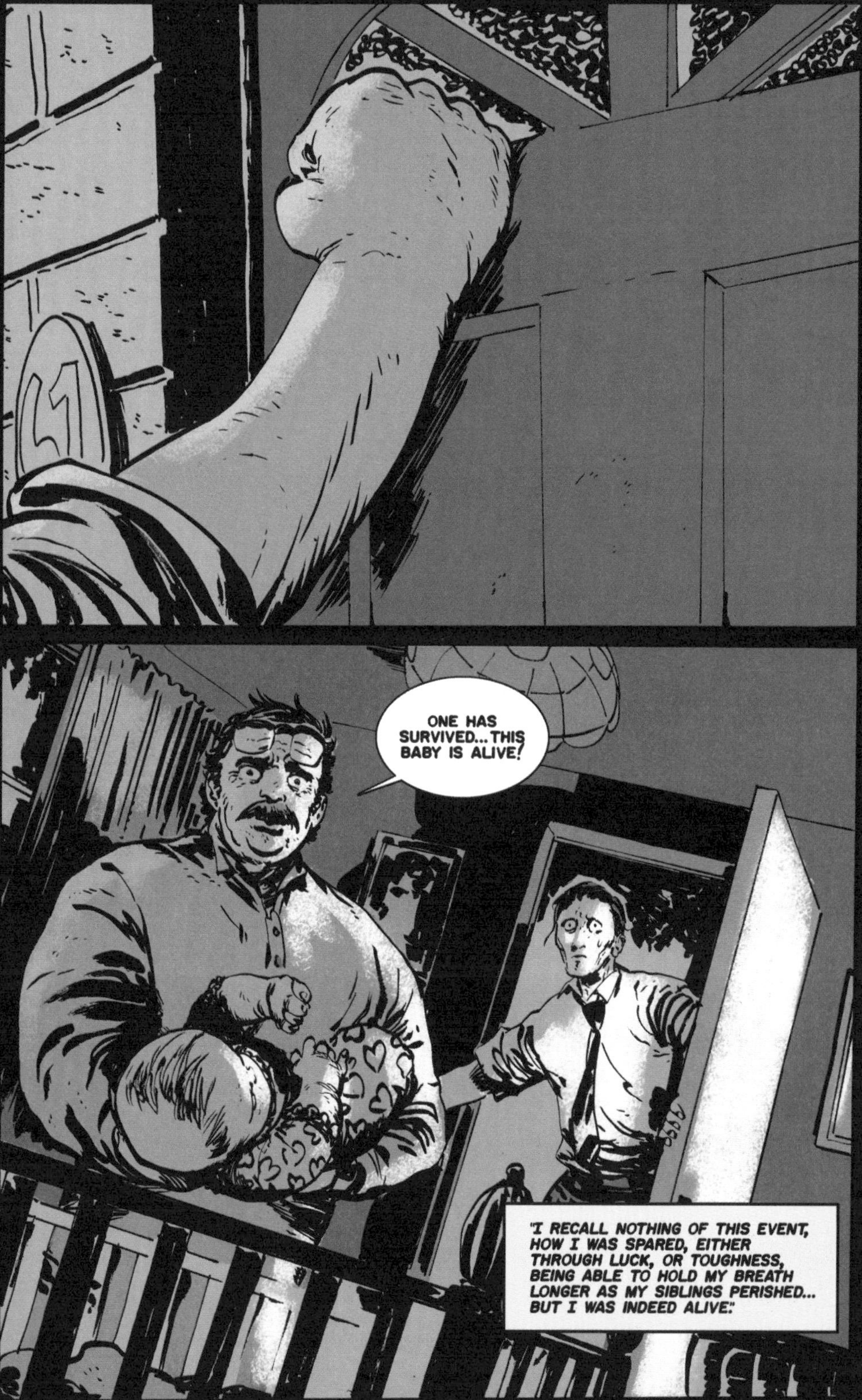
ONE HAS SURVIVED... THIS BABY IS ALIVE!
"I RECALL NOTHING OF THIS EVENT, HOW I WAS SPARED, EITHER THROUGH LUCK, OR TOUGHNESS, BEING ABLE TO HOLD MY BREATH LONGER AS MY SIBLINGS PERISHED... BUT I WAS INDEED ALIVE."

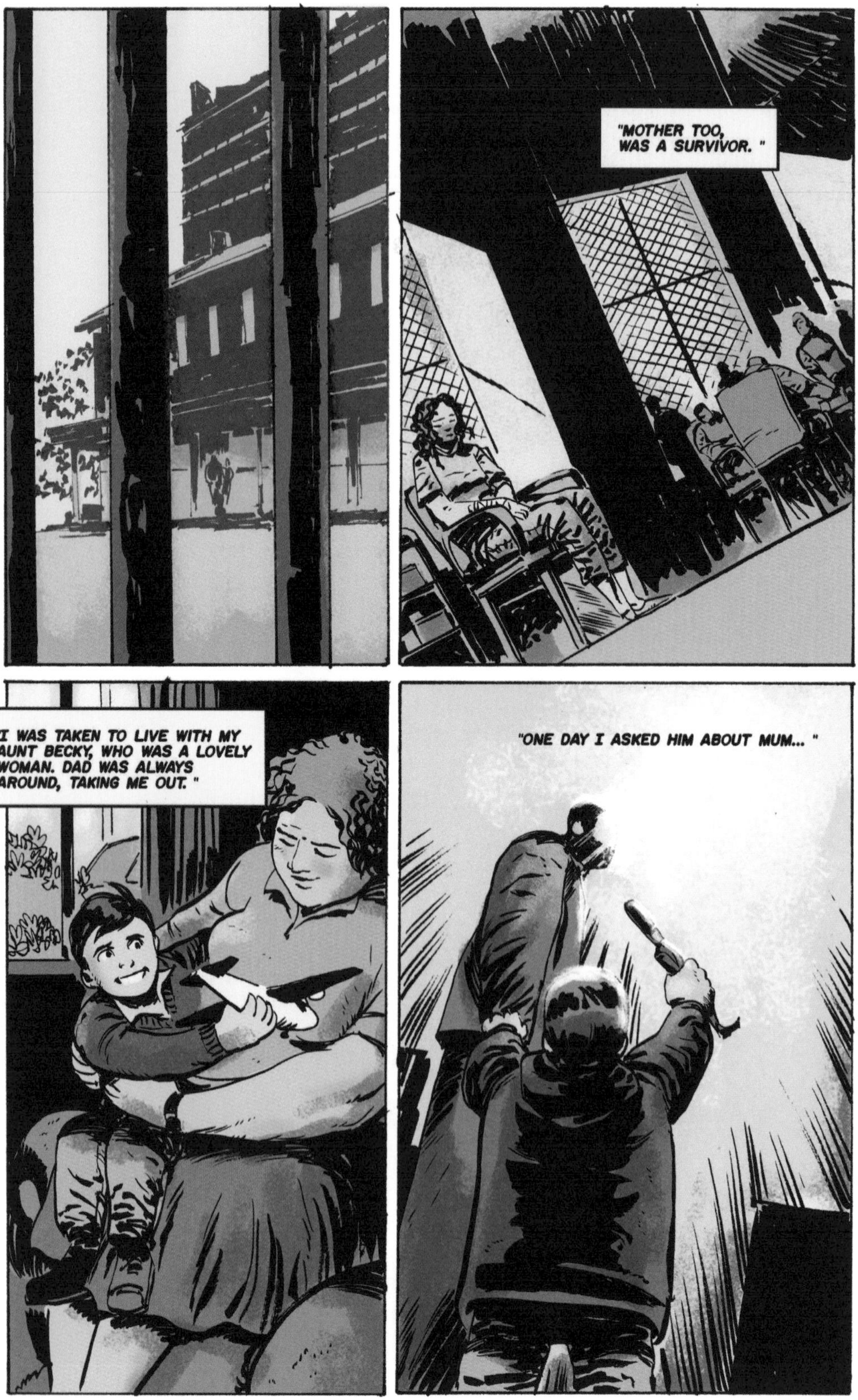
"MOTHER TOO, WAS A SURVIVOR. "
"I WAS TAKEN TO LIVE WITH MY AUNT BECKY, WHO WAS A LOVELY WOMAN. DAD WAS ALWAYS AROUND, TAKING ME OUT. "
"ONE DAY I ASKED HIM ABOUT MUM... "

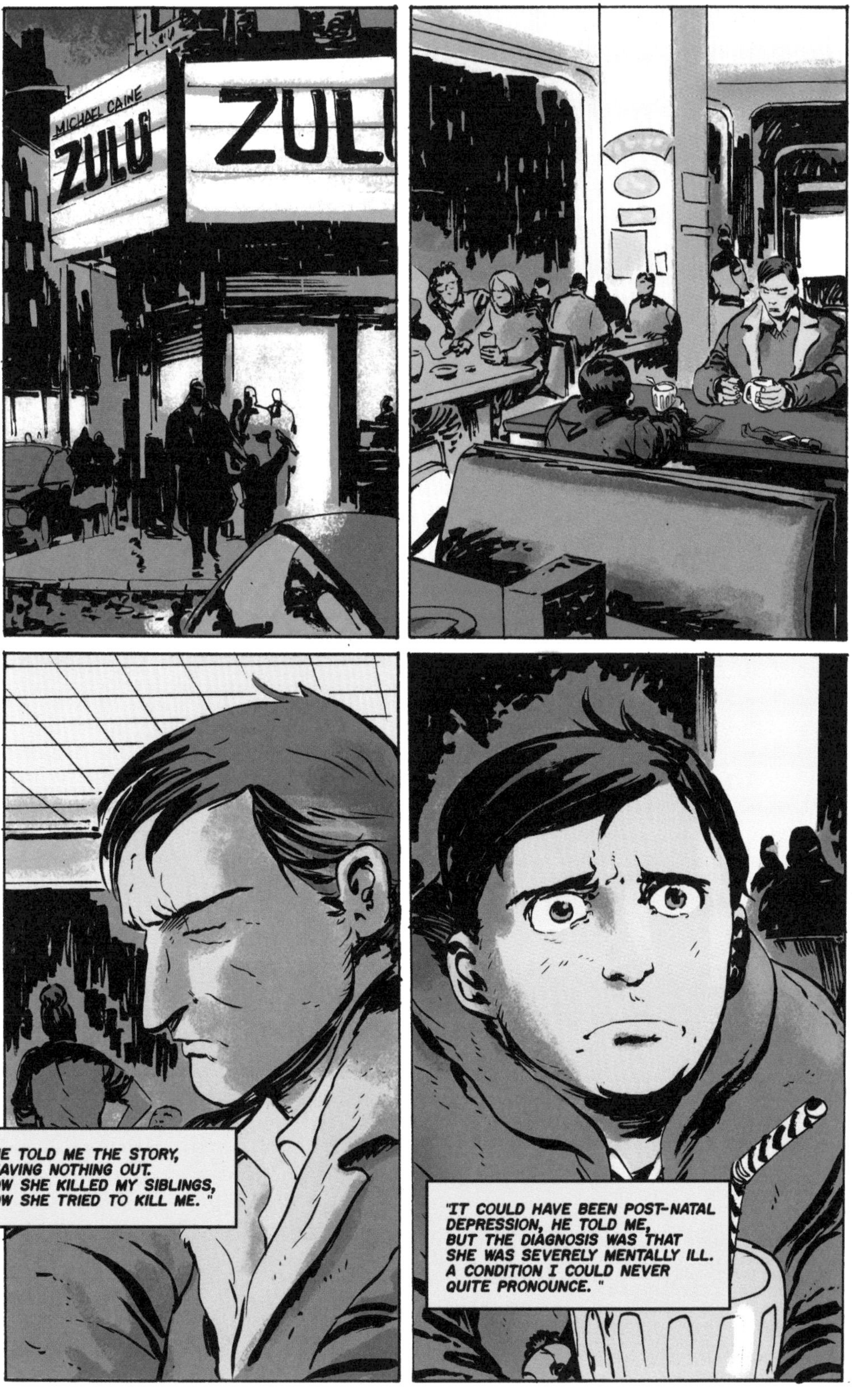
MICHAEL CAINE
ZULU
ZULU
"HE TOLD ME THE STORY, LEAVING NOTHING OUT. HOW SHE KILLED MY SIBLINGS, HOW SHE TRIED TO KILL ME."
"IT COULD HAVE BEEN POST-NATAL DEPRESSION, HE TOLD ME, BUT THE DIAGNOSIS WAS THAT SHE WAS SEVERELY MENTALLY ILL. A CONDITION I COULD NEVER QUITE PRONOUNCE."

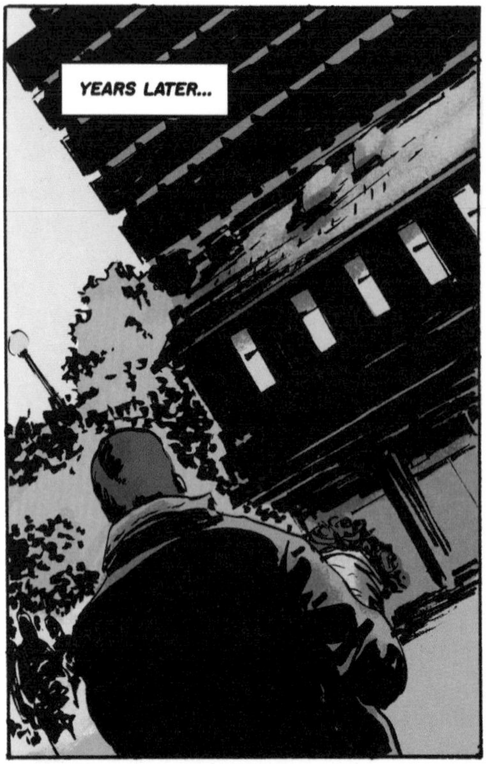
YEARS LATER...

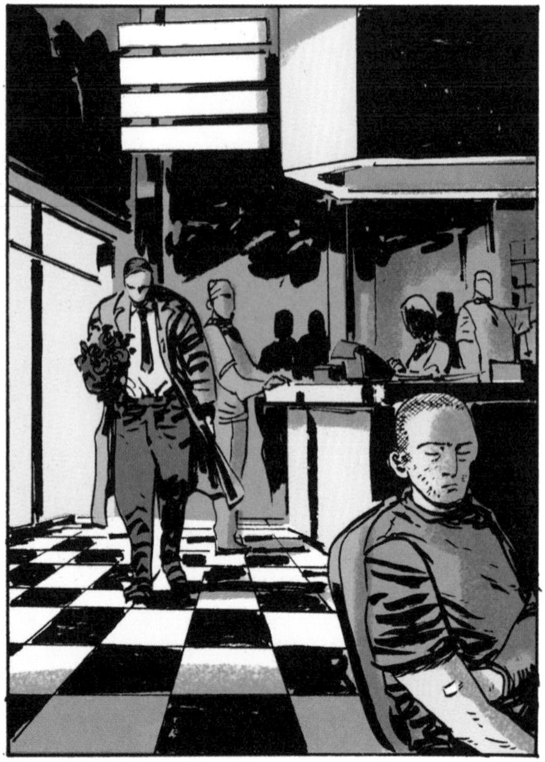

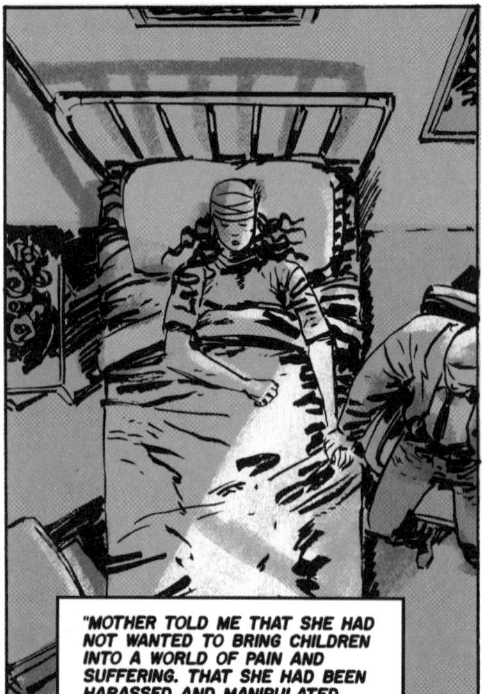
"MOTHER TOLD ME THAT SHE HAD NOT WANTED TO BRING CHILDREN INTO A WORLD OF PAIN AND SUFFERING. THAT SHE HAD BEEN HARASSED AND MANIPULATED INTO IT BY FATHER."

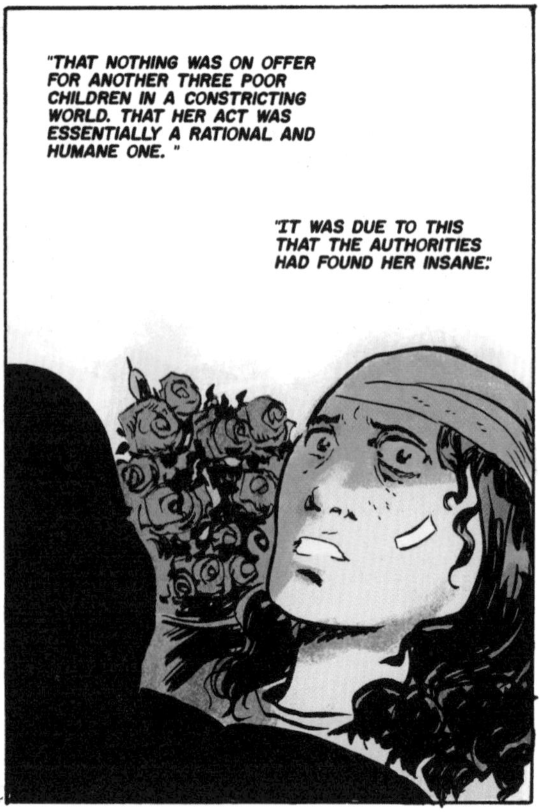
"THAT NOTHING WAS ON OFFER FOR ANOTHER THREE POOR CHILDREN IN A CONSTRICTING WORLD. THAT HER ACT WAS ESSENTIALLY A RATIONAL AND HUMANE ONE."
"IT WAS DUE TO THIS THAT THE AUTHORITIES HAD FOUND HER INSANE."

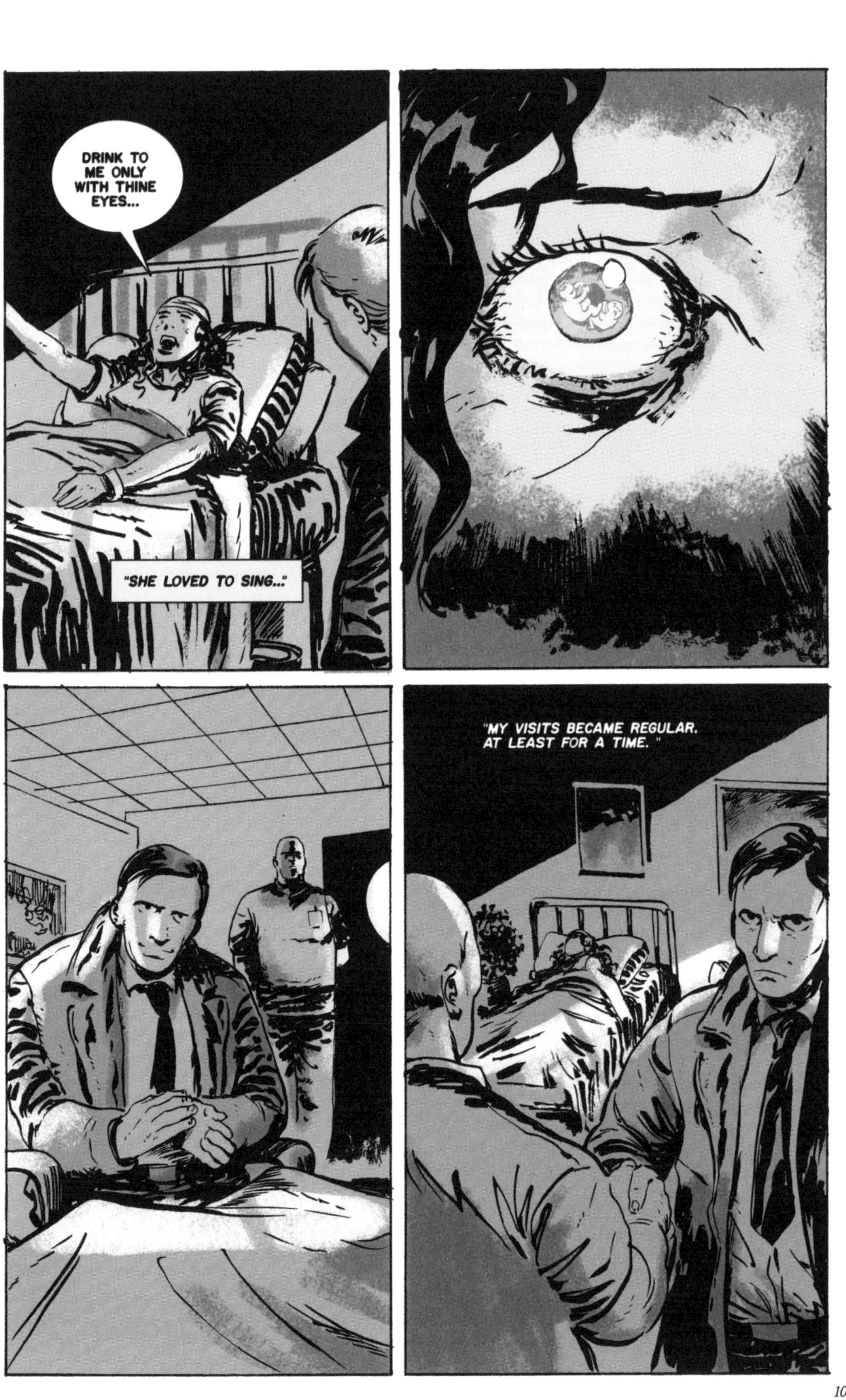
DRINK TO ME ONLY WITH THINE EYES...
"SHE LOVED TO SING..."
"MY VISITS BECAME REGULAR. AT LEAST FOR A TIME."

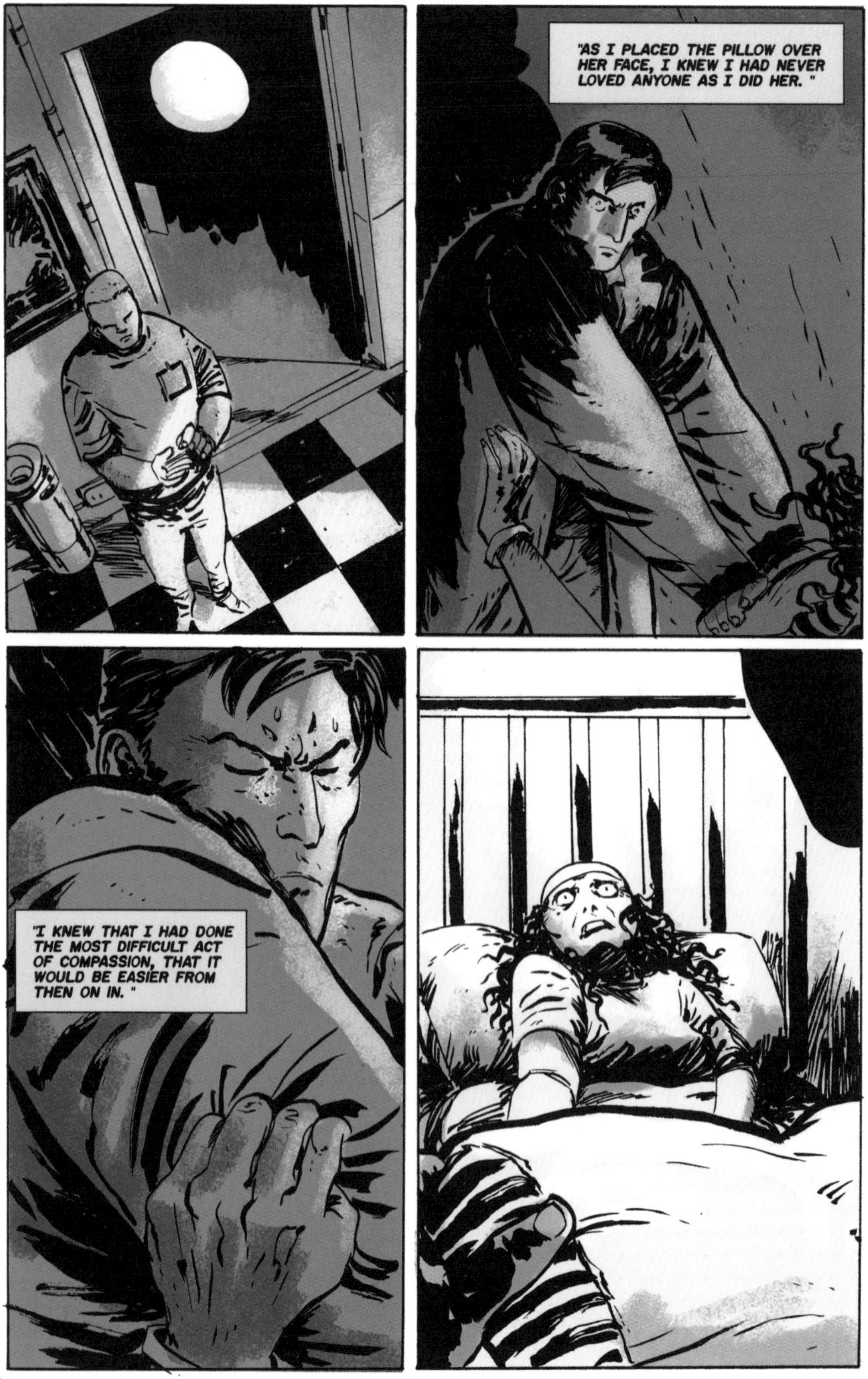
"AS I PLACED THE PILLOW OVER HER FACE, I KNEW I HAD NEVER LOVED ANYONE AS I DID HER."
"I KNEW THAT I HAD DONE THE MOST DIFFICULT ACT OF COMPASSION, THAT IT WOULD BE EASIER FROM THEN ON IN."

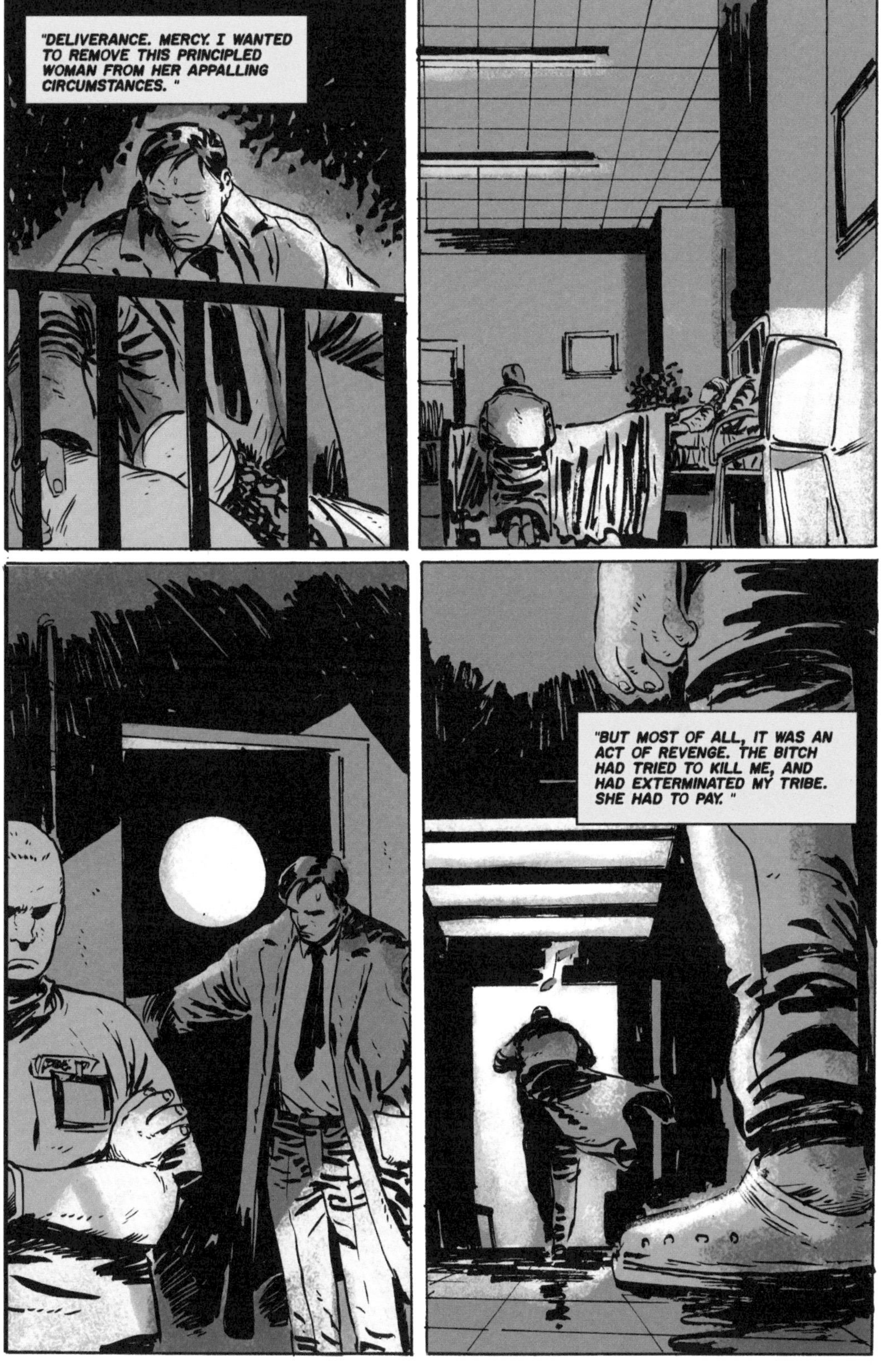
"DELIVERANCE. MERCY. I WANTED TO REMOVE THIS PRINCIPLED WOMAN FROM HER APPALLING CIRCUMSTANCES."
"BUT MOST OF ALL, IT WAS AN ACT OF REVENGE. THE BITCH HAD TRIED TO KILL ME, AND HAD EXTERMINATED MY TRIBE. SHE HAD TO PAY."

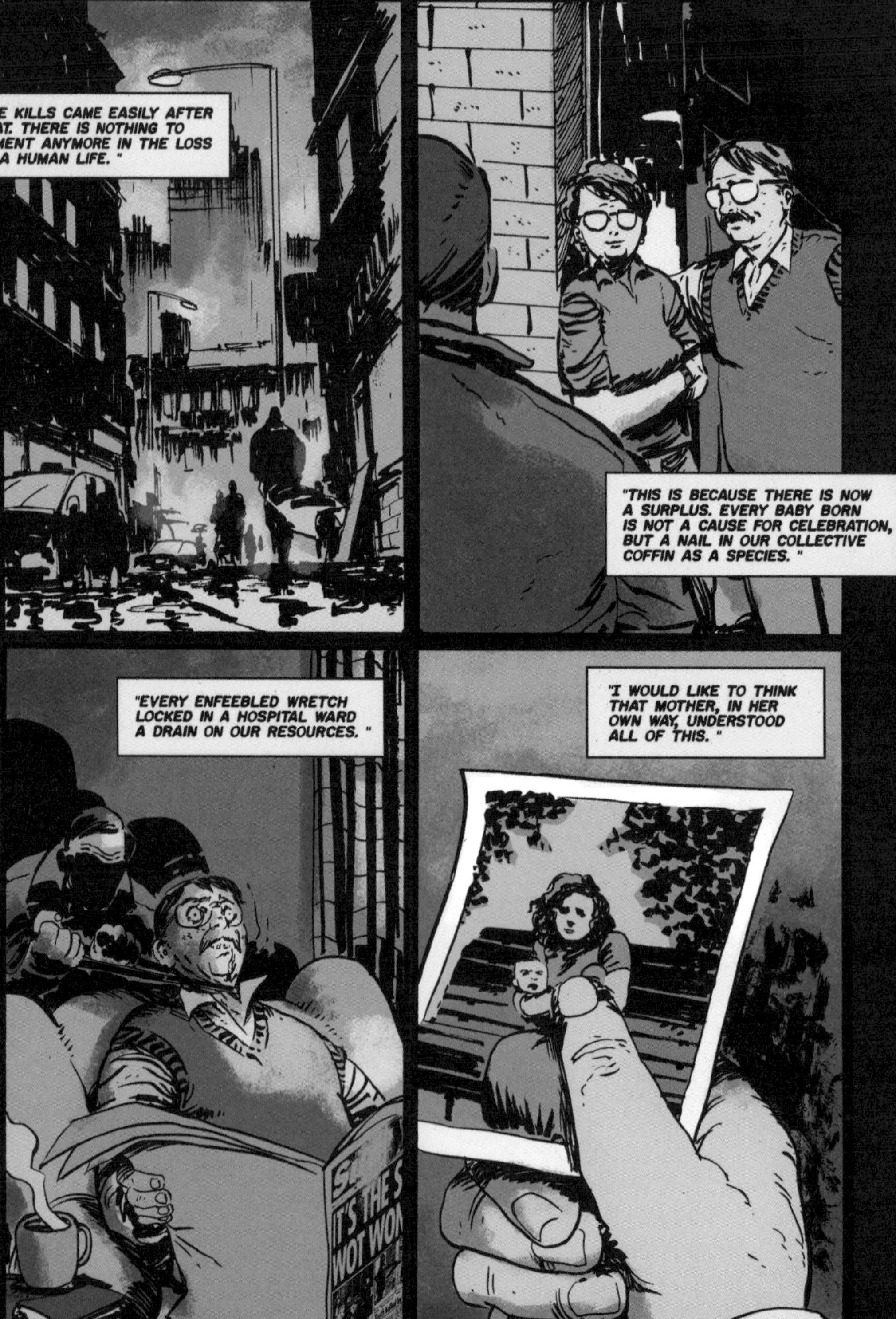
"THE KILLS CAME EASILY AFTER THAT. THERE IS NOTHING TO LAMENT ANYMORE IN THE LOSS OF A HUMAN LIFE."
"THIS IS BECAUSE THERE IS NOW A SURPLUS. EVERY BABY BORN IS NOT A CAUSE FOR CELEBRATION, BUT A NAIL IN OUR COLLECTIVE COFFIN AS A SPECIES."
"EVERY ENFEEBLED WRETCH LOCKED IN A HOSPITAL WARD A DRAIN ON OUR RESOURCES."
"I WOULD LIKE TO THINK THAT MOTHER, IN HER OWN WAY, UNDERSTOOD ALL OF THIS."

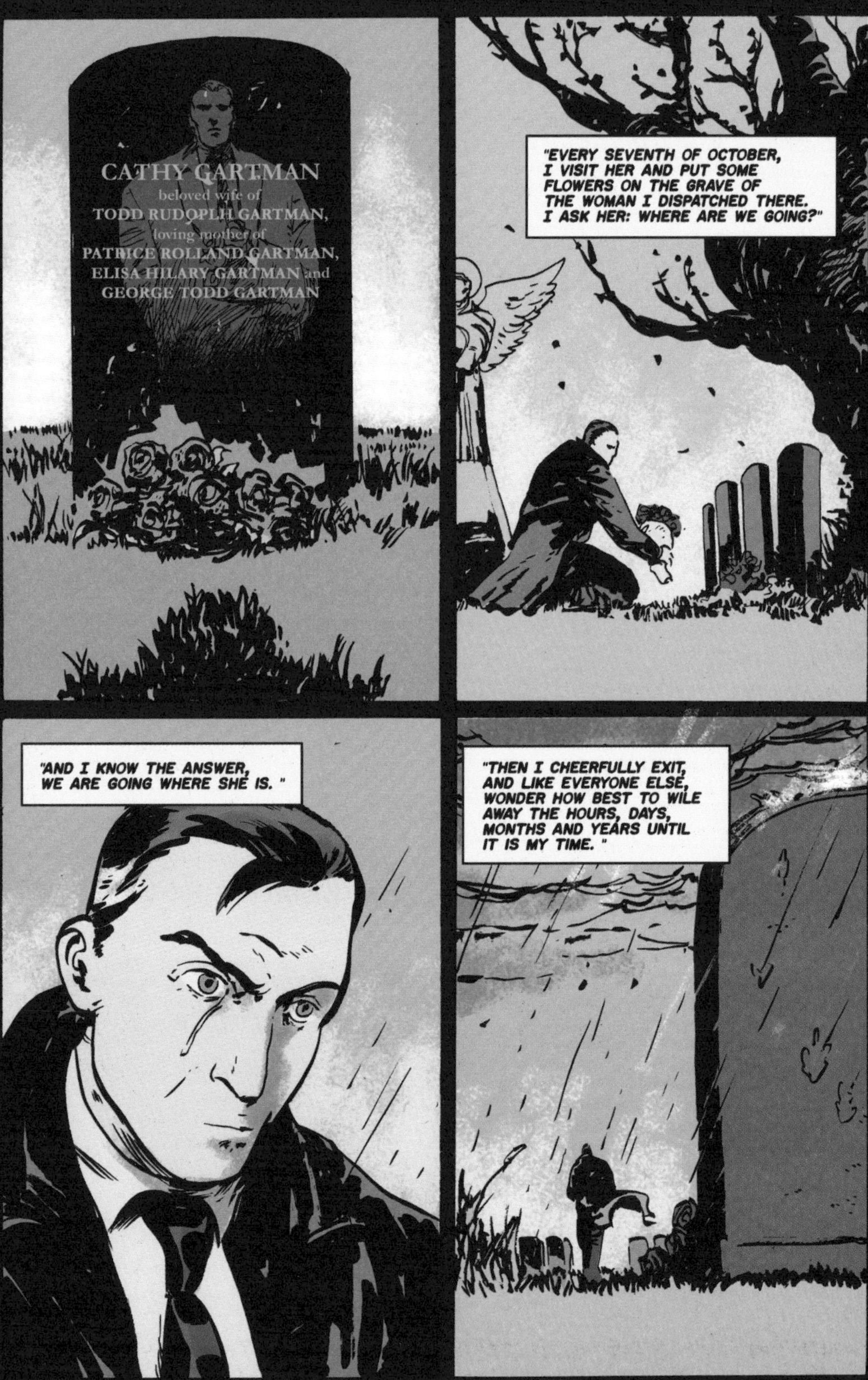
CATHY GARTMAN
beloved wife of
TODD RUDOPLH GARTMAN,
loving mother of
PATRICE ROLLAND GARTMAN,
ELISA HILARY GARTMAN and
GEORGE TODD GARTMAN
"EVERY SEVENTH OF OCTOBER, I VISIT HER AND PUT SOME FLOWERS ON THE GRAVE OF THE WOMAN I DISPATCHED THERE. I ASK HER: WHERE ARE WE GOING?"
"AND I KNOW THE ANSWER, WE ARE GOING WHERE SHE IS."
"THEN I CHEERFULLY EXIT, AND LIKE EVERYONE ELSE, WONDER HOW BEST TO WILE AWAY THE HOURS, DAYS, MONTHS AND YEARS UNTIL IT IS MY TIME."

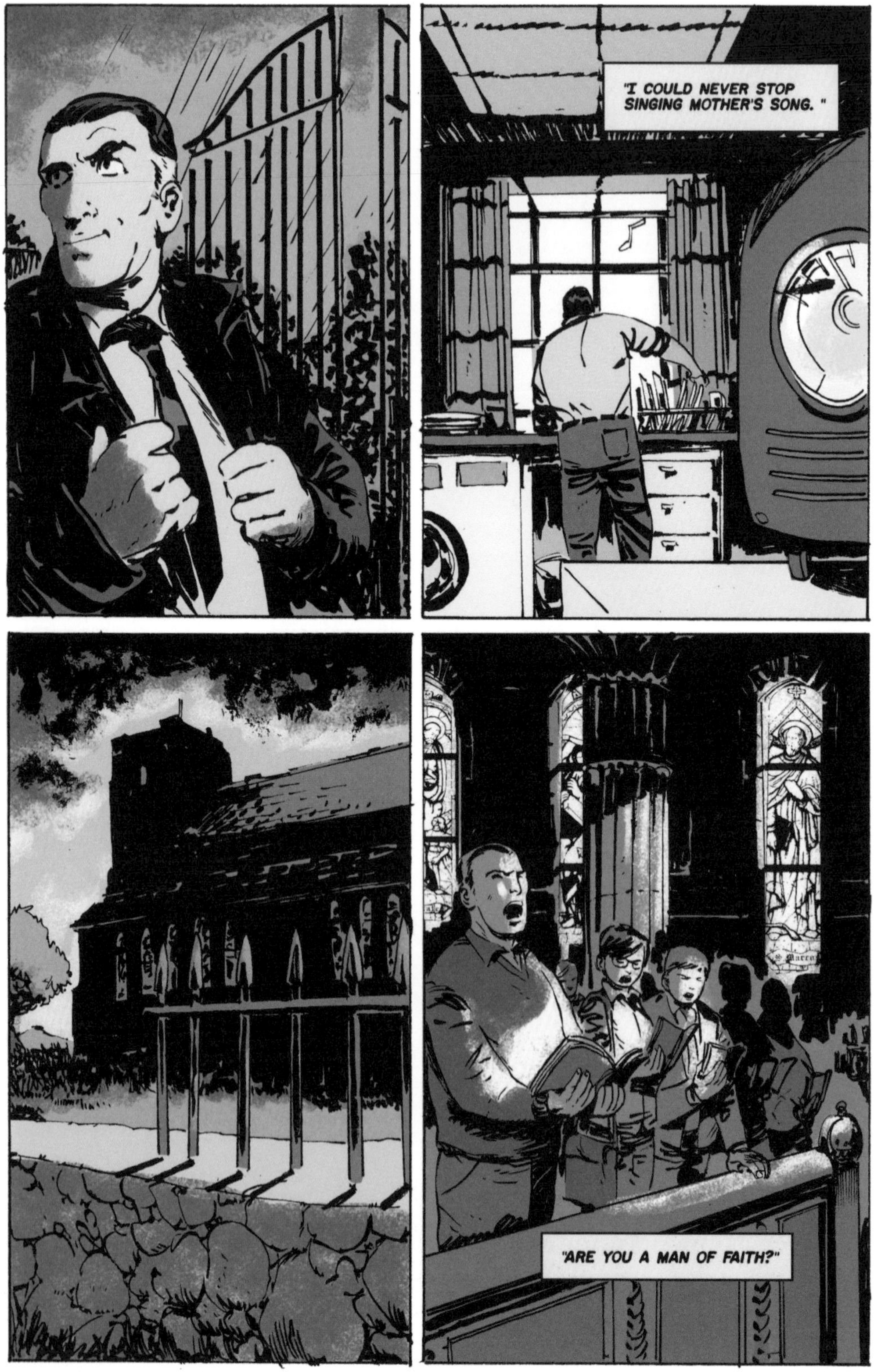
"I COULD NEVER STOP SINGING MOTHER'S SONG."
"ARE YOU A MAN OF FAITH?"

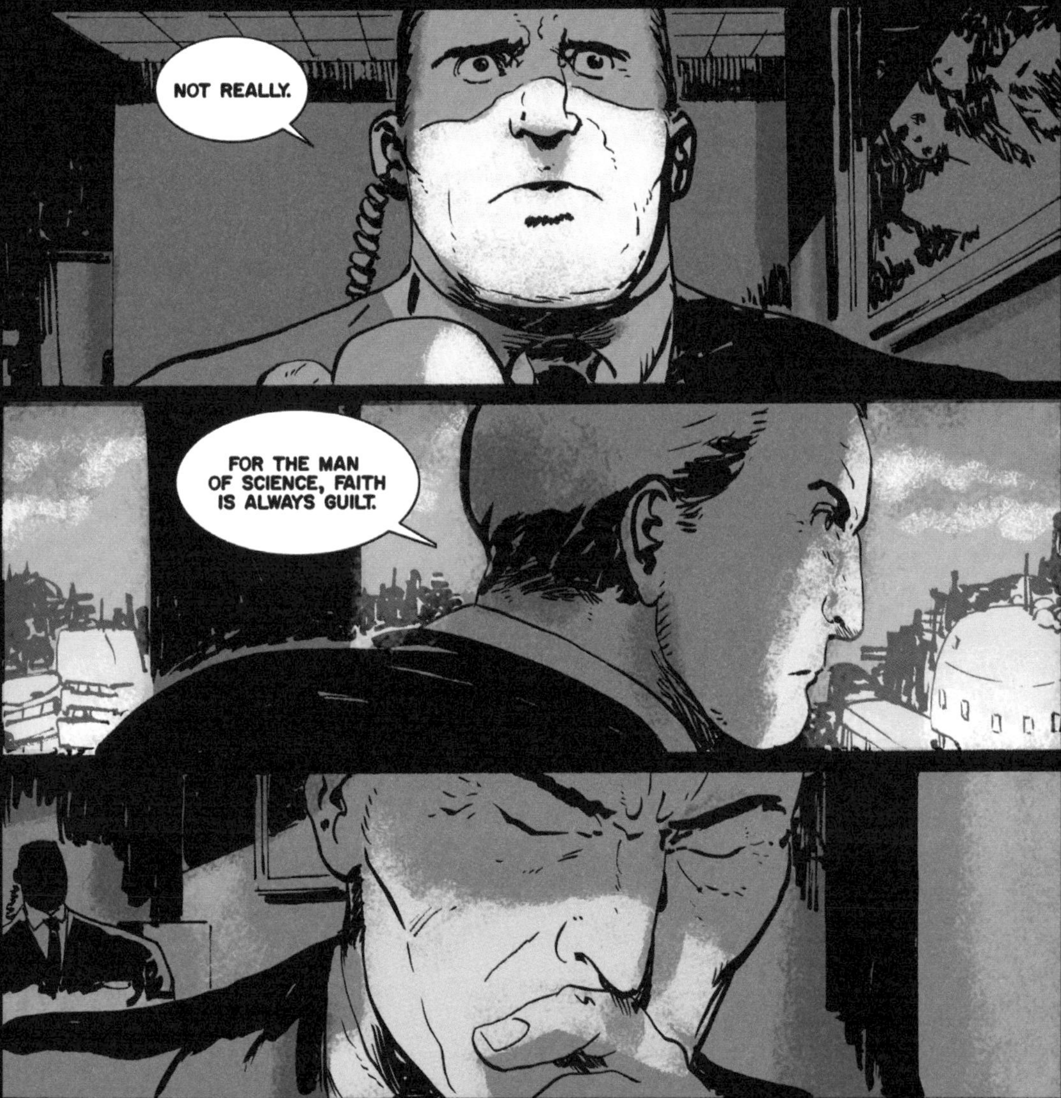
NOT REALLY.
FOR THE MAN OF SCIENCE, FAITH IS ALWAYS GUILT.

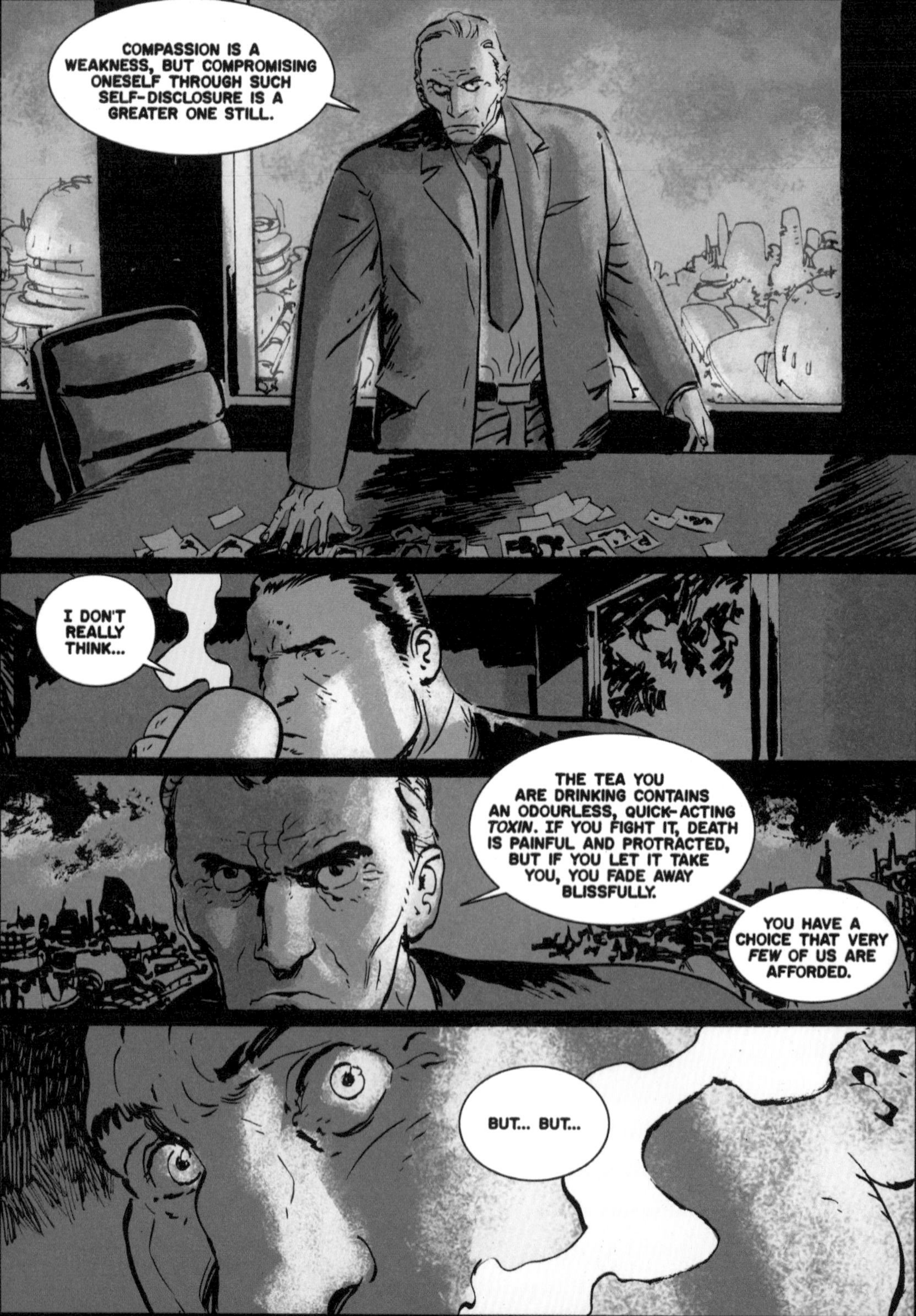
COMPASSION IS A WEAKNESS, BUT COMPROMISING ONESELF THROUGH SUCH SELF-DISCLOSURE IS A GREATER ONE STILL.
I DON'T REALLY THINK...
THE TEA YOU ARE DRINKING CONTAINS AN ODOURLESS, QUICK-ACTING *TOXIN*. IF YOU FIGHT IT, DEATH IS PAINFUL AND PROTRACTED, BUT IF YOU LET IT TAKE YOU, YOU FADE AWAY BLISSFULLY.
YOU HAVE A CHOICE THAT VERY *FEW* OF US ARE AFFORDED.
BUT... BUT...

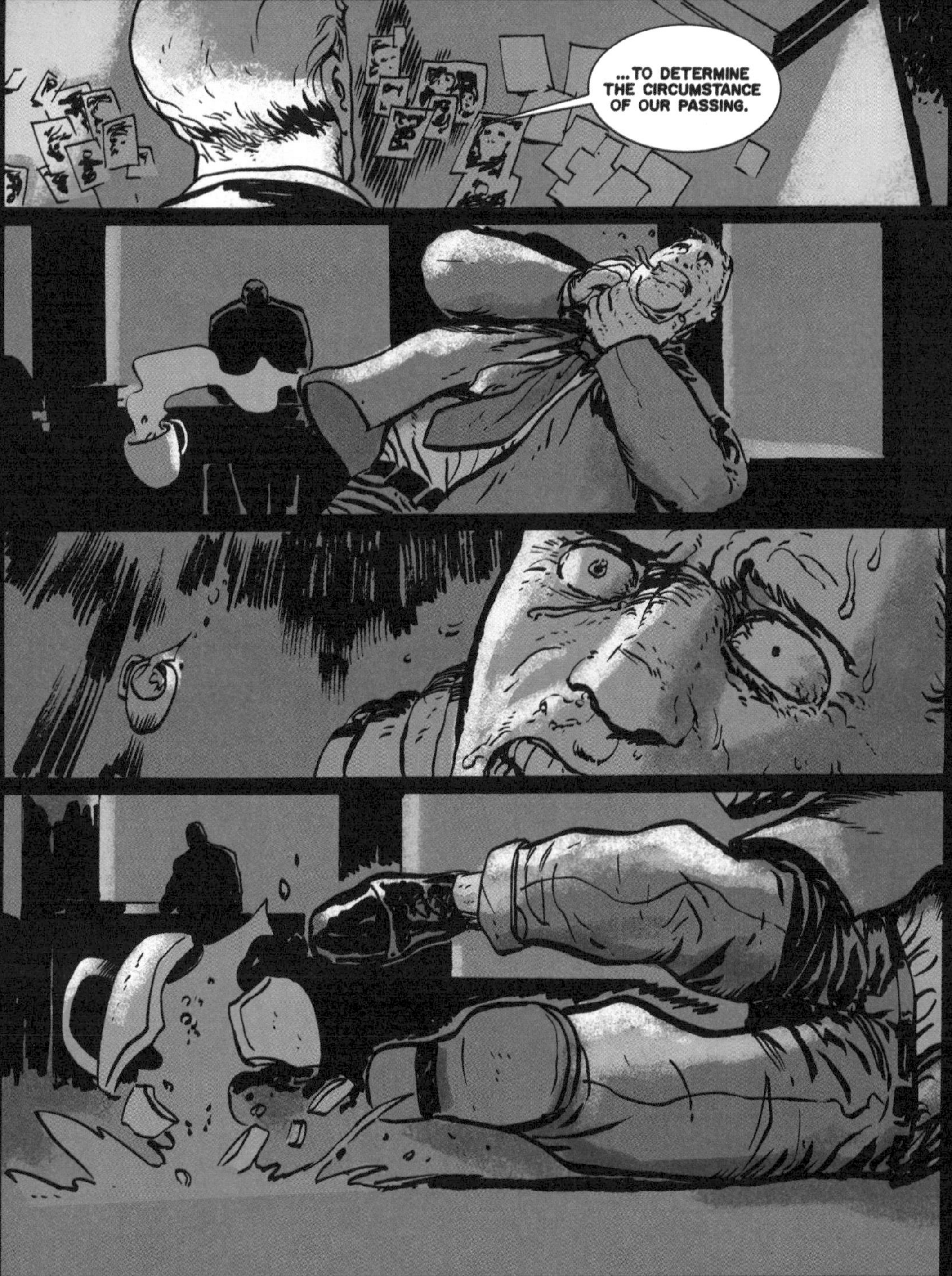
...TO DETERMINE THE CIRCUMSTANCE OF OUR PASSING.

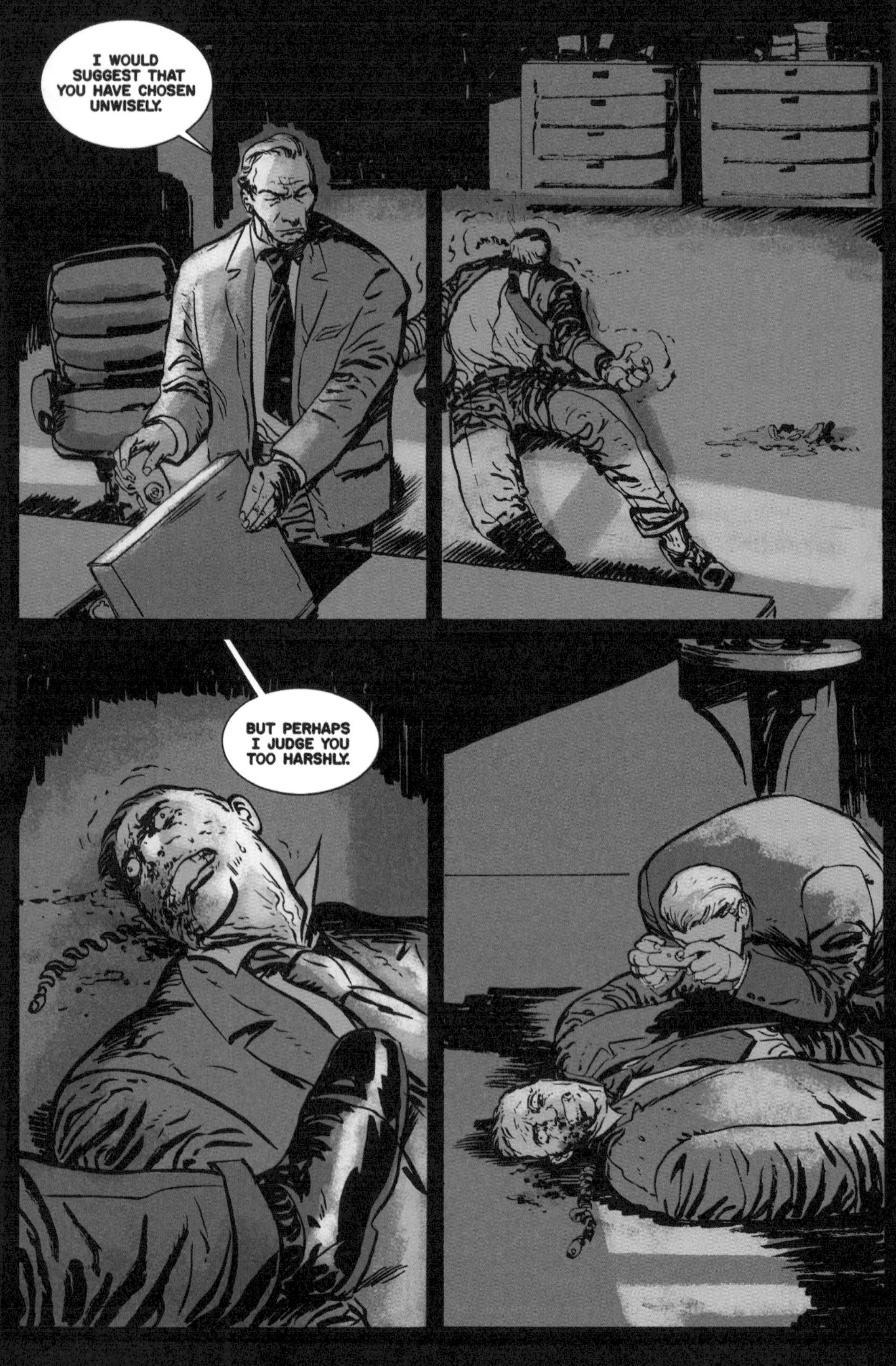
I WOULD SUGGEST THAT YOU HAVE CHOSEN UNWISELY.
BUT PERHAPS I JUDGE YOU TOO HARSHLY.

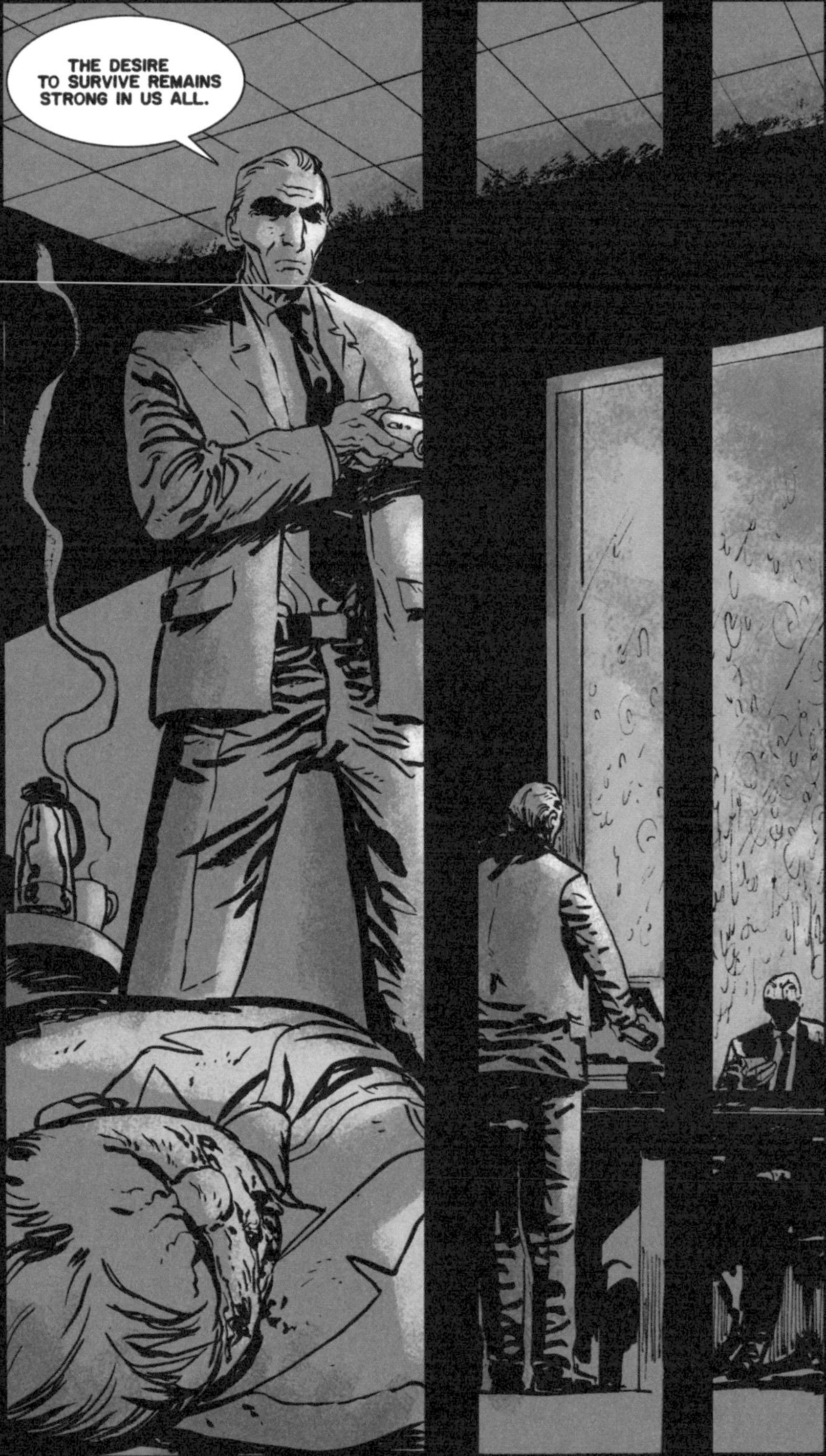
THE DESIRE TO SURVIVE REMAINS STRONG IN US ALL.

IDP: 2043

Chapter 5

Denise Mina & Barroux

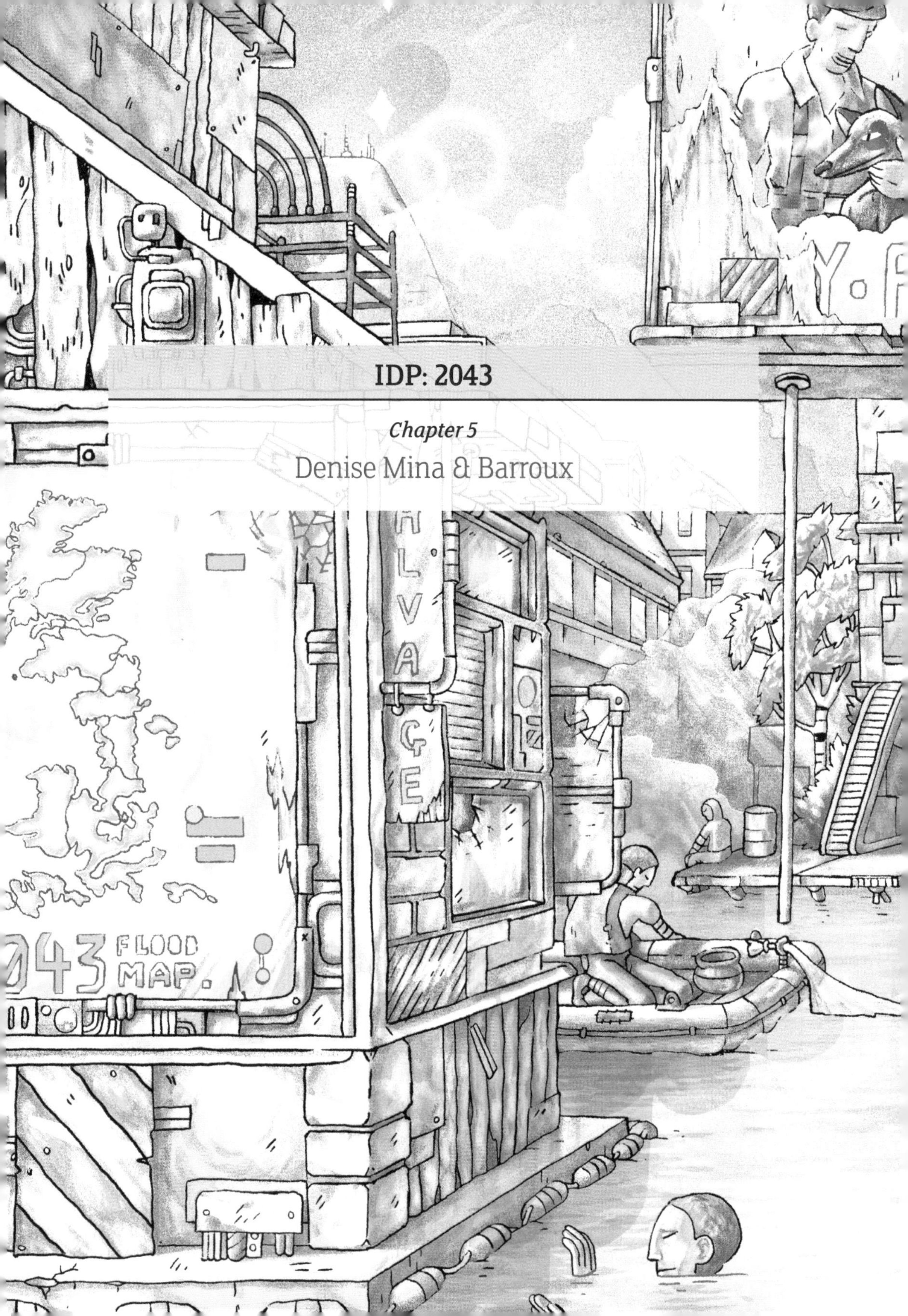
043 FLOOD
MAP.

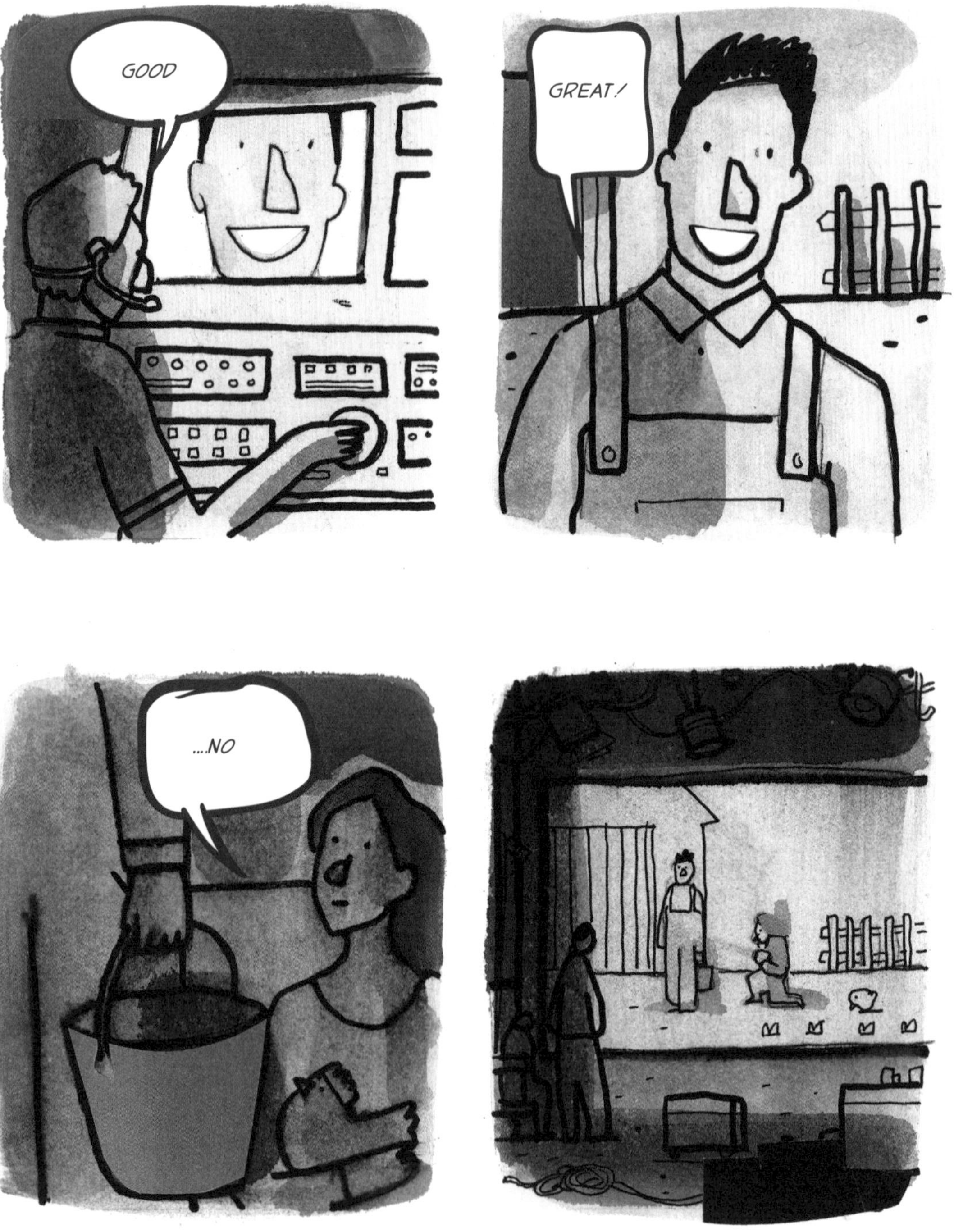
GOOD
GREAT!
...NO

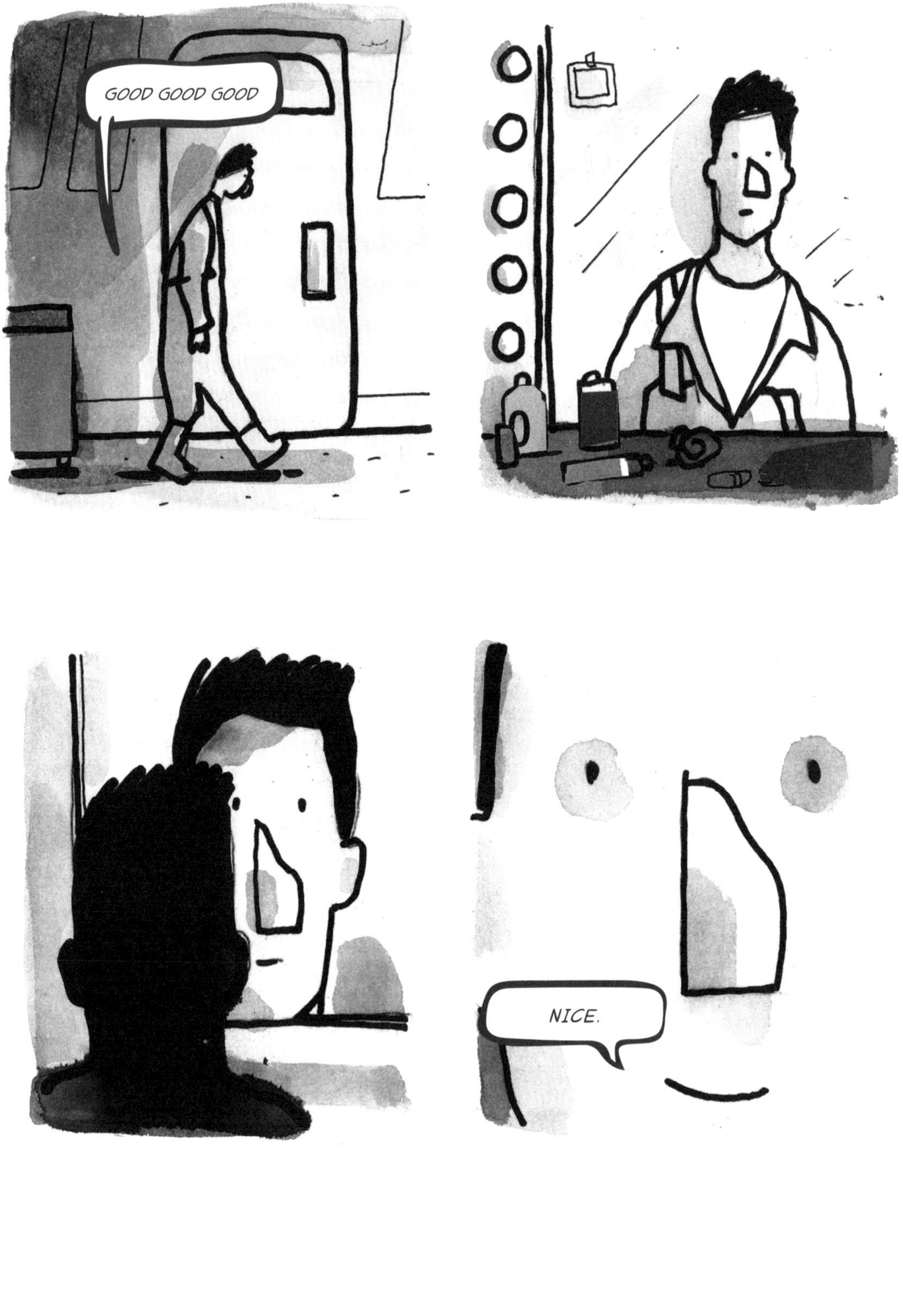
GOOD GOOD GOOD
NICE.

REC

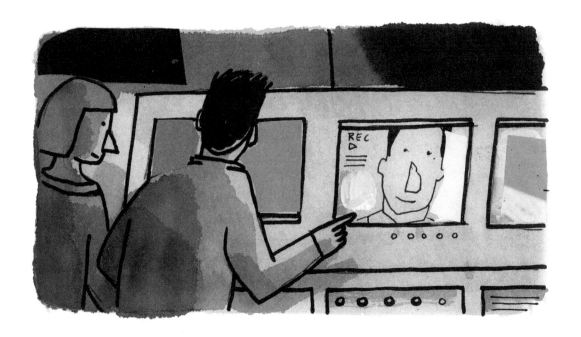

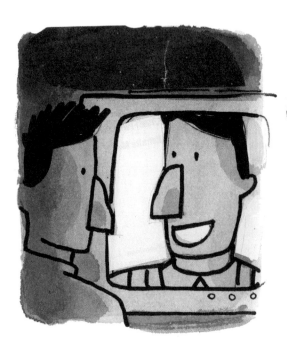

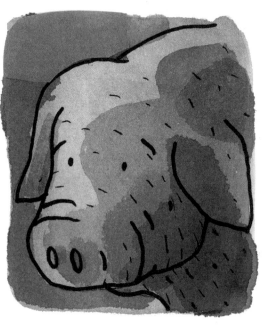

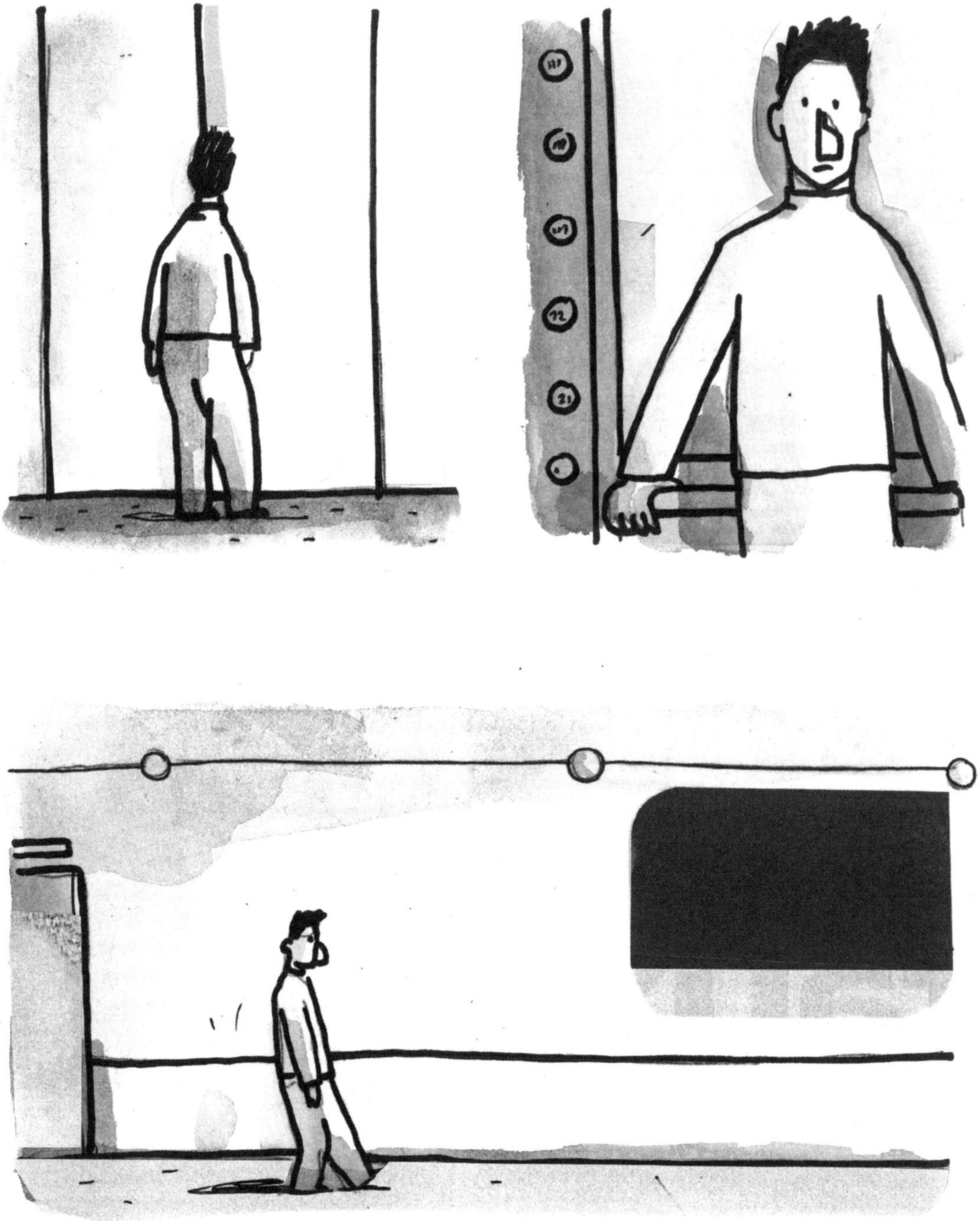

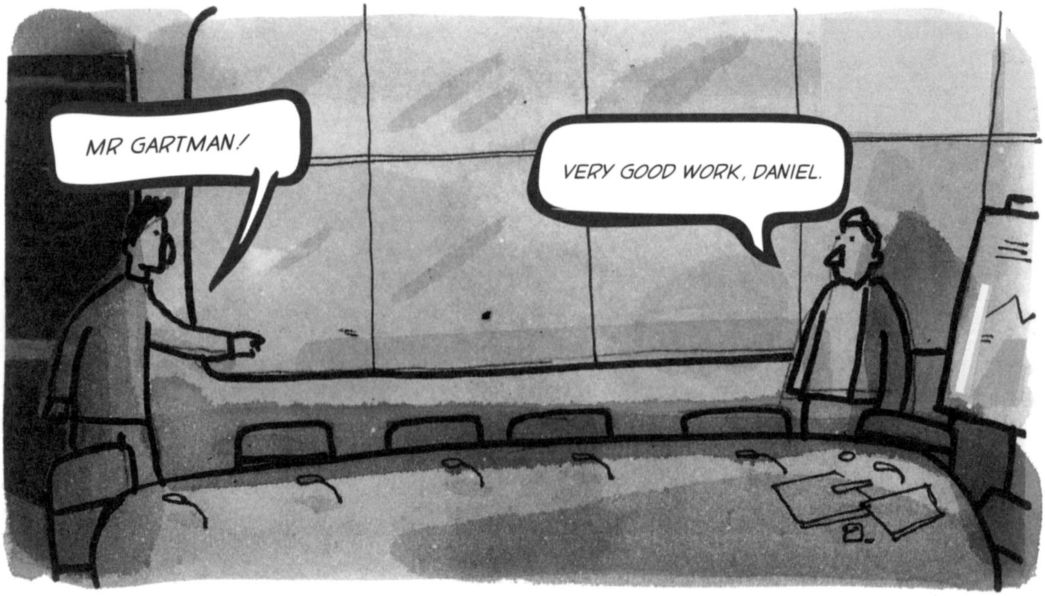
MR GARTMAN!
VERY GOOD WORK, DANIEL.

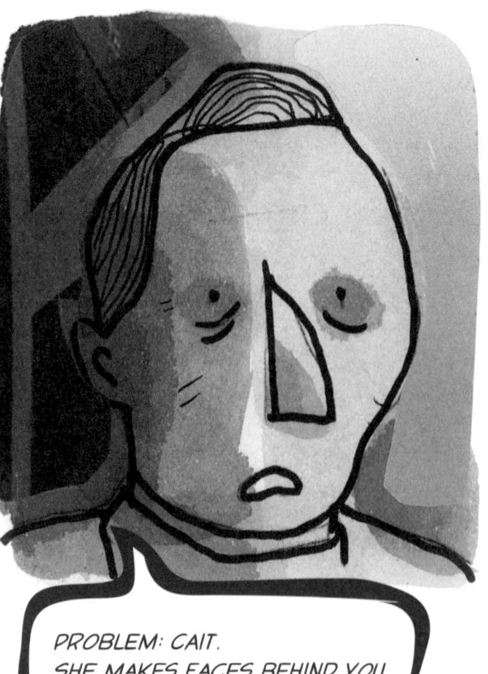
PROBLEM: CAIT.
SHE MAKES FACES BEHIND YOU.

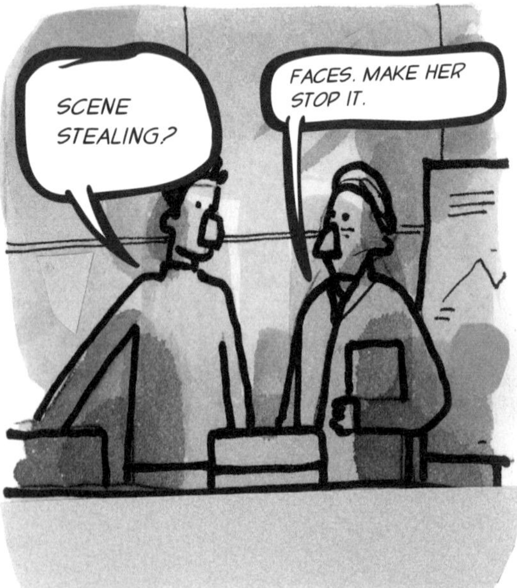
SCENE STEALING?
FACES. MAKE HER STOP IT.

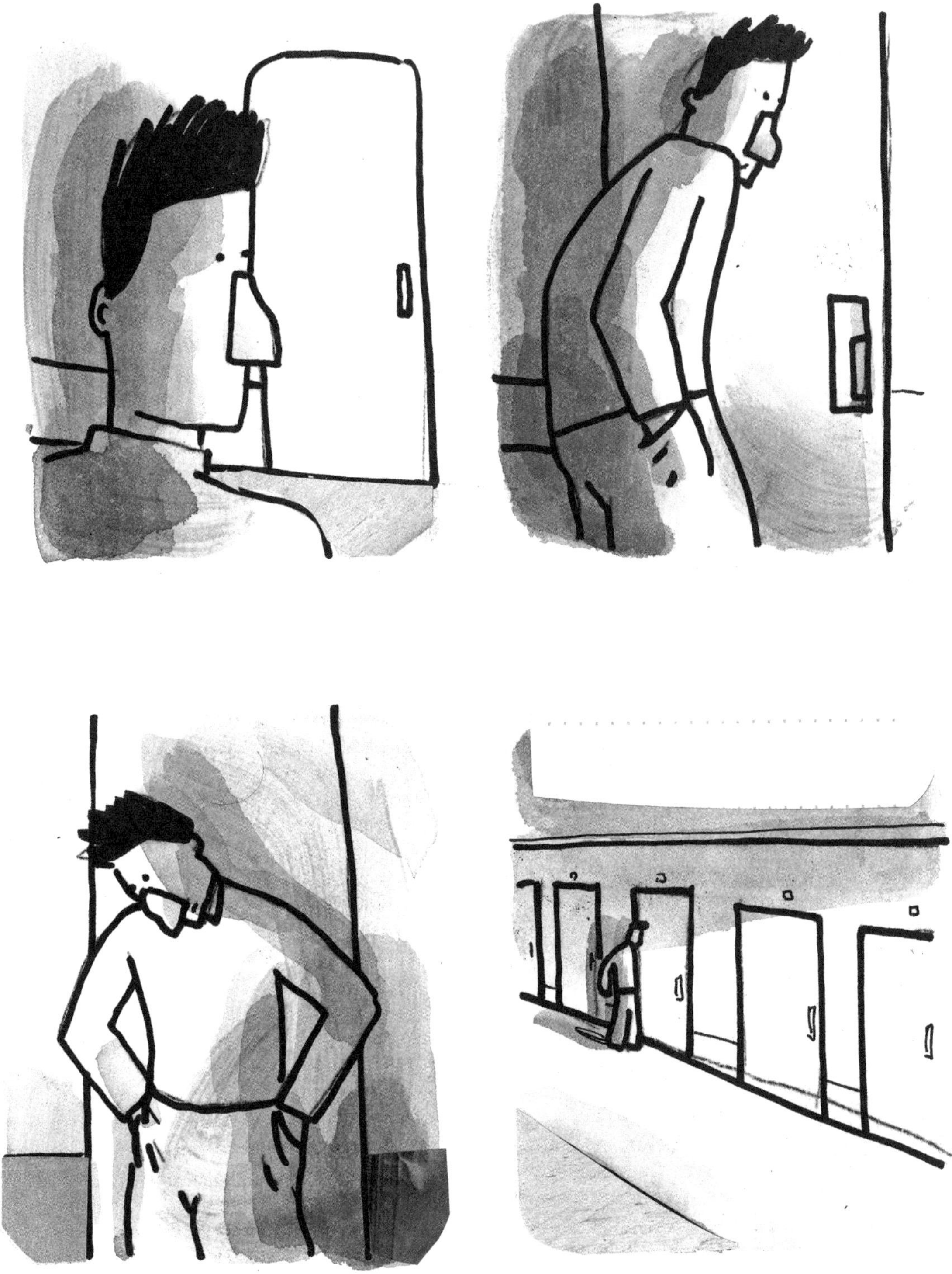

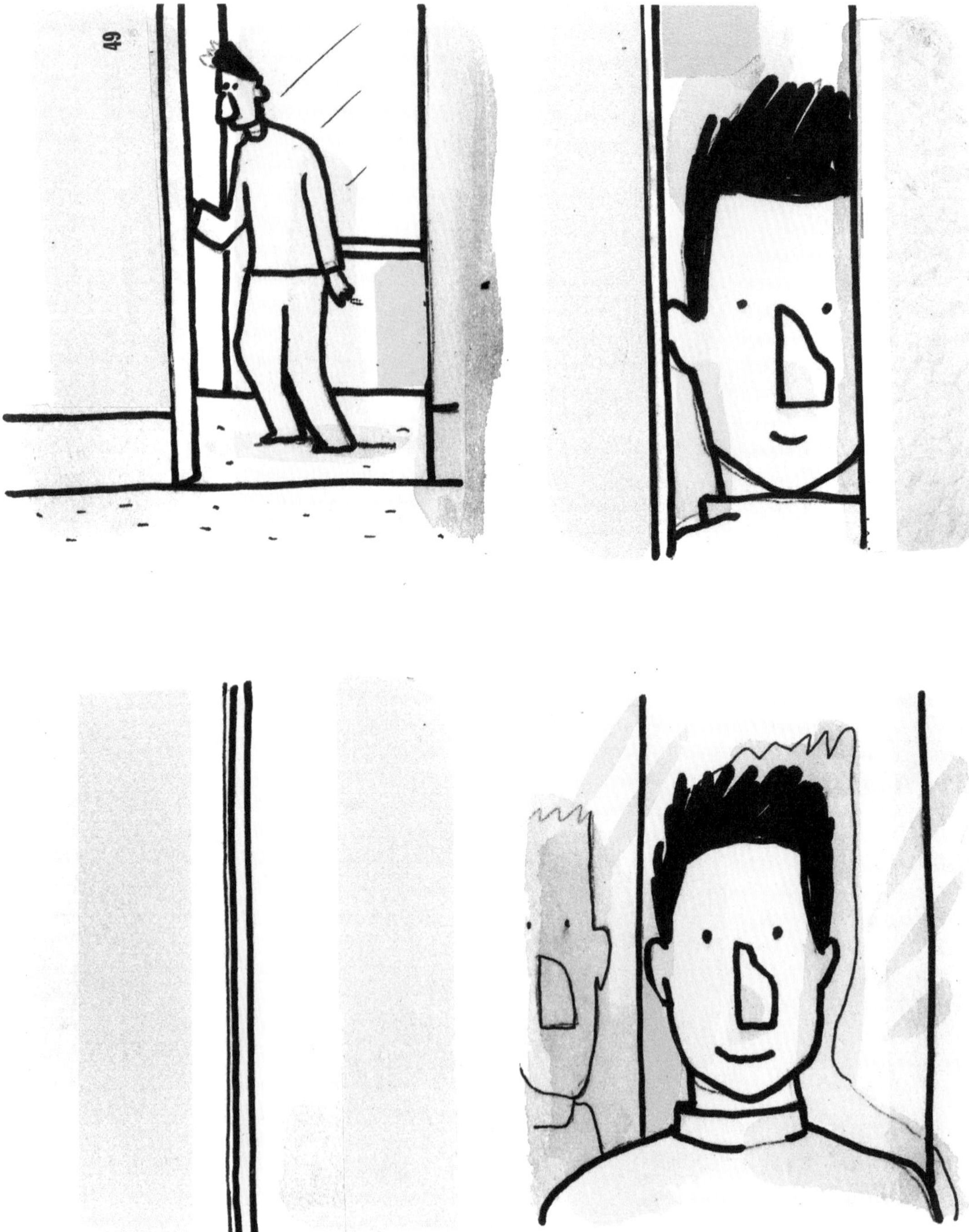

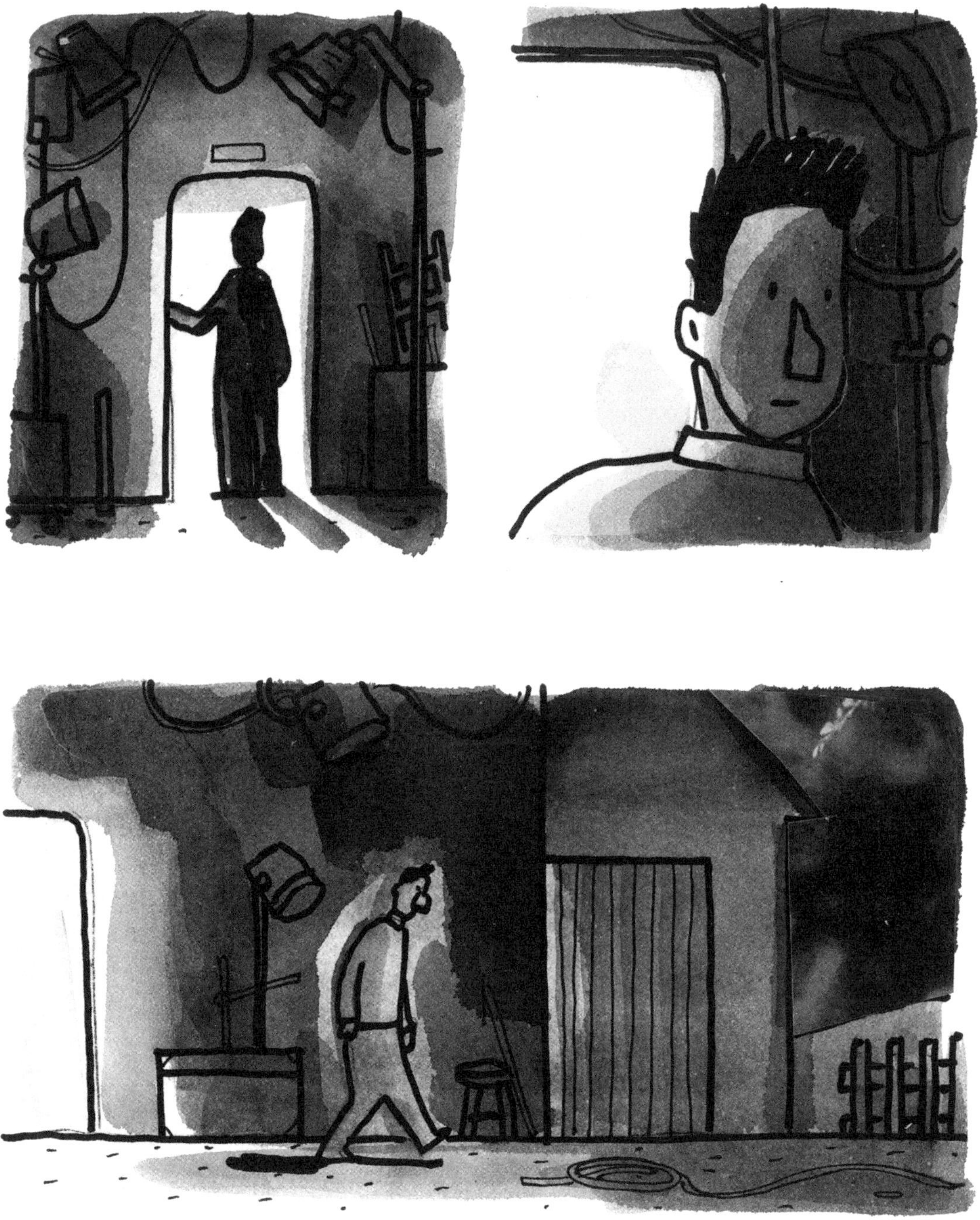

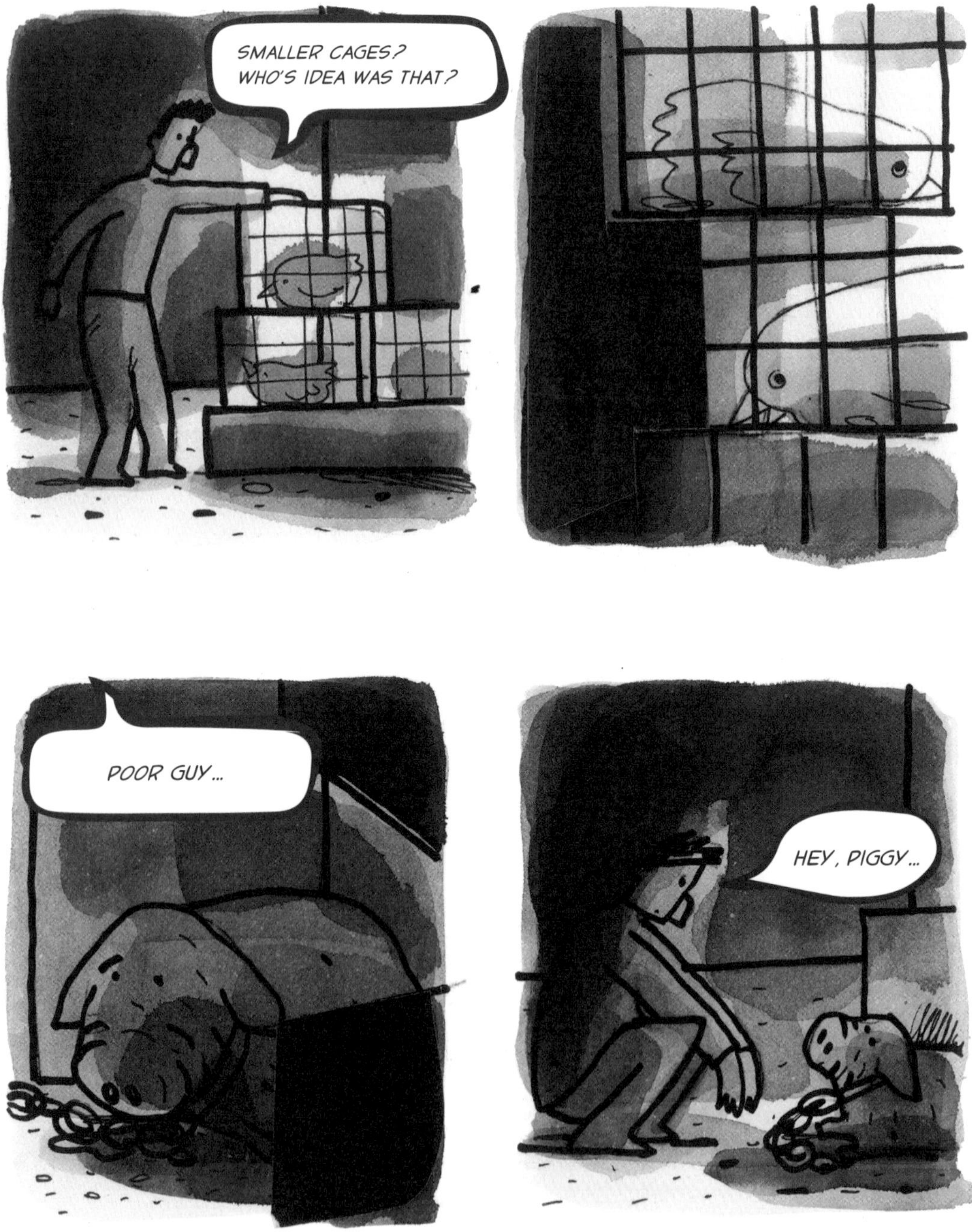
SMALLER CAGES?
WHO'S IDEA WAS THAT?
POOR GUY...
HEY, PIGGY...

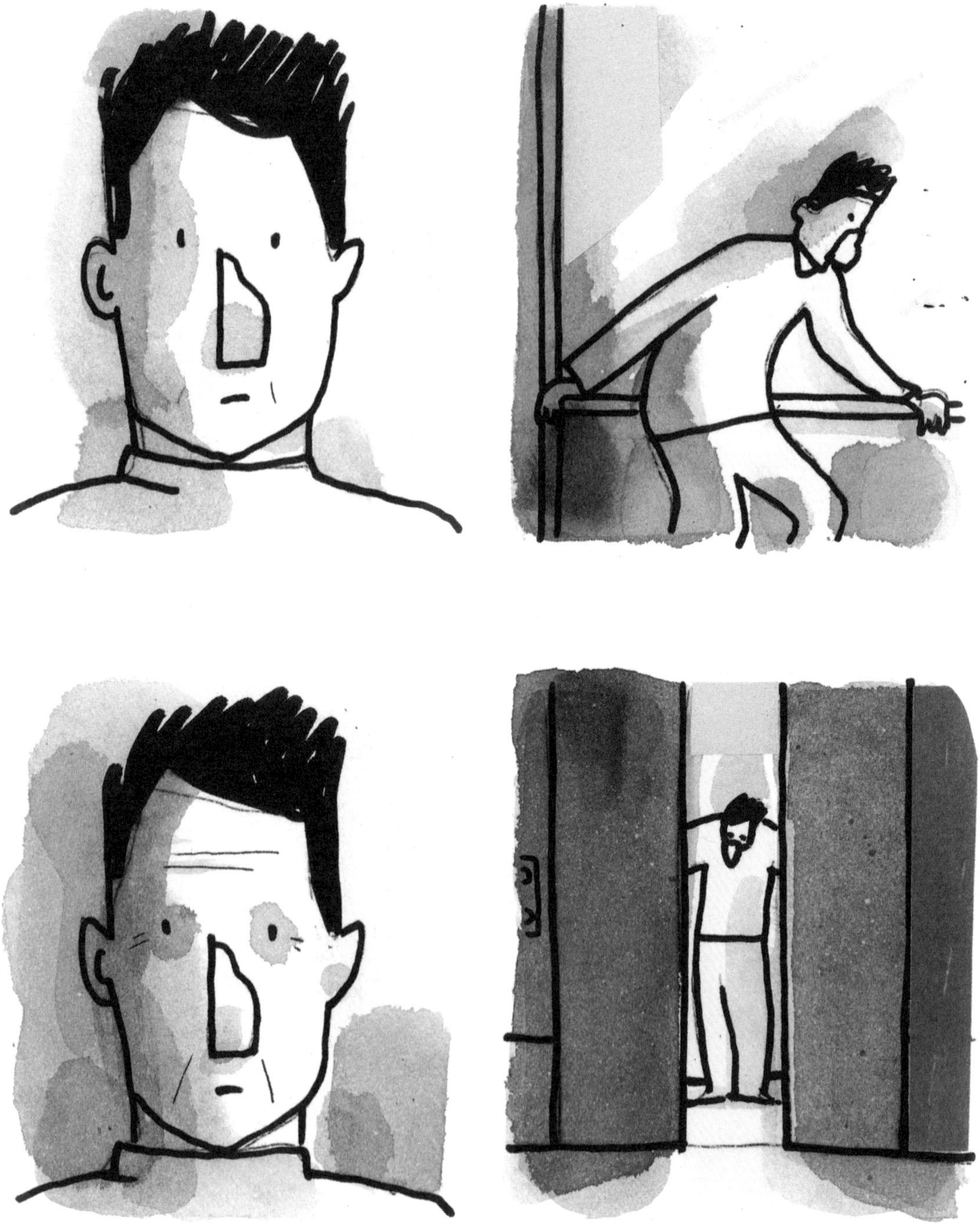

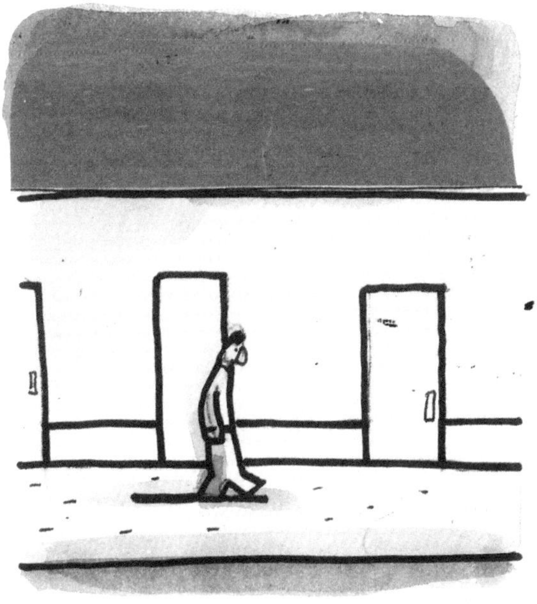

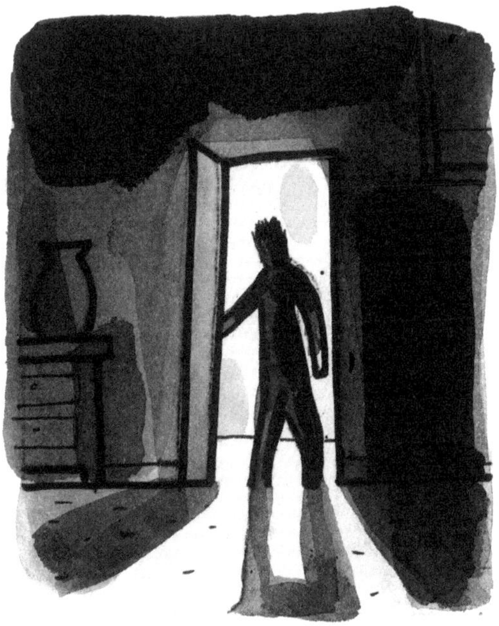

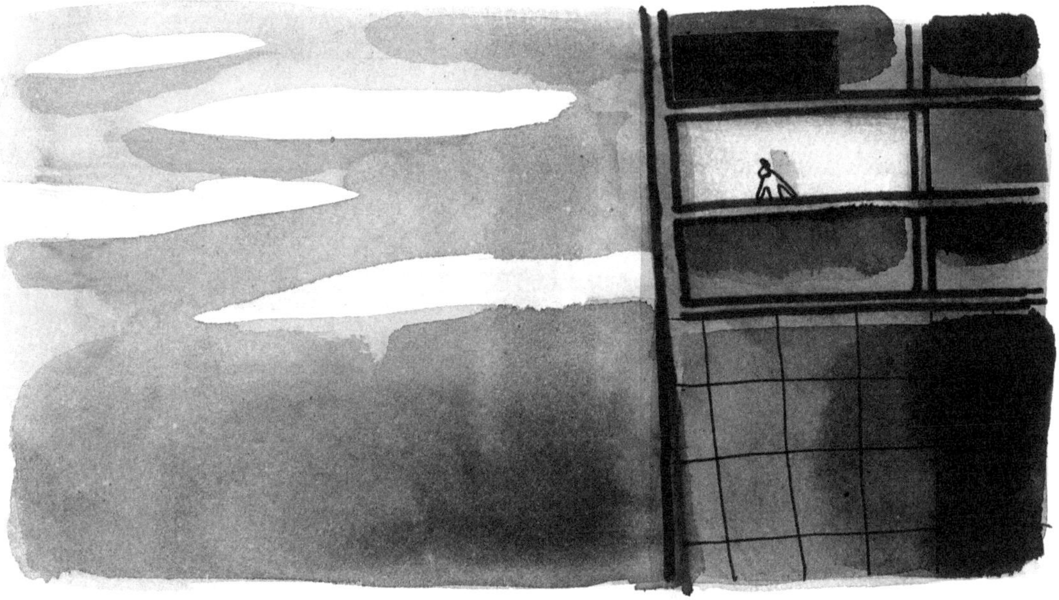

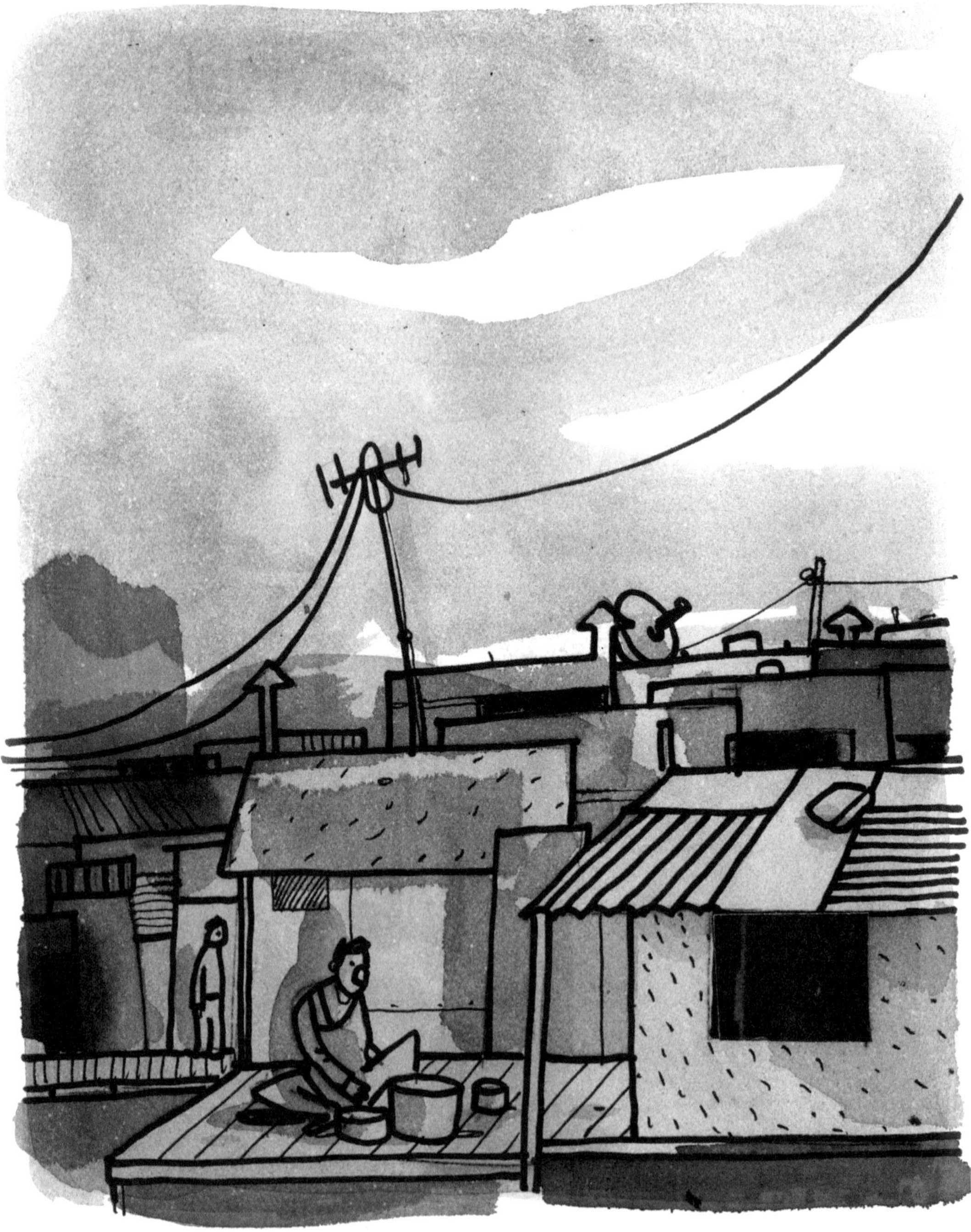

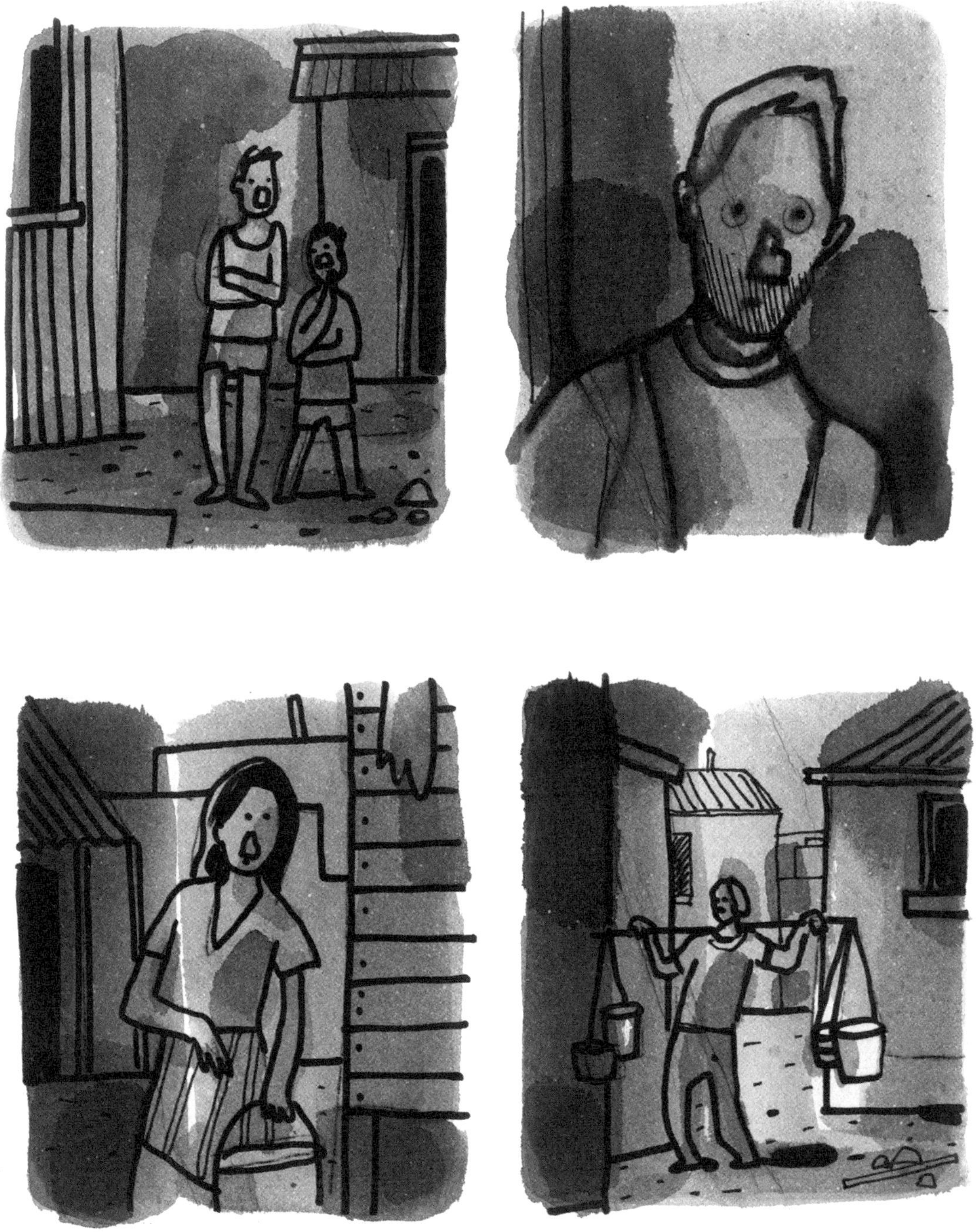

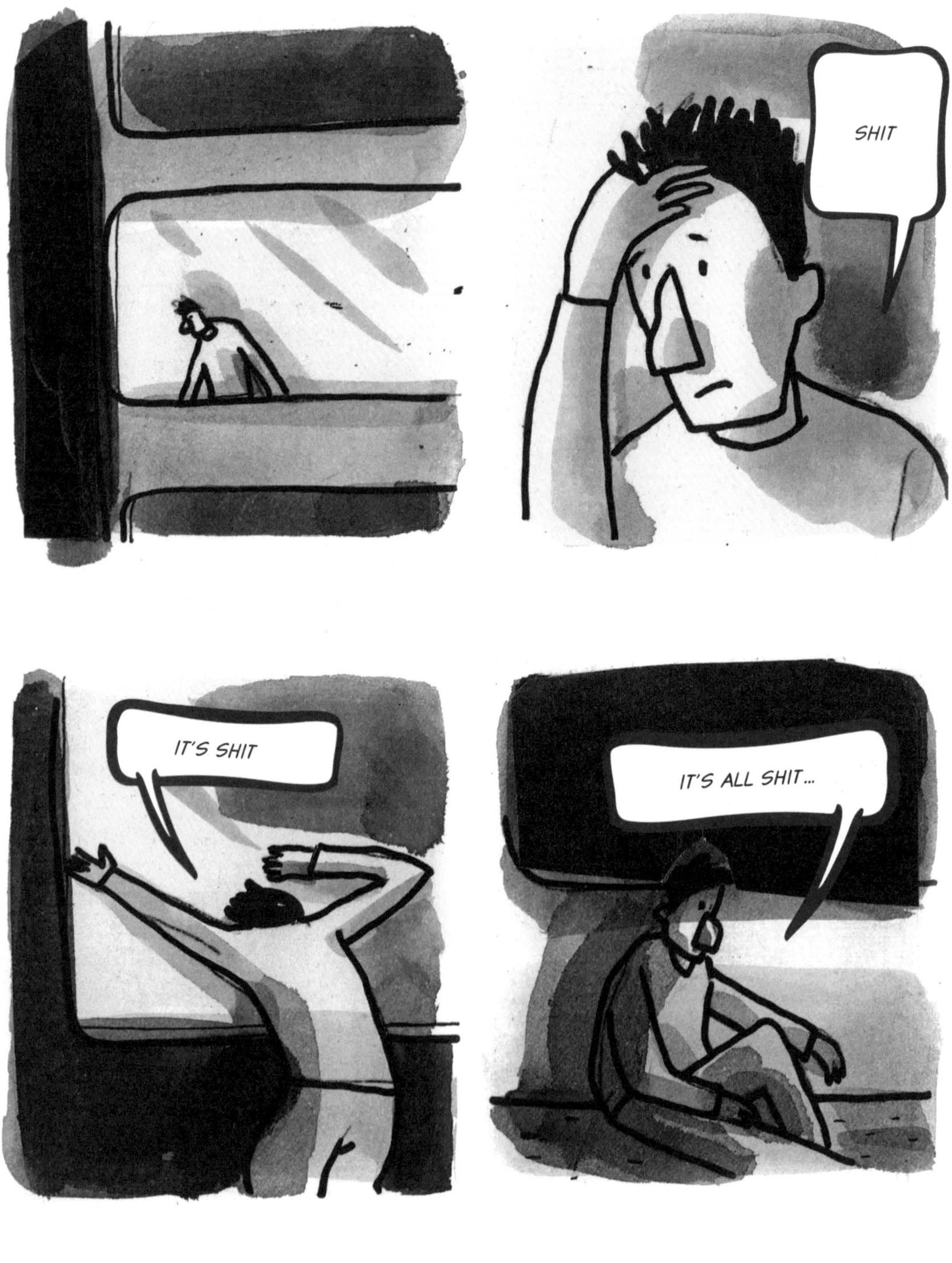
SHIT
IT'S SHIT
IT'S ALL SHIT...

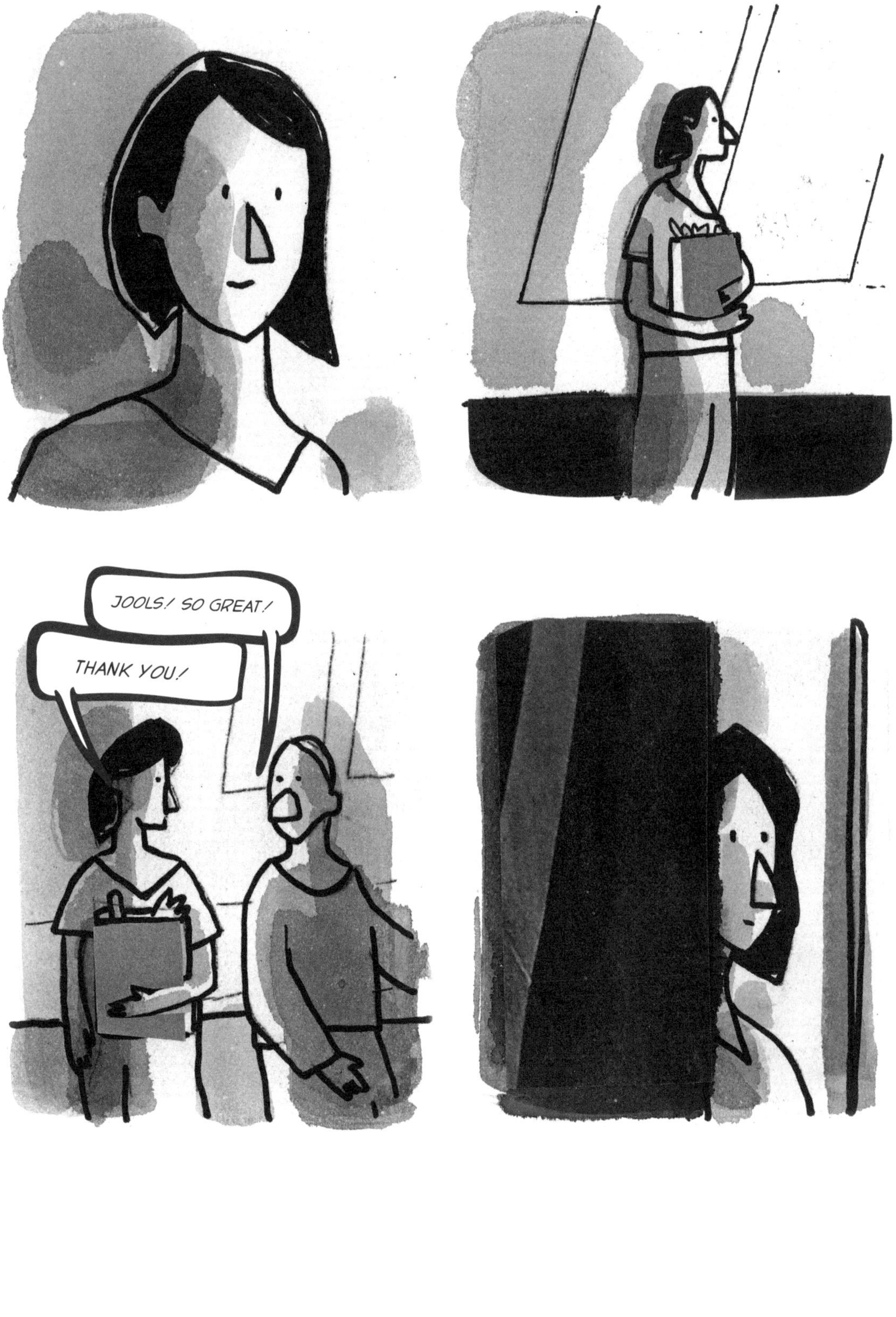
JOOLS! SO GREAT!
THANK YOU!

FOOD?

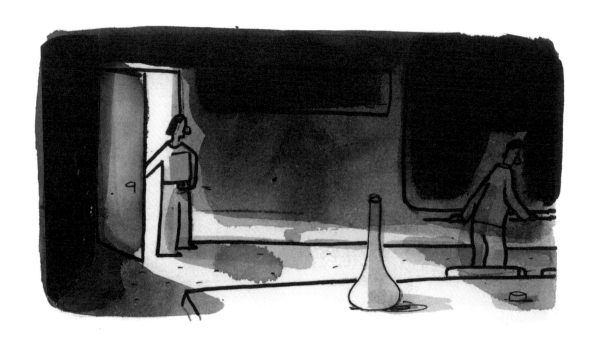

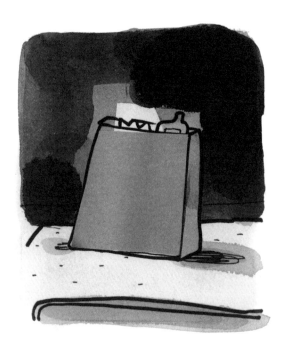

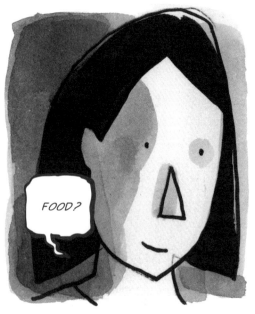

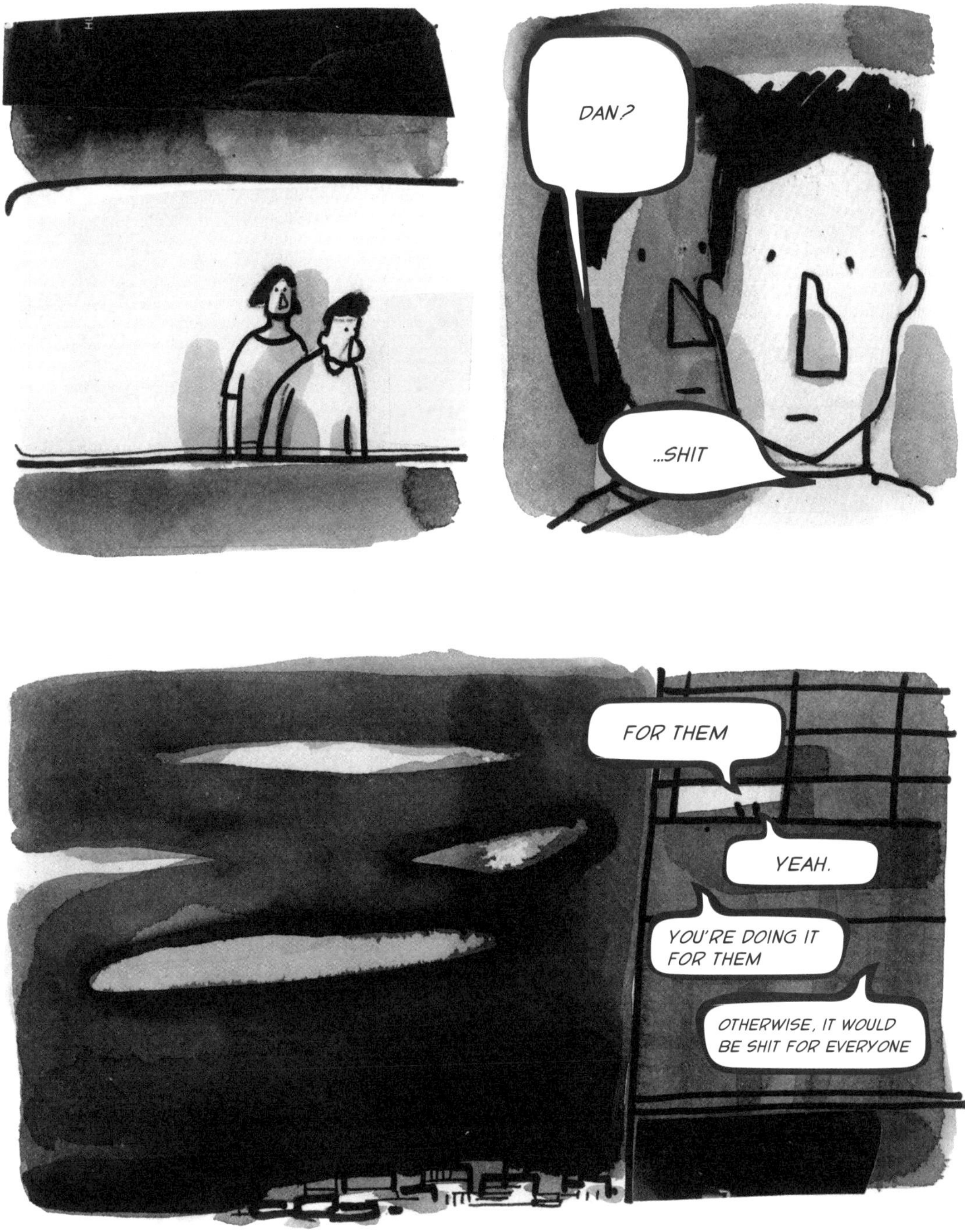
DAN?
...SHIT
FOR THEM
YEAH.
YOU'RE DOING IT
FOR THEM
OTHERWISE, IT WOULD
BE SHIT FOR EVERYONE

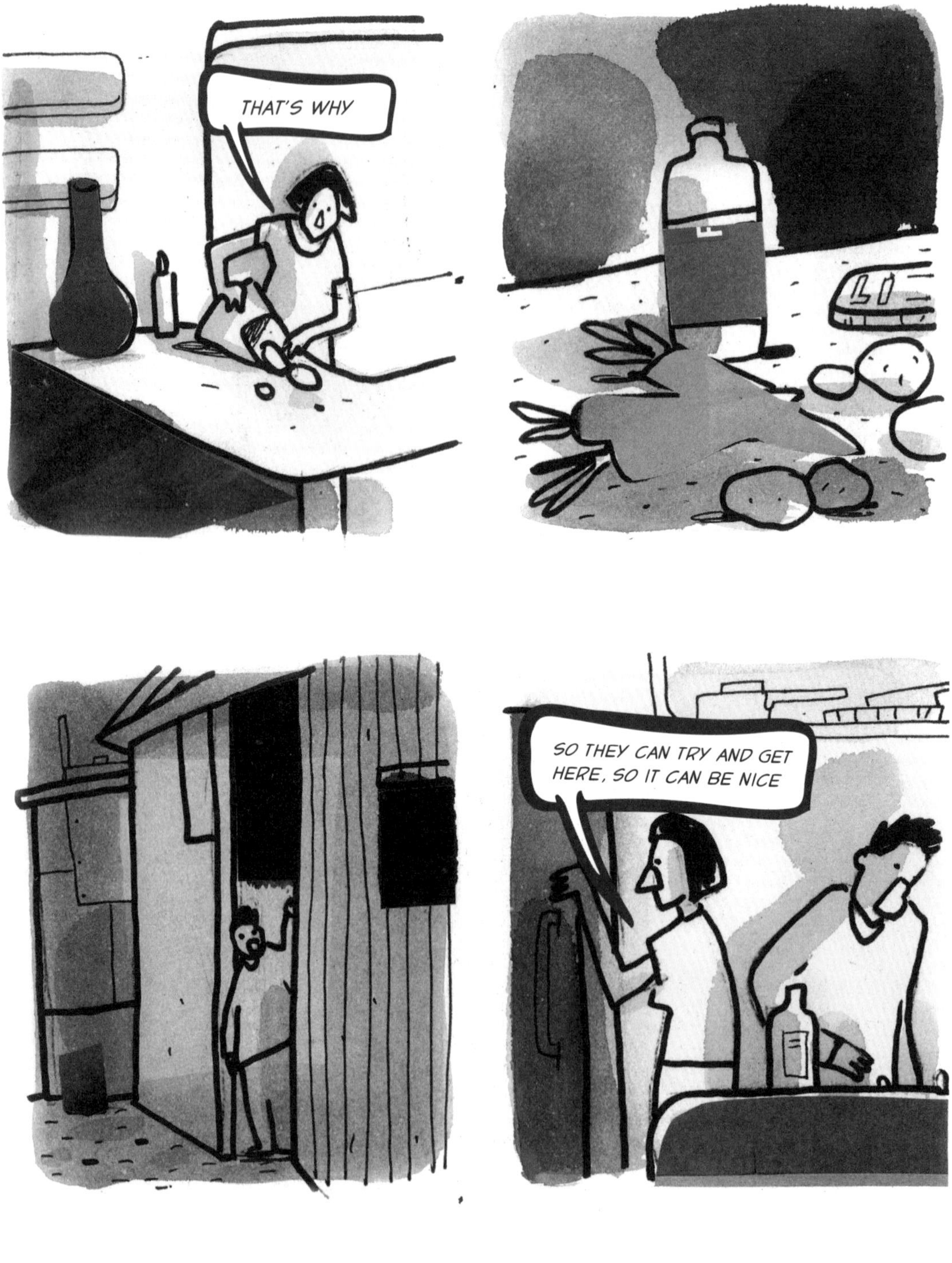
THAT'S WHY
SO THEY CAN TRY AND GET HERE, SO IT CAN BE NICE

NICE CARROTS.
YEAH
NICE BREAD

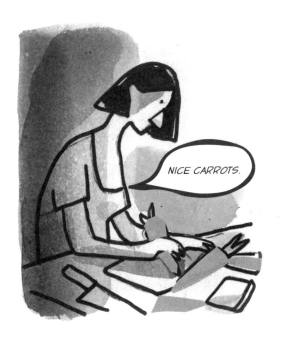

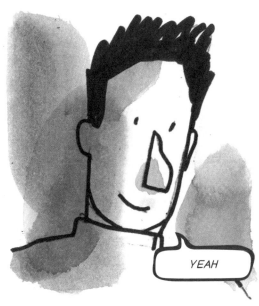

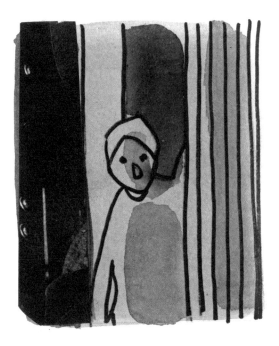

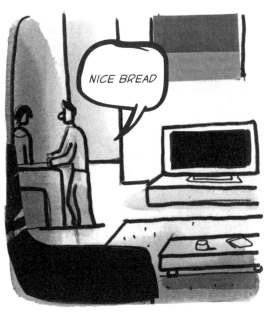

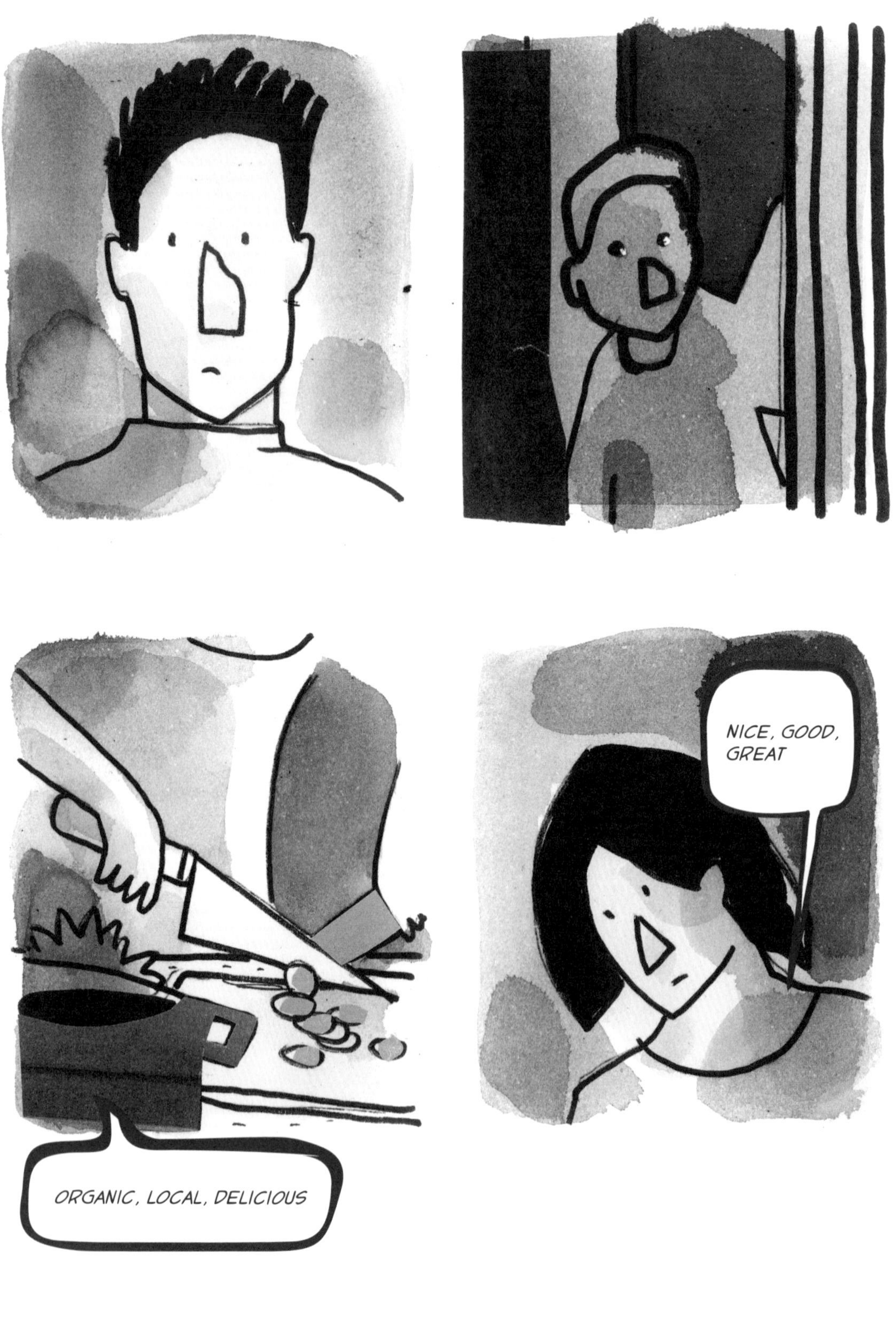
ORGANIC, LOCAL, DELICIOUS
NICE, GOOD, GREAT

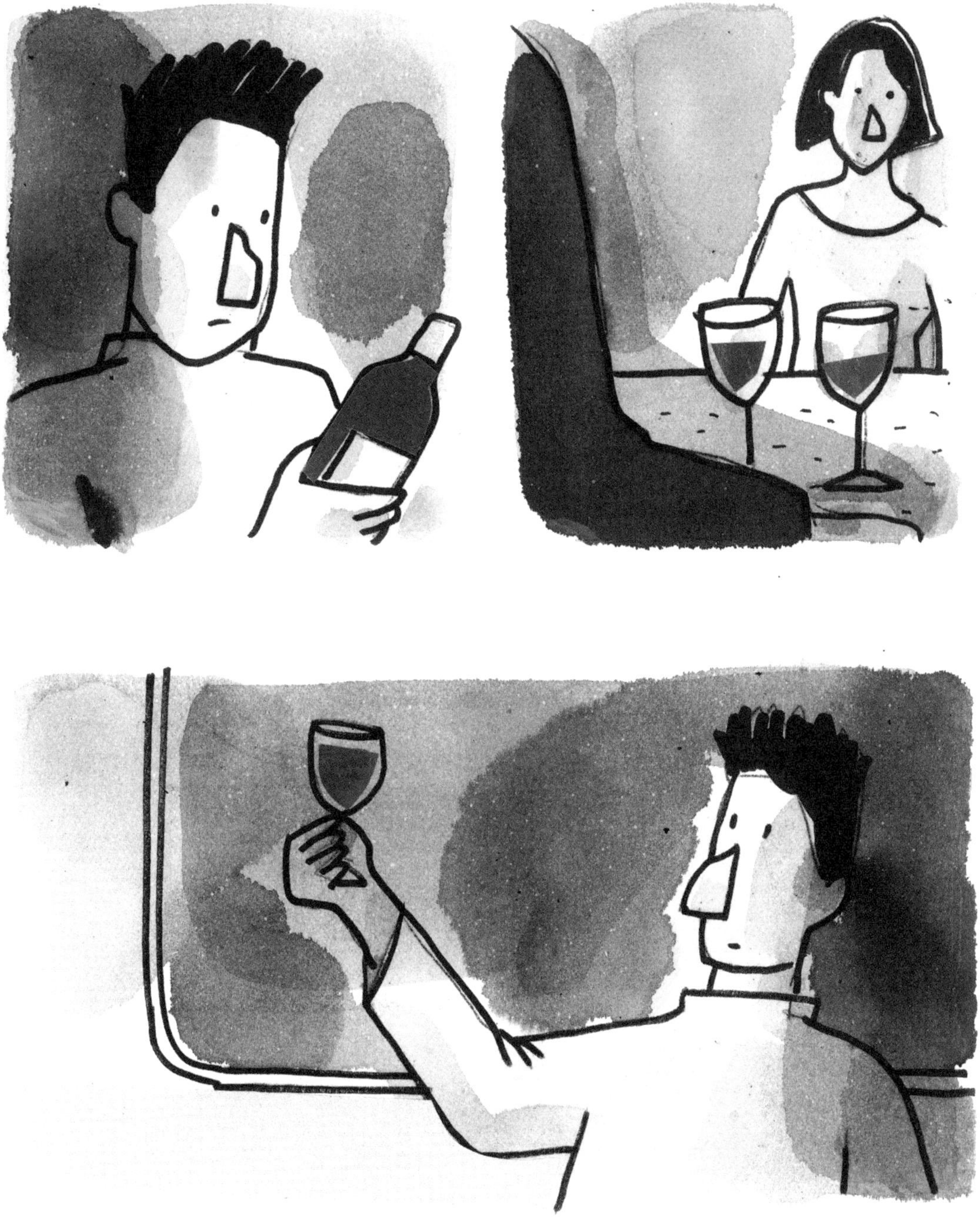

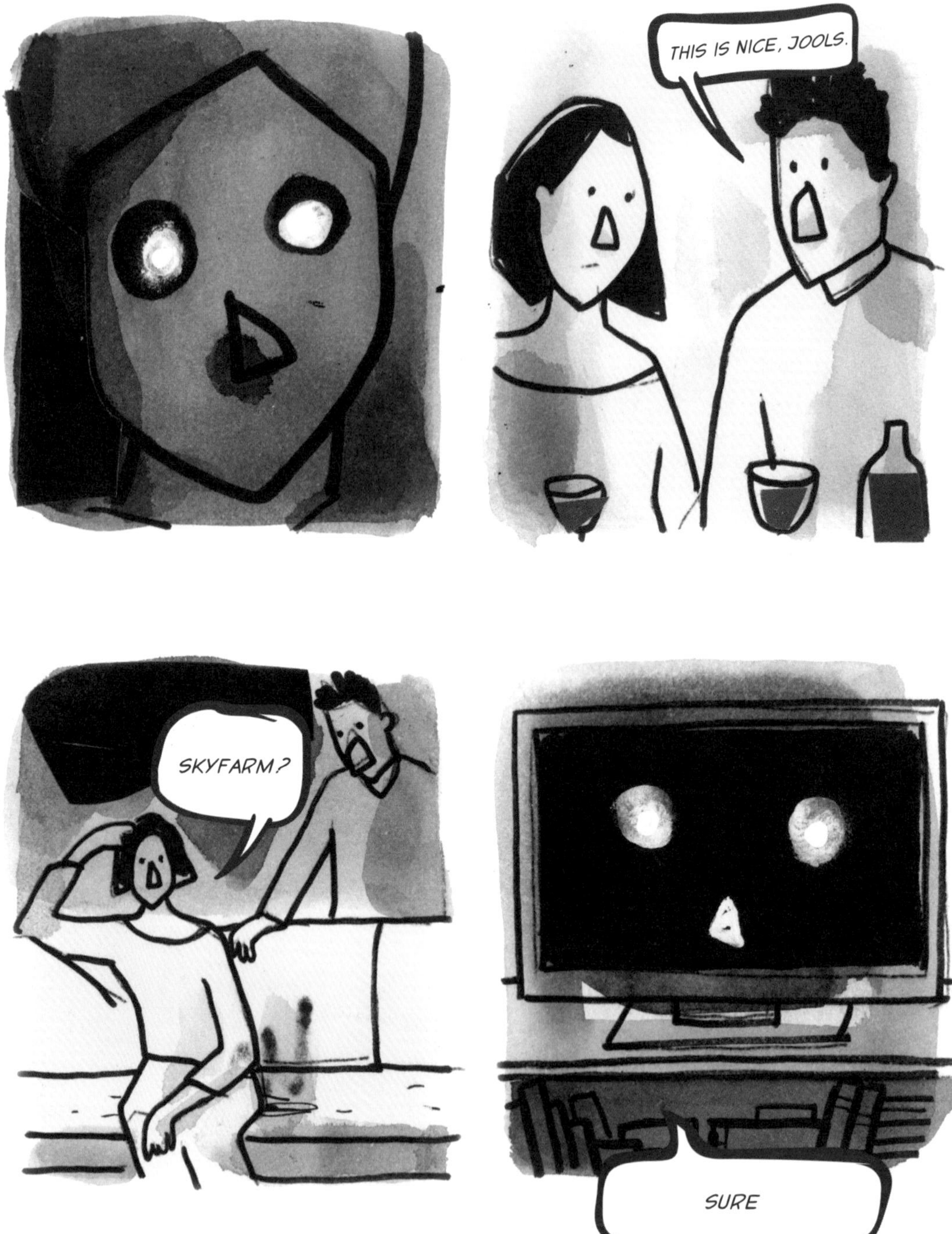
THIS IS NICE, JOOLS.
SKYFARM?
SURE

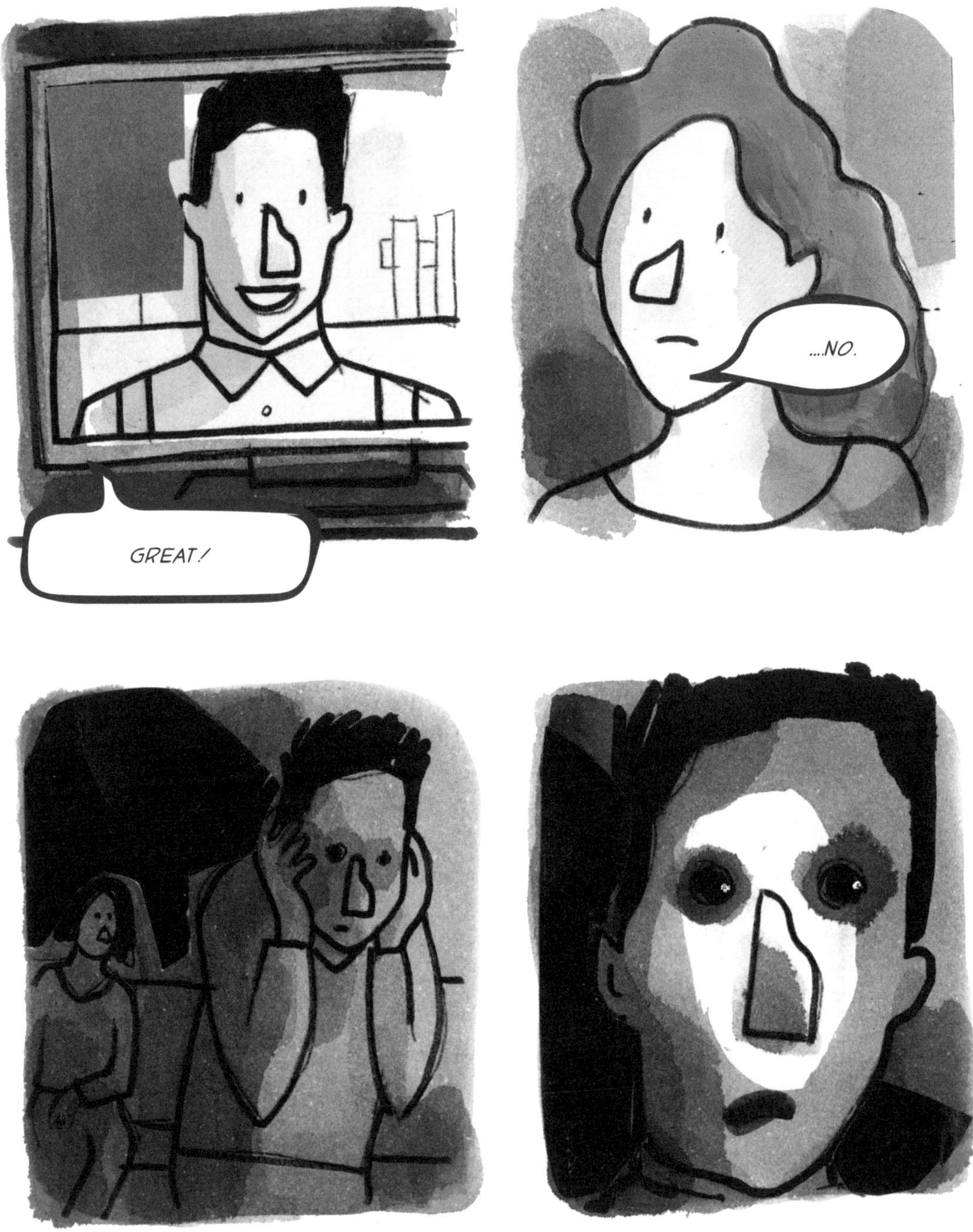
GREAT!
...NO.

IDP: 2043

Chapter 6

Mary Talbot & Kate Charlesworth

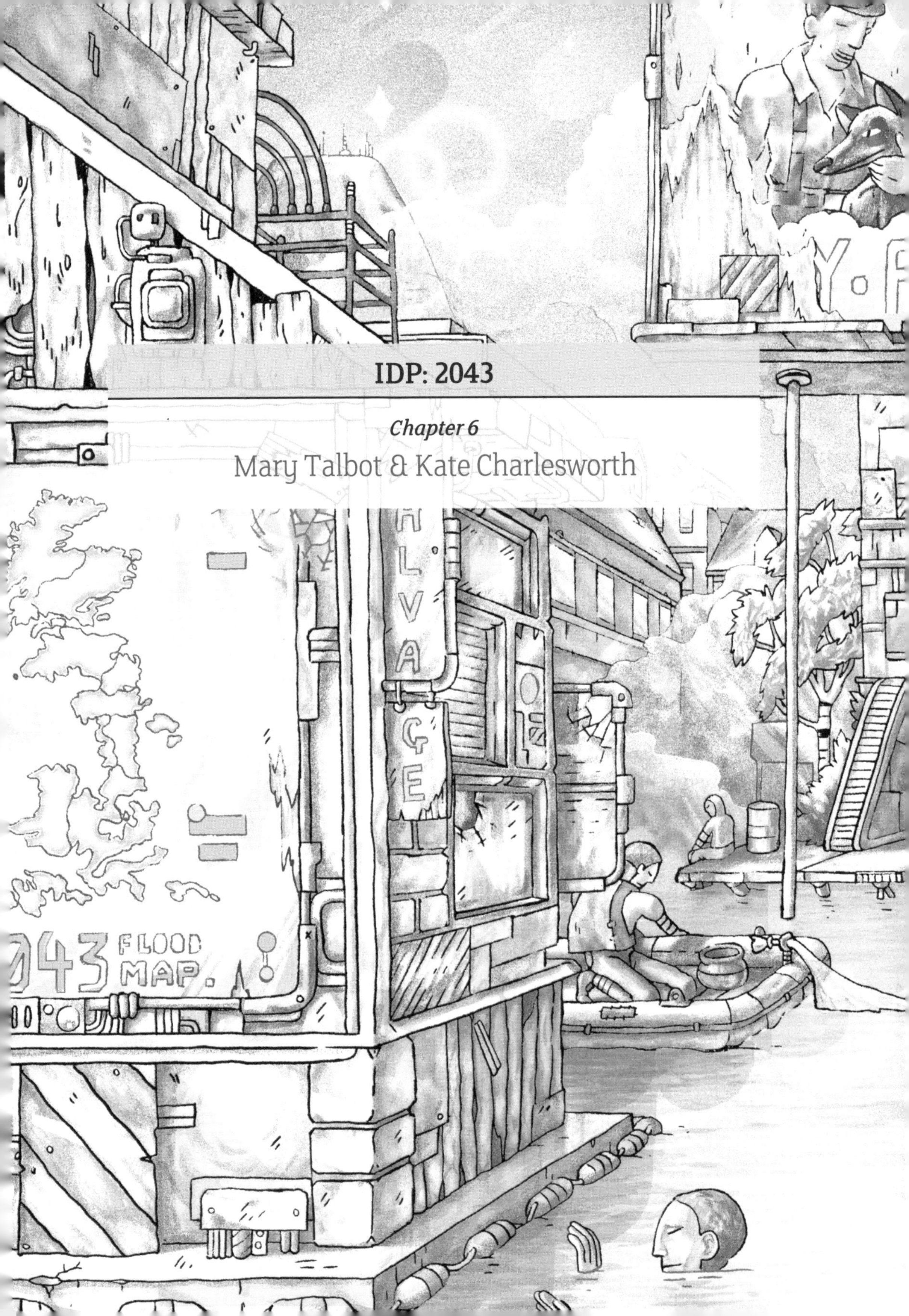
FLOOD MAP.

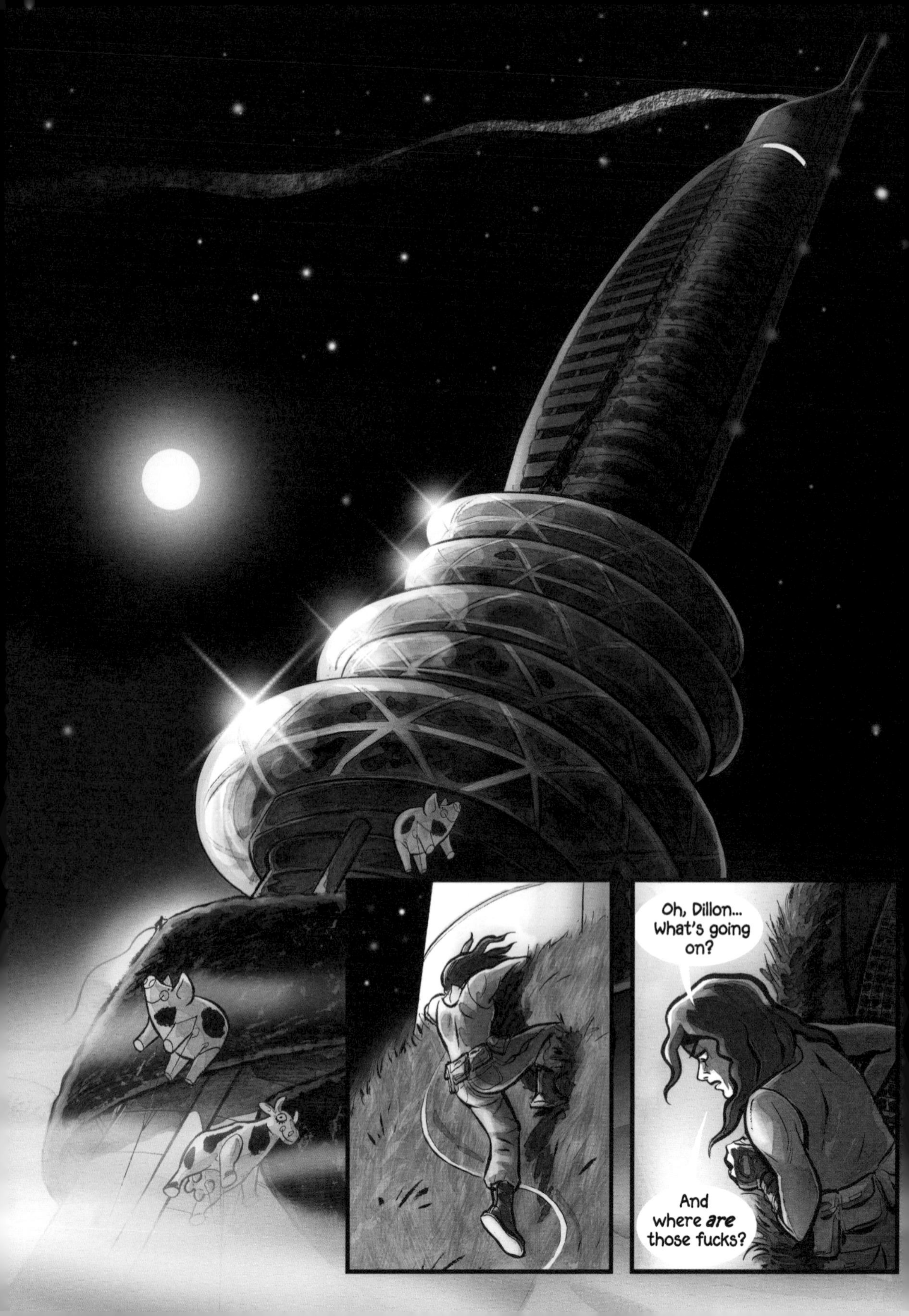
Oh, Dillon...
What's going on?
And where *are* those fucks?

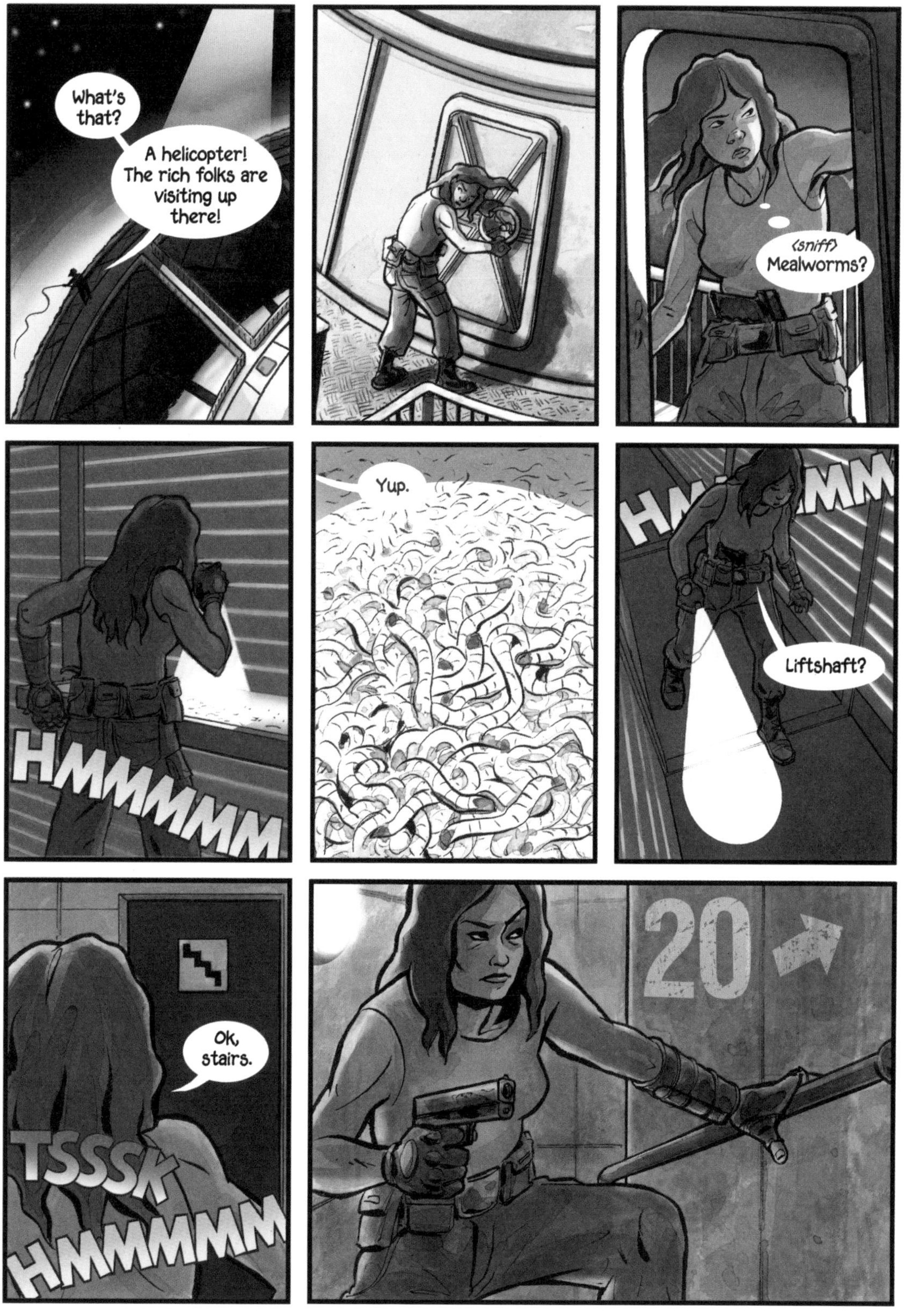
What's that?
A helicopter! The rich folks are visiting up there!
‹sniff› Mealworms?
HMMMMMM
Yup.
Liftshaft?
Ok, stairs.
TSSSK
HMMMMM
20

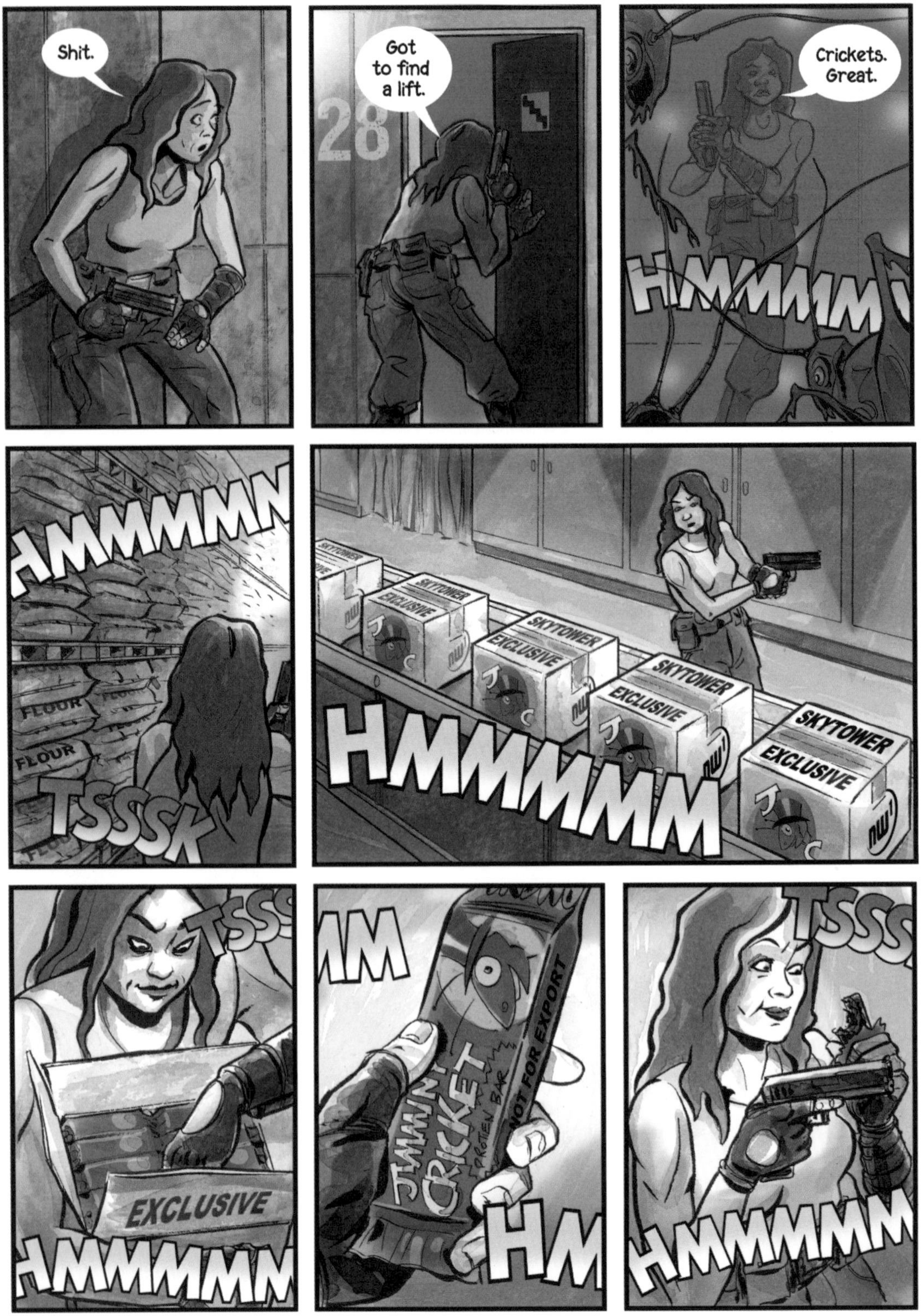
Shit.
Got to find a lift.
28
Crickets. Great.
HMMMMM
HMMMMN
FLOUR
TSSSK
SKYTOWER EXCLUSIVE
HMMMMMM
TSSS
EXCLUSIVE
HMMMMM
MM
JIMMINY CRICKET
PROTIEN BAR
NOT FOR EXPORT
HM
TSSS
HMMMMM

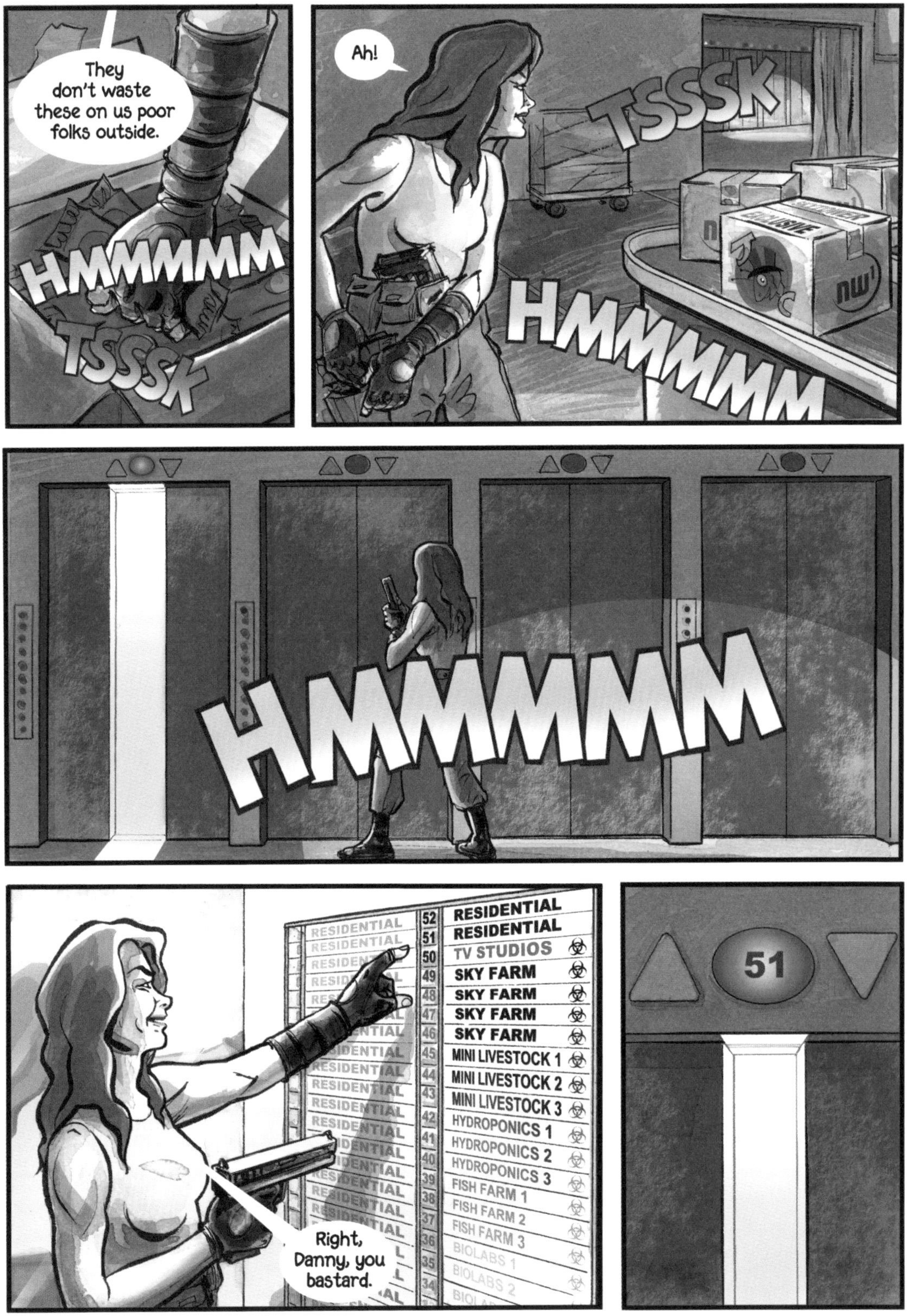
They don't waste these on us poor folks outside.
HMMMMM
TSSSK
Ah!
TSSSK
HMMMMMM
HMMMMMM
52 RESIDENTIAL
51 RESIDENTIAL
50 TV STUDIOS
49 SKY FARM
48 SKY FARM
47 SKY FARM
46 SKY FARM
45 MINI LIVESTOCK 1
44 MINI LIVESTOCK 2
43 MINI LIVESTOCK 3
42 HYDROPONICS 1
41 HYDROPONICS 2
40 HYDROPONICS 3
39 FISH FARM 1
38 FISH FARM 2
37 FISH FARM 3
36 BIOLABS 1
35 BIOLABS 2
Right, Danny, you bastard.
51

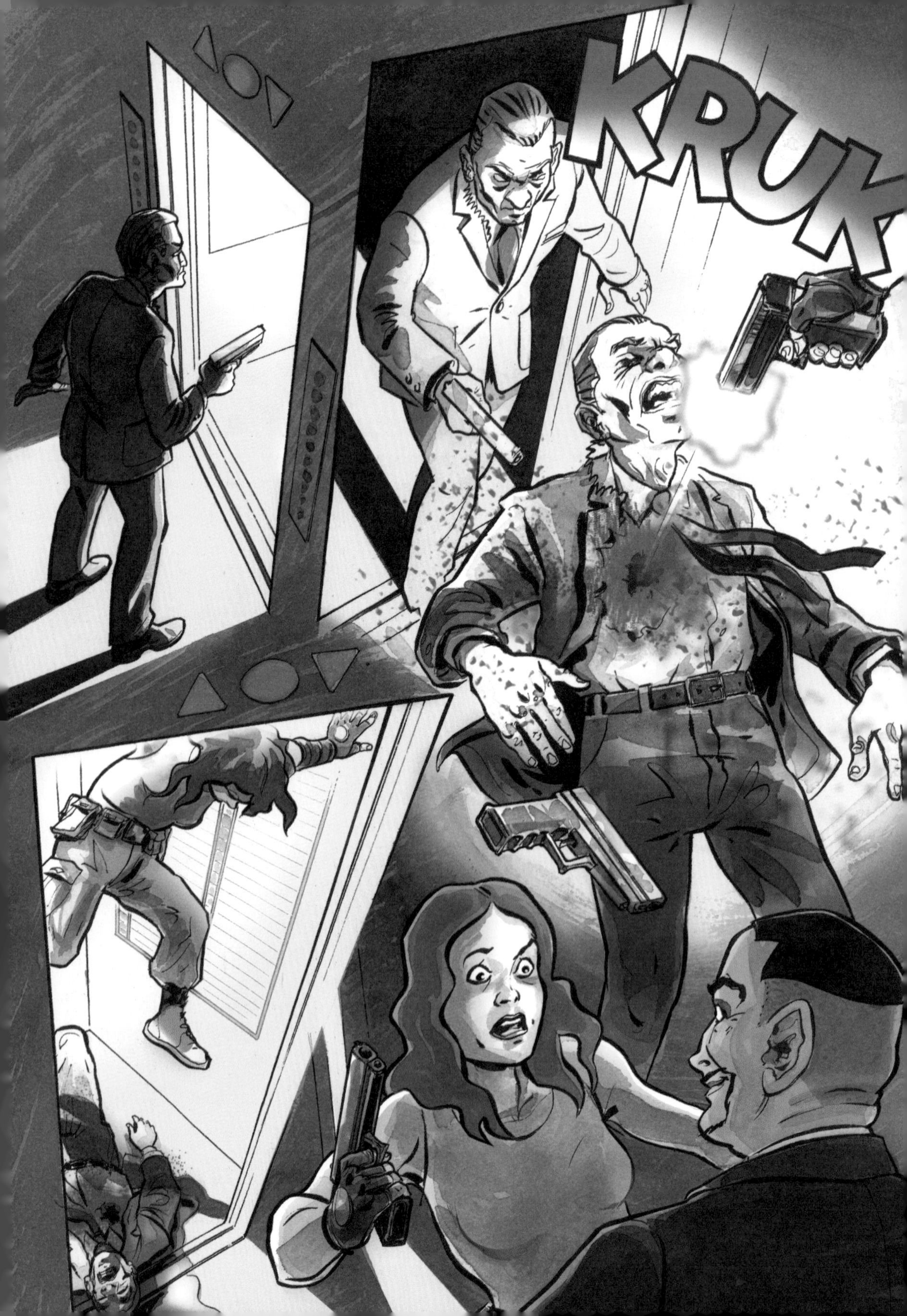
KRUK

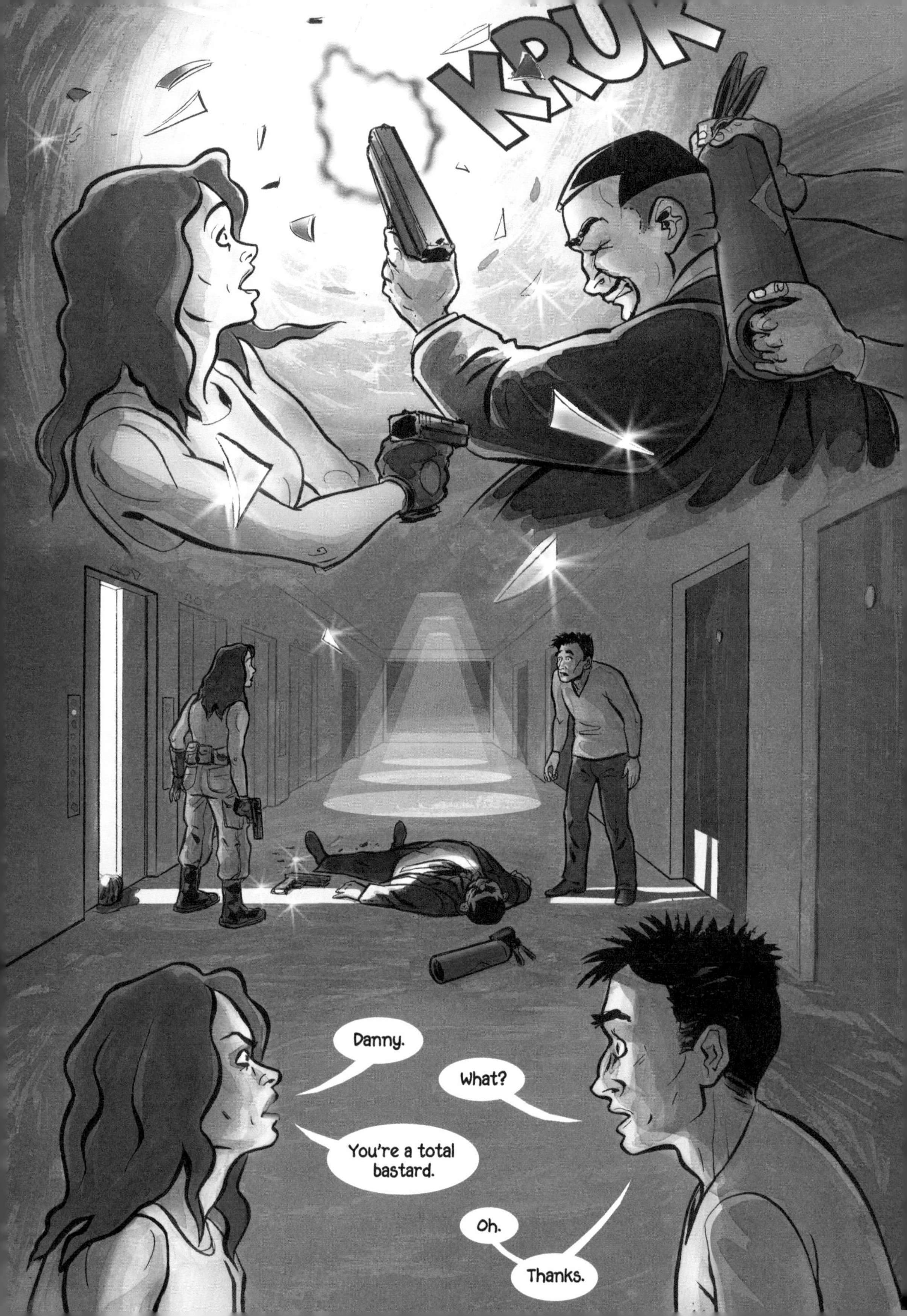
KRUK
Danny.
What?
You're a total bastard.
Oh.
Thanks.

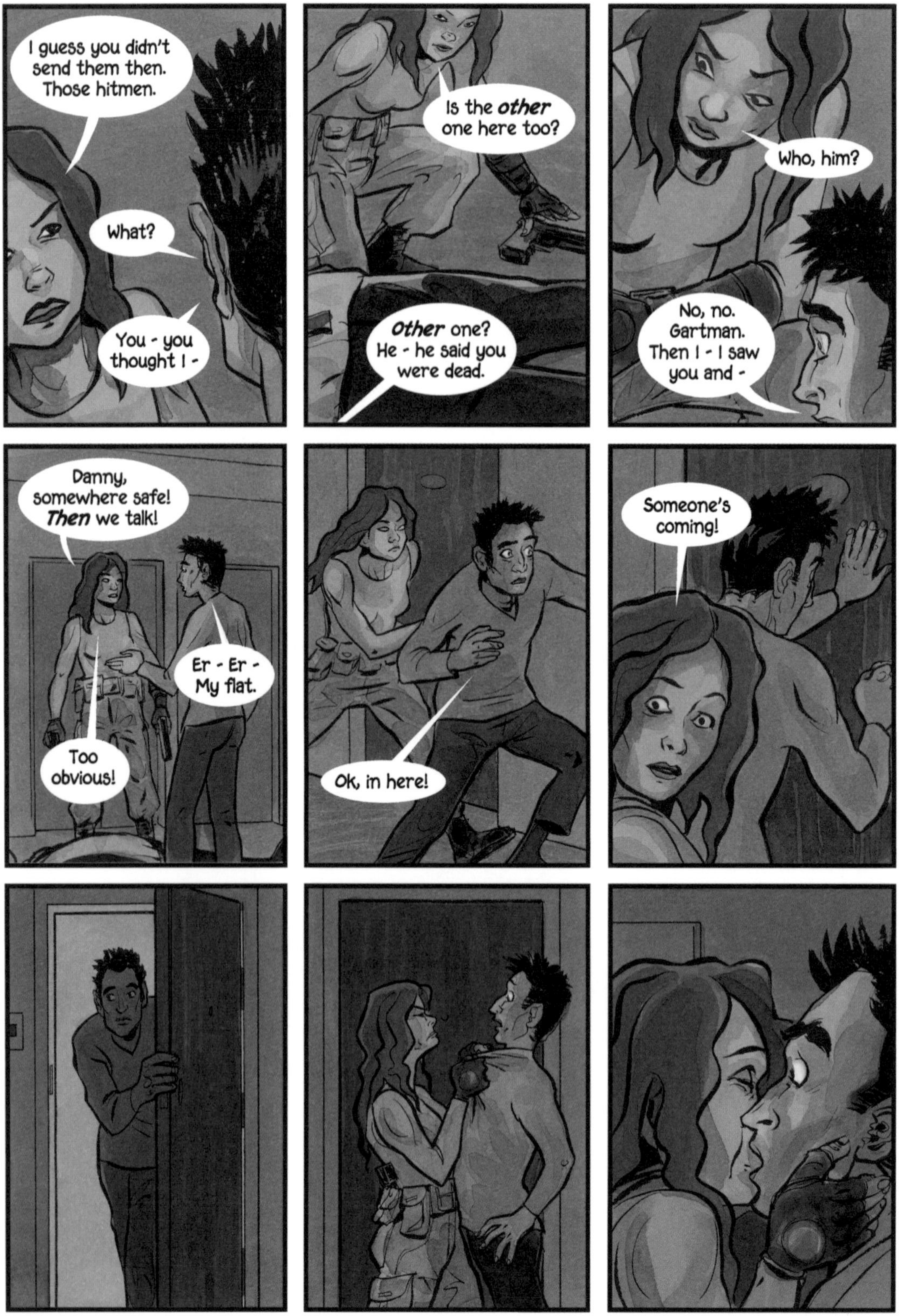
I guess you didn't send them then. Those hitmen.
What?
You - you thought I -
Is the *other* one here too?
Other one? He - he said you were dead.
Who, him?
No, no. Gartman. Then I - I saw you and -
Danny, somewhere safe! *Then* we talk!
Er - Er - My flat.
Too obvious!
Ok, in here!
Someone's coming!

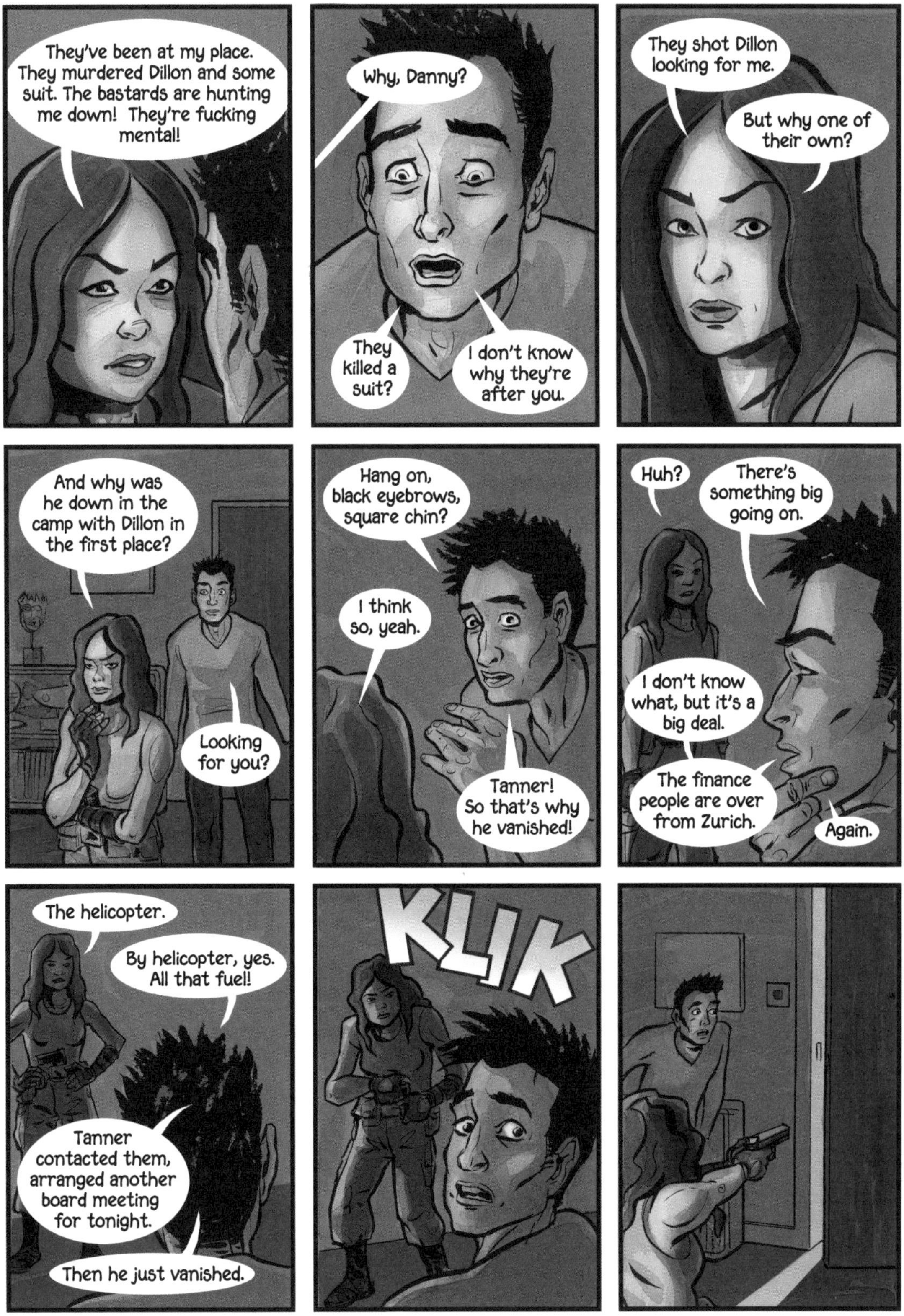
They've been at my place. They murdered Dillon and some suit. The bastards are hunting me down! They're fucking mental!
Why, Danny?
They killed a suit?
I don't know why they're after you.
They shot Dillon looking for me.
But why one of their own?
And why was he down in the camp with Dillon in the first place?
Looking for you?
Hang on, black eyebrows, square chin?
I think so, yeah.
Tanner! So that's why he vanished!
Huh?
There's something big going on.
I don't know what, but it's a big deal.
The finance people are over from Zurich.
Again.
The helicopter.
By helicopter, yes. All that fuel!
Tanner contacted them, arranged another board meeting for tonight.
Then he just vanished.
KLIK

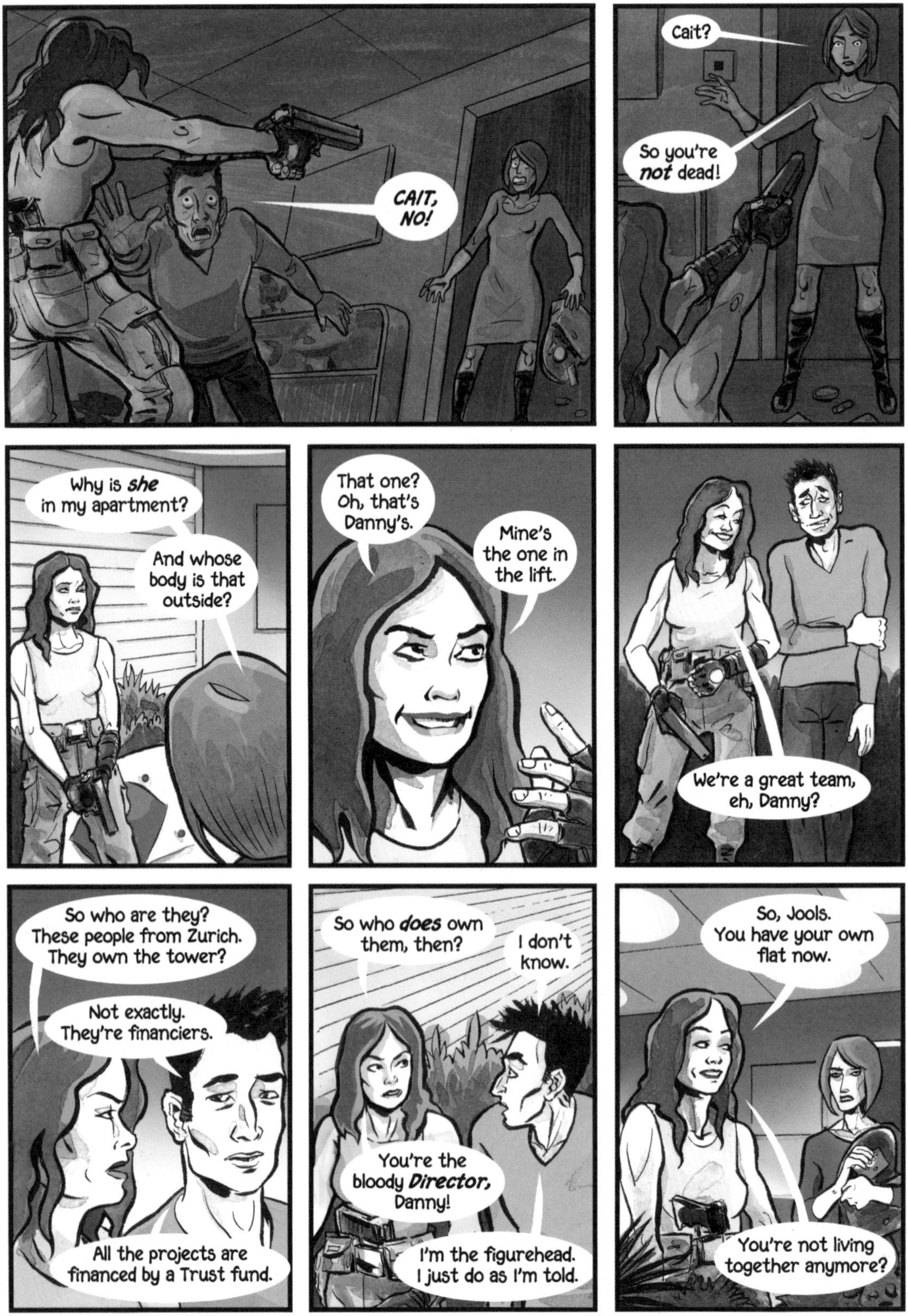
CAIT, NO!
Cait?
So you're *not* dead!
Why is *she* in my apartment?
And whose body is that outside?
That one? Oh, that's Danny's.
Mine's the one in the lift.
We're a great team, eh, Danny?
So who are they? These people from Zurich. They own the tower?
Not exactly. They're financiers.
All the projects are financed by a Trust fund.
So who *does* own them, then?
I don't know.
You're the bloody *Director,* Danny!
I'm the figurehead. I just do as I'm told.
So, Jools. You have your own flat now.
You're not living together anymore?

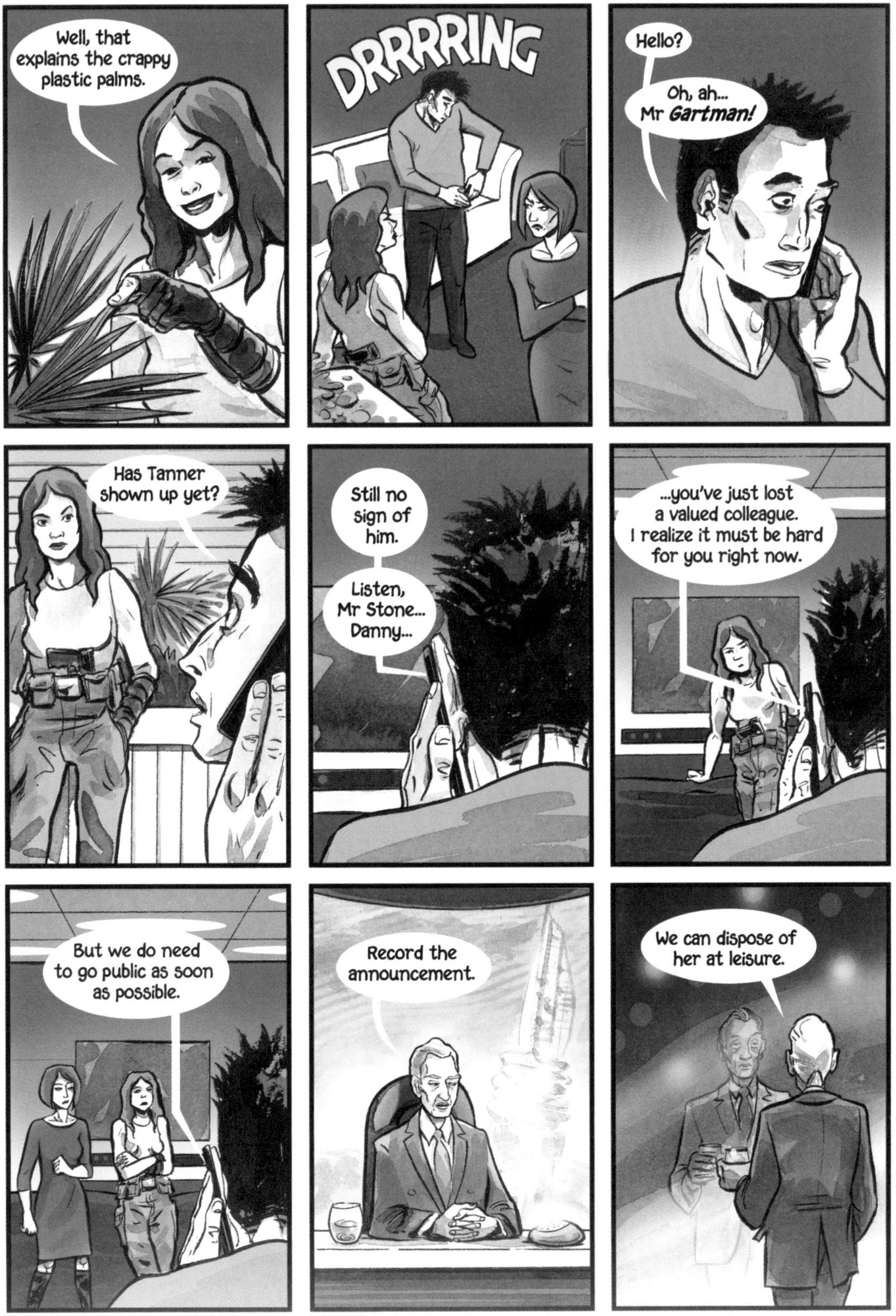
Well, that explains the crappy plastic palms.
DRRRRING
Hello?
Oh, ah... Mr *Gartman!*
Has Tanner shown up yet?
Still no sign of him.
Listen, Mr Stone... Danny...
...you've just lost a valued colleague. I realize it must be hard for you right now.
But we do need to go public as soon as possible.
Record the announcement.
We can dispose of her at leisure.

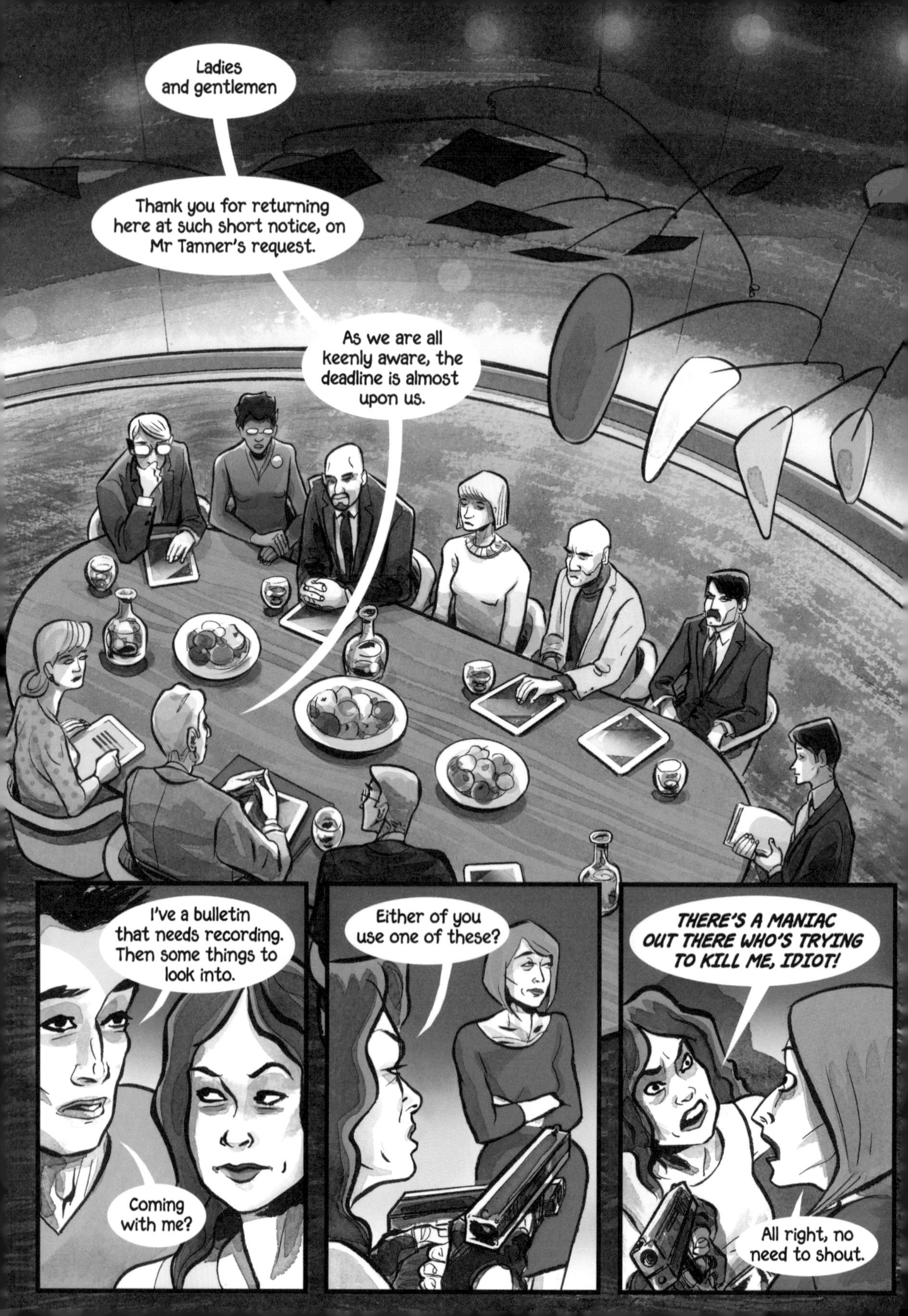
Ladies and gentlemen
Thank you for returning here at such short notice, on Mr Tanner's request.
As we are all keenly aware, the deadline is almost upon us.
I've a bulletin that needs recording. Then some things to look into.
Coming with me?
Either of you use one of these?
THERE'S A MANIAC OUT THERE WHO'S TRYING TO KILL ME, IDIOT!
All right, no need to shout.

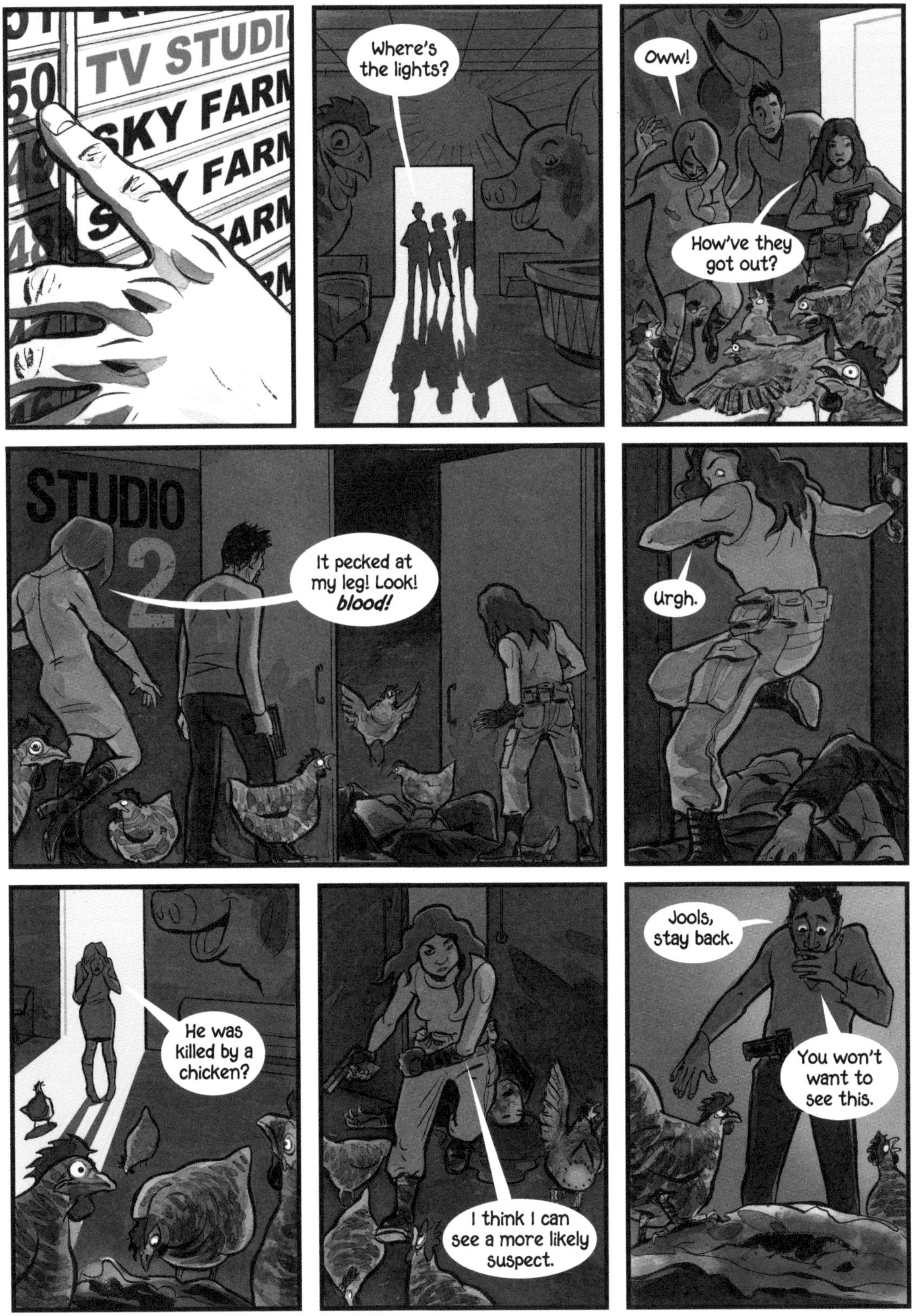
50
49
48
TV STUDIO
SKY FARM
SKY FARM
SKY FARM
Where's the lights?
Oww!
How've they got out?
STUDIO 2
It pecked at my leg! Look! ***blood!***
Urgh.
He was killed by a chicken?
I think I can see a more likely suspect.
Jools, stay back.
You won't want to see this.

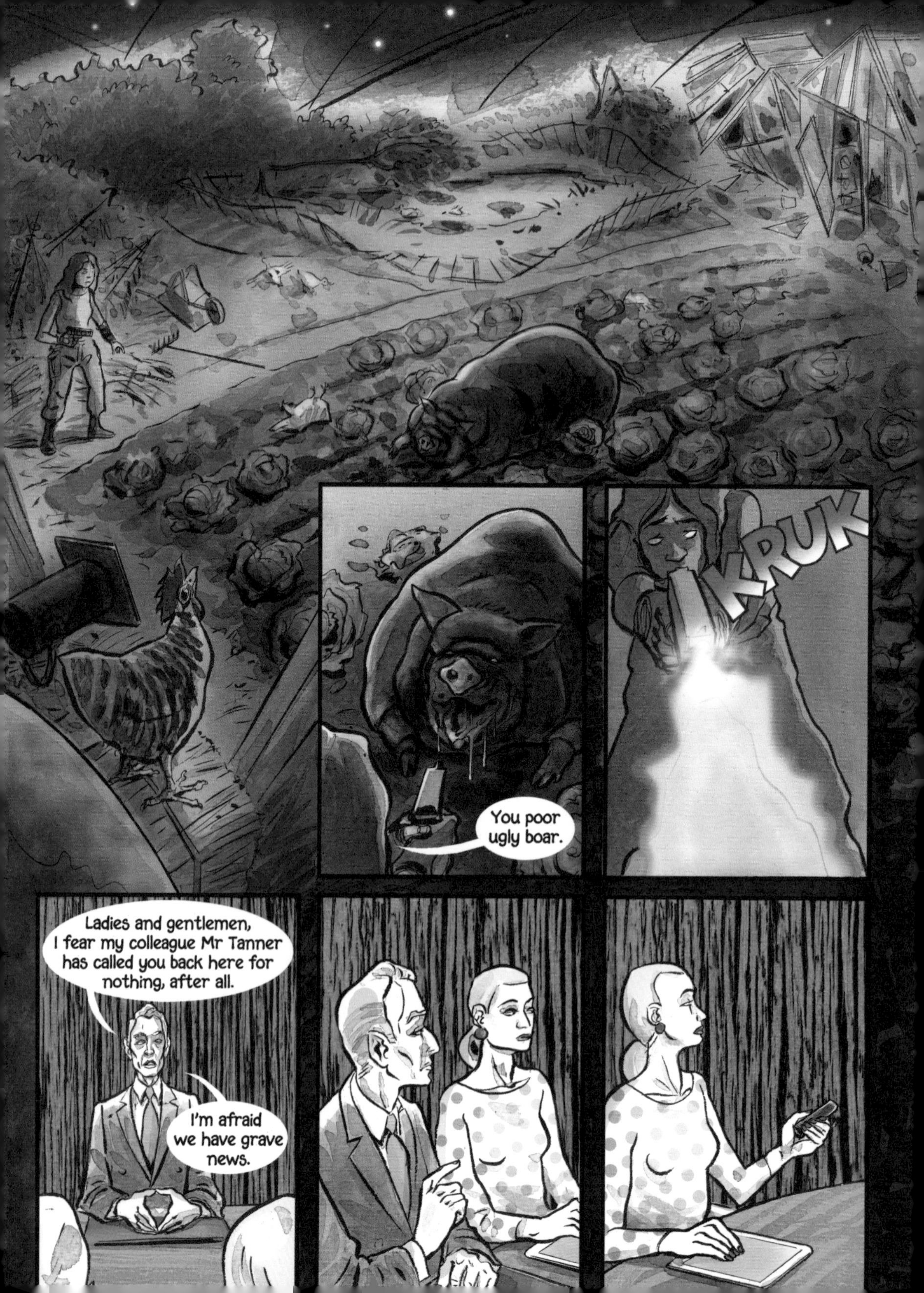
You poor ugly boar.
KRUK
Ladies and gentlemen, I fear my colleague Mr Tanner has called you back here for nothing, after all.
I'm afraid we have grave news.

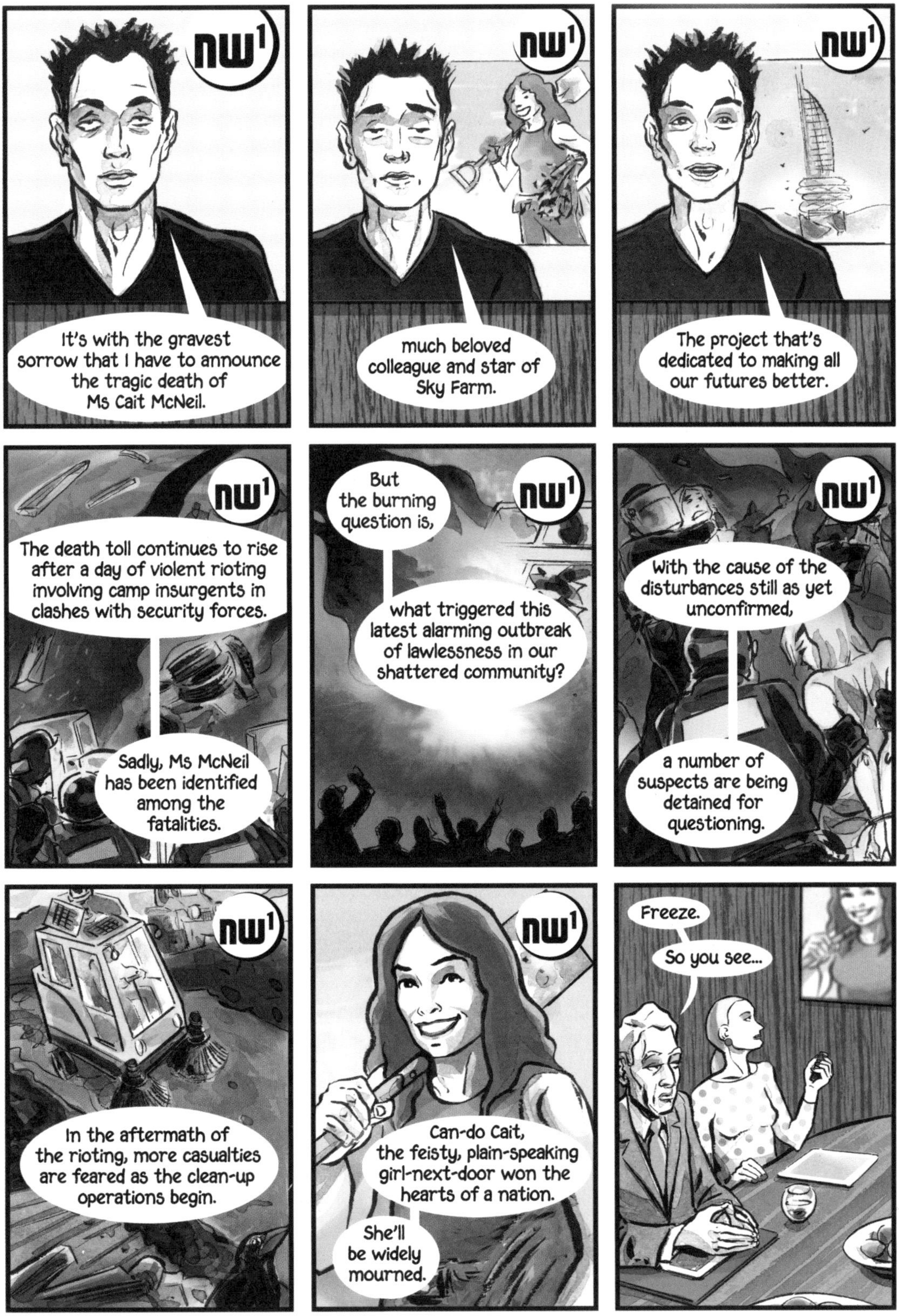
NW1
It's with the gravest sorrow that I have to announce the tragic death of Ms Cait McNeil.
much beloved colleague and star of Sky Farm.
The project that's dedicated to making all our futures better.
The death toll continues to rise after a day of violent rioting involving camp insurgents in clashes with security forces.
Sadly, Ms McNeil has been identified among the fatalities.
But the burning question is,
what triggered this latest alarming outbreak of lawlessness in our shattered community?
With the cause of the disturbances still as yet unconfirmed,
a number of suspects are being detained for questioning.
In the aftermath of the rioting, more casualties are feared as the clean-up operations begin.
Can-do Cait, the feisty, plain-speaking girl-next-door won the hearts of a nation.
She'll be widely mourned.
Freeze.
So you see...

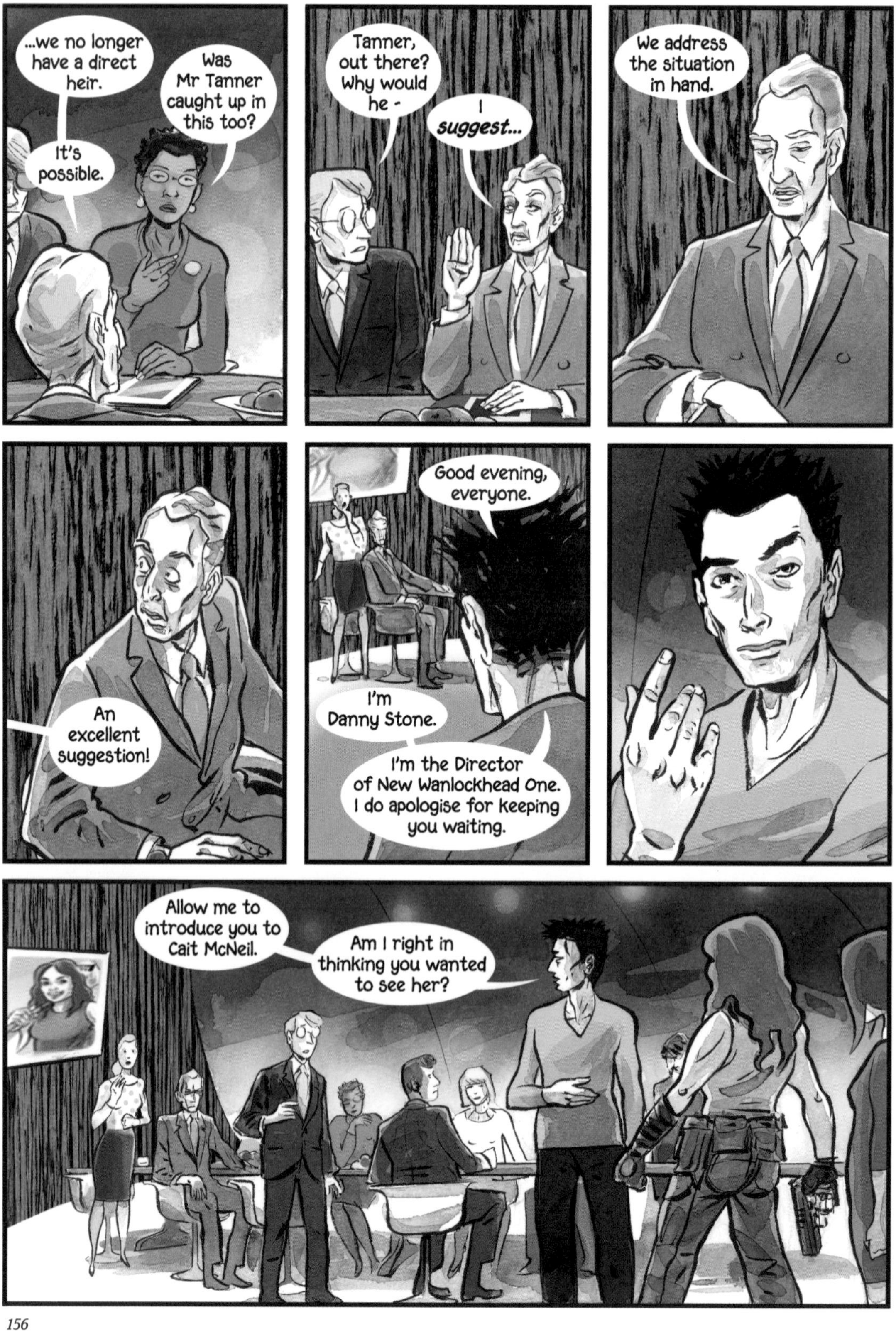
...we no longer have a direct heir.
Was Mr Tanner caught up in this too?
It's possible.
Tanner, out there? Why would he -
I *suggest...*
We address the situation in hand.
An excellent suggestion!
Good evening, everyone.
I'm Danny Stone.
I'm the Director of New Wanlockhead One. I do apologise for keeping you waiting.
Allow me to introduce you to Cait McNeil.
Am I right in thinking you wanted to see her?

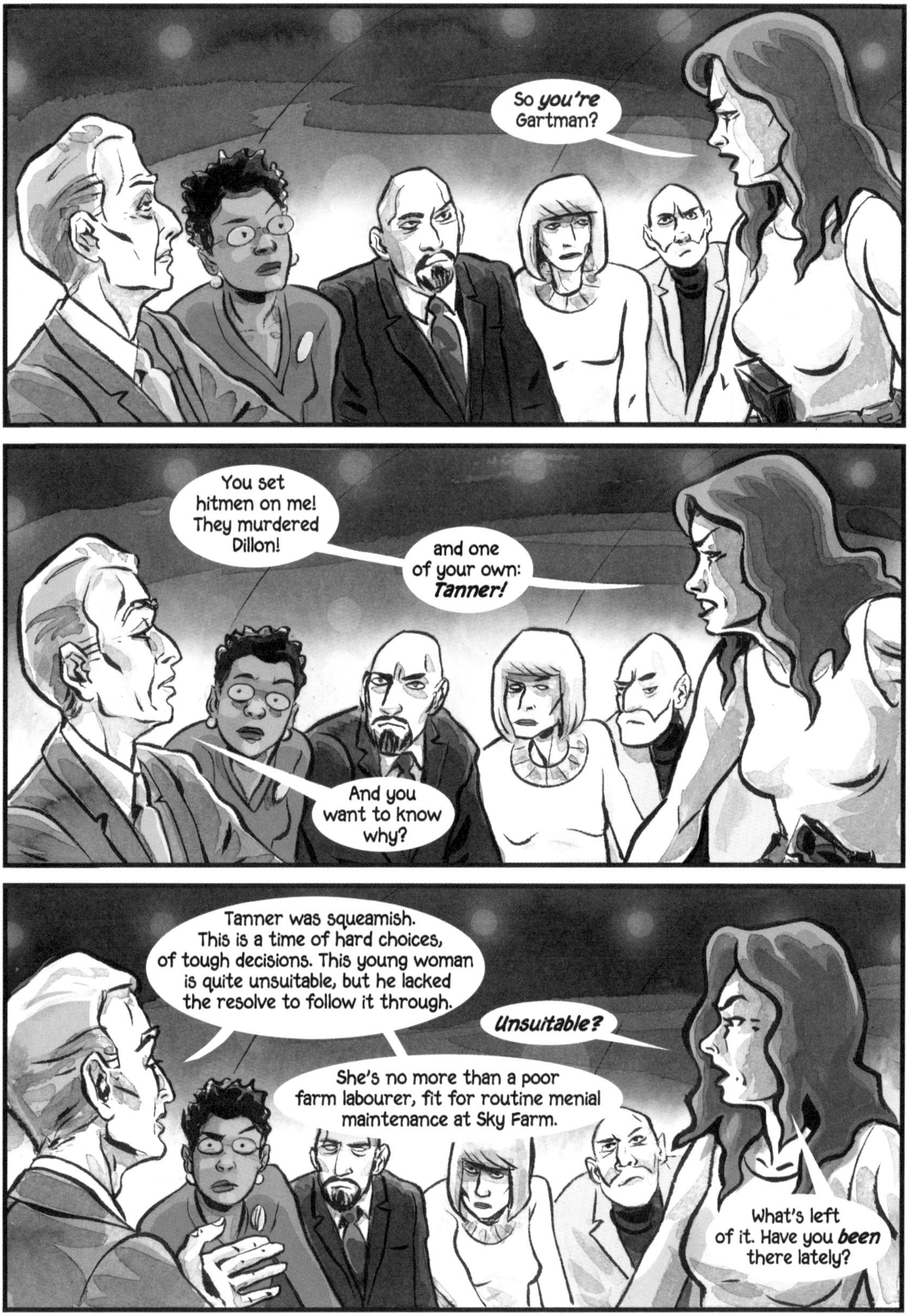
So *you're* Gartman?
You set hitmen on me! They murdered Dillon!
and one of your own: ***Tanner!***
And you want to know why?
Tanner was squeamish. This is a time of hard choices, of tough decisions. This young woman is quite unsuitable, but he lacked the resolve to follow it through.
Unsuitable?
She's no more than a poor farm labourer, fit for routine menial maintenance at Sky Farm.
What's left of it. Have you ***been*** there lately?

Those mutant monsters have all died in convulsions, but not before trashing the whole place.

They've been feeding the stock with growth hormones that haven't been tested properly.

It's grotesque.

There *is* no Sky Farm.

What's this?

This raises major concerns about profitability.

We've had assurances from you that this first tower project was approaching cost effectiveness. If this isn't the case, then we will have to reconsider the viability of Phases Two and Three.

Cait's right, but it's not only the growth hormones. The labs aren't producing enough results.

And the hydroponics are running into big problems too. The automation's working fine but the yield's nothing like what we were promised.

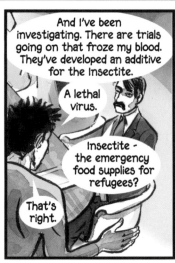

And I've been investigating. There are trials going on that froze my blood. They've developed an additive for the Insectite.

A lethal virus.

Insectite - the emergency food supplies for refugees?

That's right.

It's only a matter of stabilising an antidote to safeguard people in the towers, then it goes out.

A couple of months, max.

I don't recall your corporate strategy extending to the elimination of segments of the population.

I'm assuming that this *is* the purpose of this additive?

Indeed it is.

Are you aware of this undertaking, Mr Gartman?

Ah, yes.

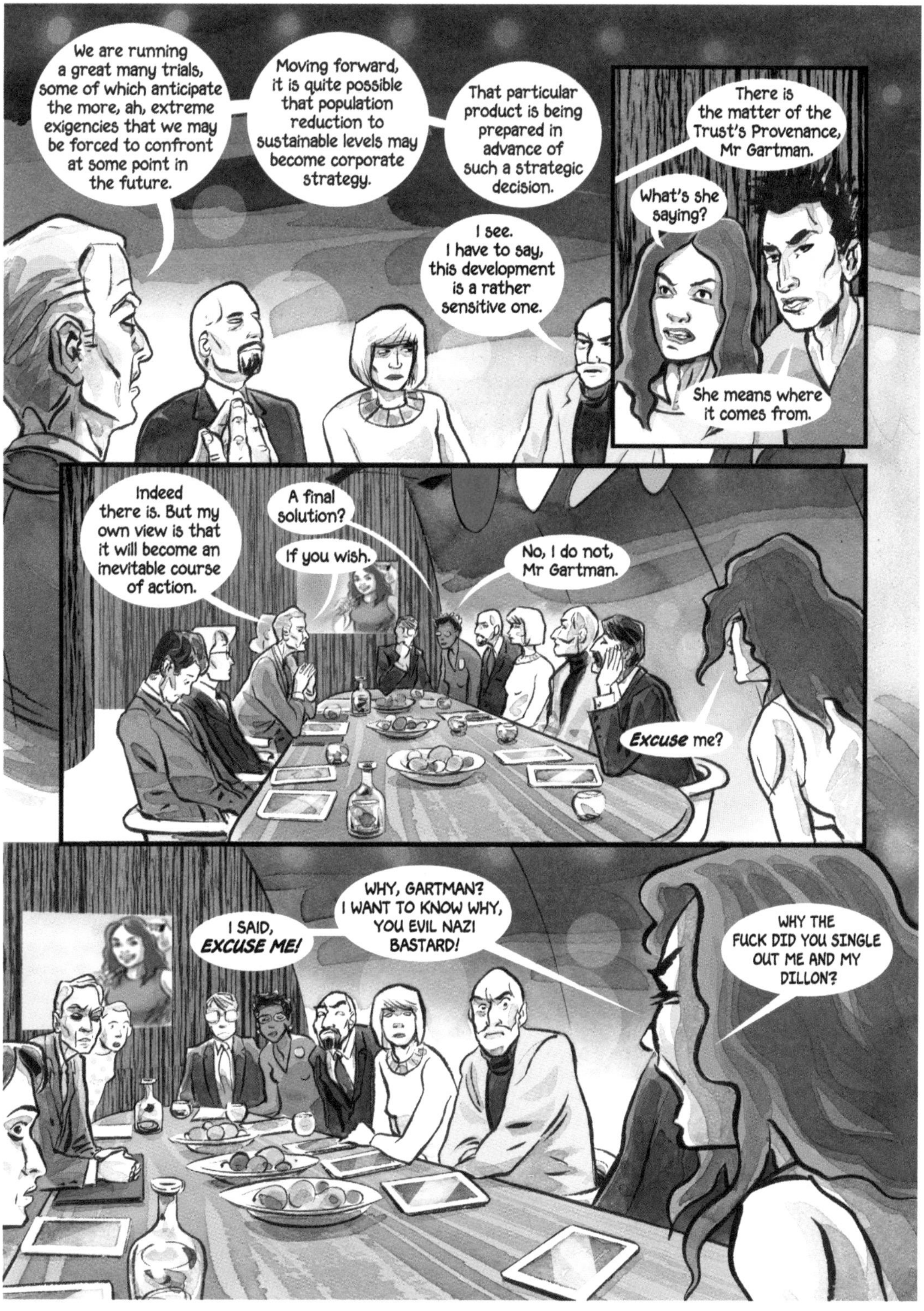

We are running a great many trials, some of which anticipate the more, ah, extreme exigencies that we may be forced to confront at some point in the future.
Moving forward, it is quite possible that population reduction to sustainable levels may become corporate strategy.
That particular product is being prepared in advance of such a strategic decision.
I see. I have to say, this development is a rather sensitive one.
There is the matter of the Trust's Provenance, Mr Gartman.
What's she saying?
She means where it comes from.
Indeed there is. But my own view is that it will become an inevitable course of action.
A final solution?
If you wish.
No, I do not, Mr Gartman.
Excuse me?
I SAID, ***EXCUSE ME!***
WHY, GARTMAN? I WANT TO KNOW WHY, YOU EVIL NAZI BASTARD!
WHY THE FUCK DID YOU SINGLE OUT ME AND MY DILLON?

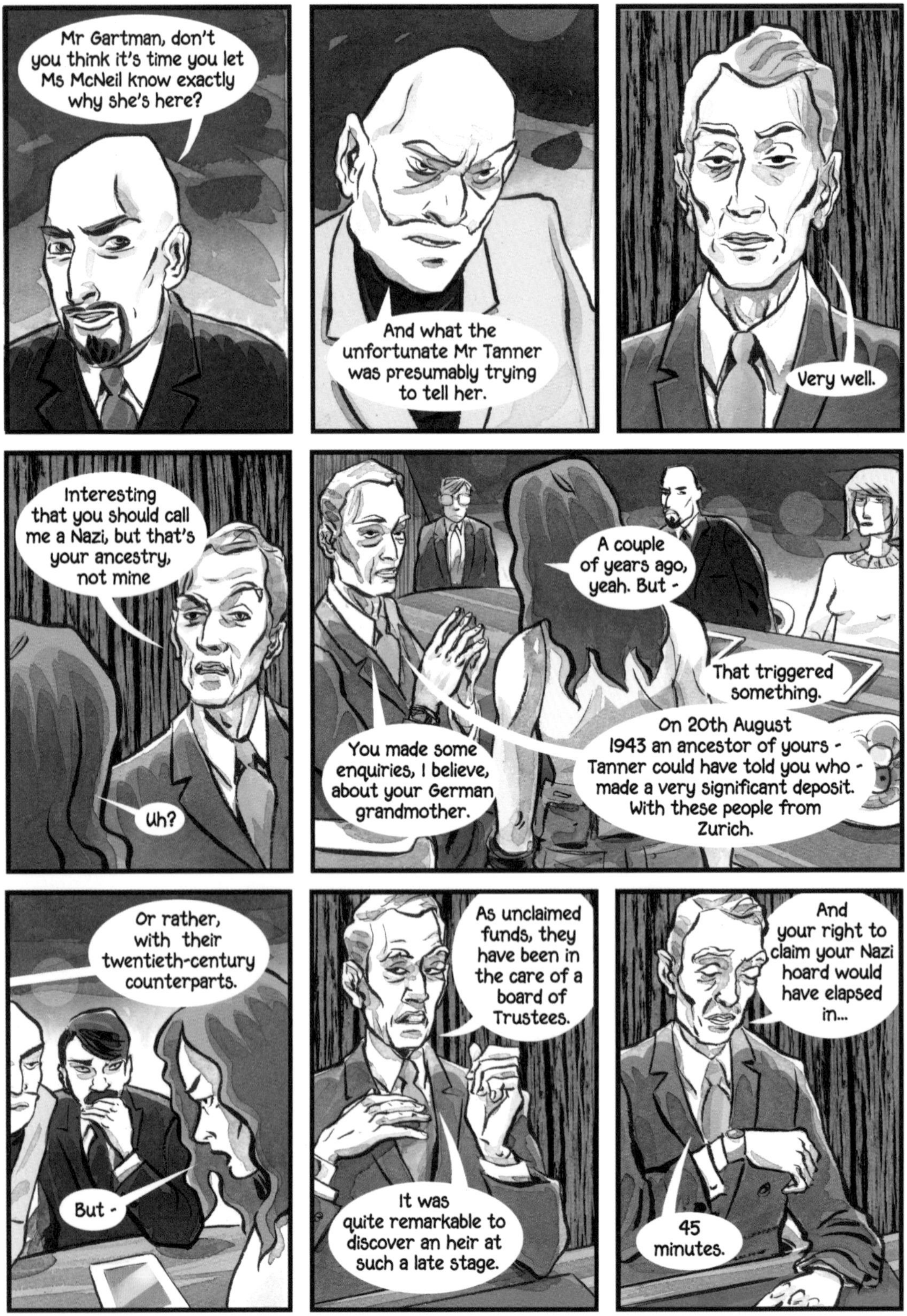
Mr Gartman, don't you think it's time you let Ms McNeil know exactly why she's here?
And what the unfortunate Mr Tanner was presumably trying to tell her.
Very well.
Interesting that you should call me a Nazi, but that's your ancestry, not mine
Uh?
A couple of years ago, yeah. But -
You made some enquiries, I believe, about your German grandmother.
That triggered something.
On 20th August 1943 an ancestor of yours - Tanner could have told you who - made a very significant deposit. With these people from Zurich.
Or rather, with their twentieth-century counterparts.
But -
As unclaimed funds, they have been in the care of a board of Trustees.
It was quite remarkable to discover an heir at such a late stage.
And your right to claim your Nazi hoard would have elapsed in...
45 minutes.

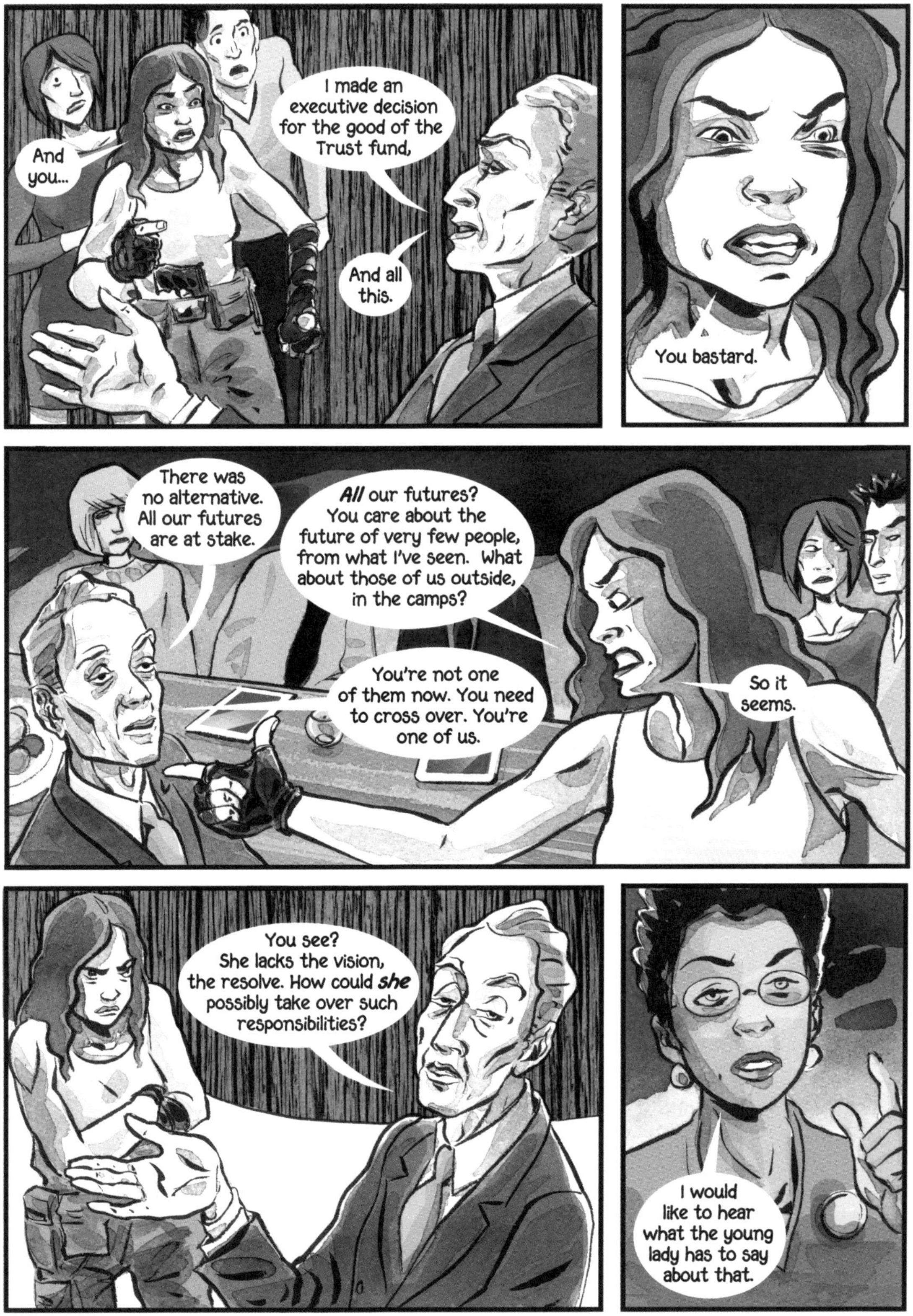
And you...
I made an executive decision for the good of the Trust fund,
And all this.
You bastard.
There was no alternative. All our futures are at stake.
All our futures? You care about the future of very few people, from what I've seen. What about those of us outside, in the camps?
You're not one of them now. You need to cross over. You're one of us.
So it seems.
You see? She lacks the vision, the resolve. How could *she* possibly take over such responsibilities?
I would like to hear what the young lady has to say about that.

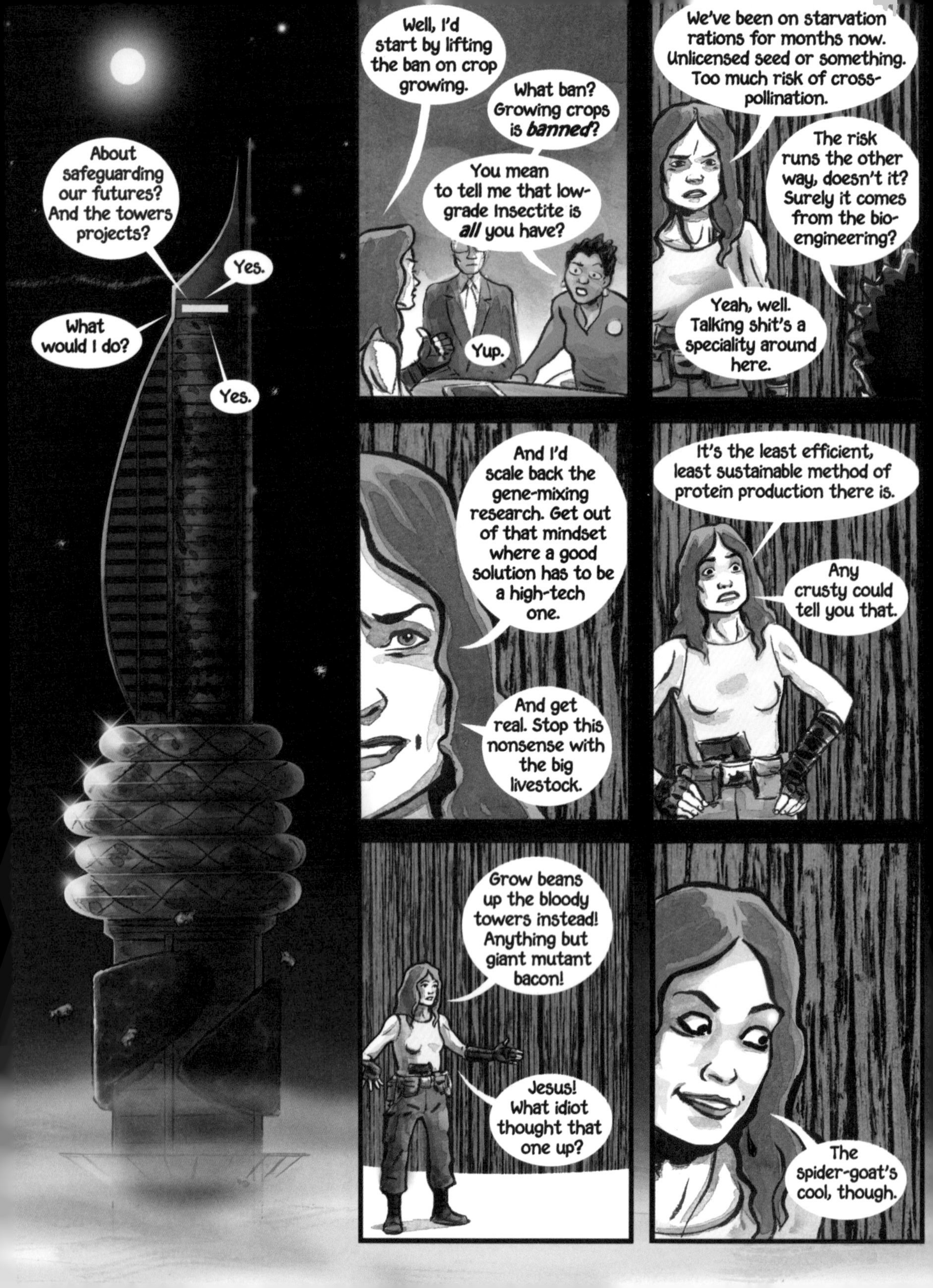
About safeguarding our futures? And the towers projects?
Yes.
What would I do?
Yes.
Well, I'd start by lifting the ban on crop growing.
What ban? Growing crops is *banned*?
You mean to tell me that low-grade Insectite is *all* you have?
Yup.
We've been on starvation rations for months now. Unlicensed seed or something. Too much risk of cross-pollination.
The risk runs the other way, doesn't it? Surely it comes from the bio-engineering?
Yeah, well. Talking shit's a speciality around here.
And I'd scale back the gene-mixing research. Get out of that mindset where a good solution has to be a high-tech one.
And get real. Stop this nonsense with the big livestock.
It's the least efficient, least sustainable method of protein production there is.
Any crusty could tell you that.
Grow beans up the bloody towers instead! Anything but giant mutant bacon!
Jesus! What idiot thought that one up?
The spider-goat's cool, though.

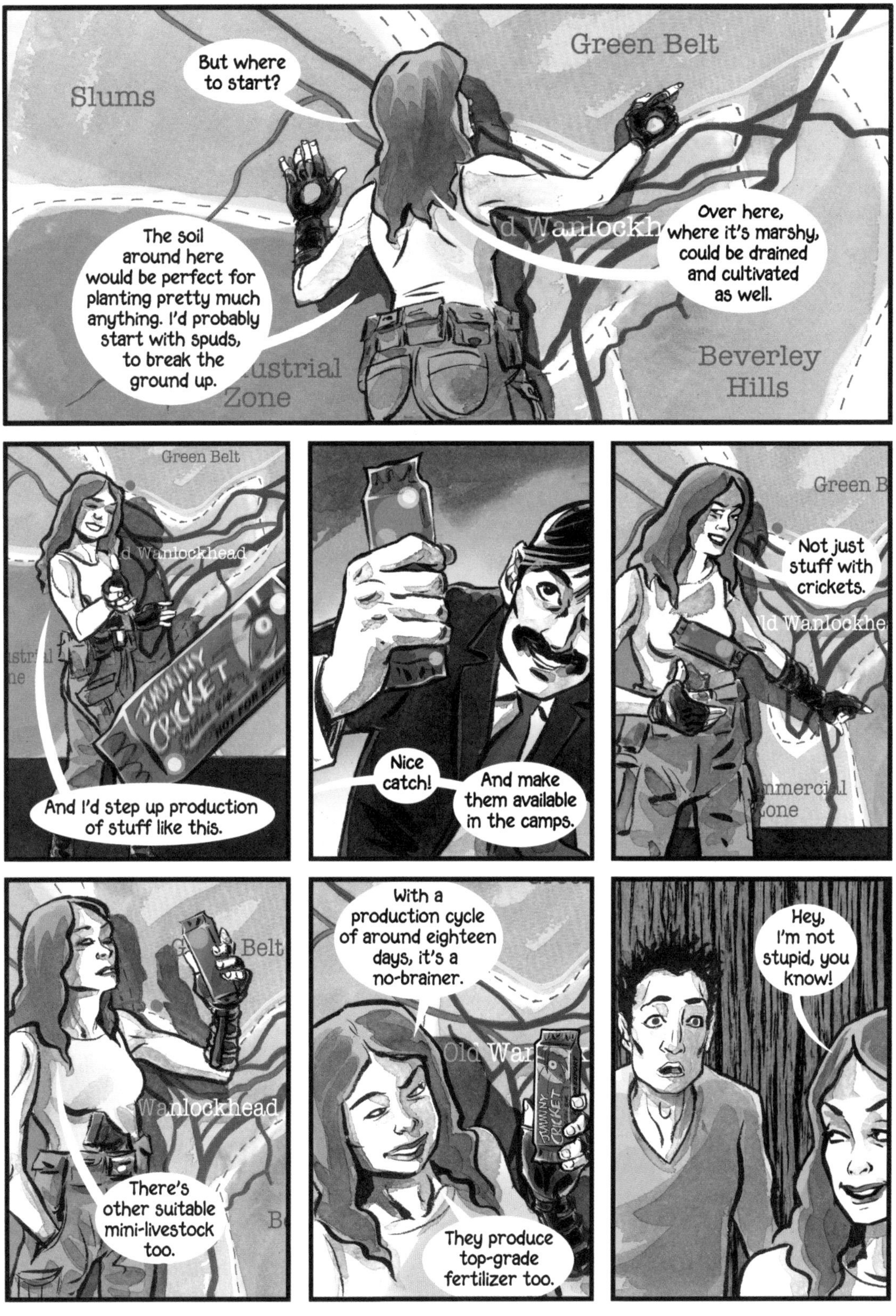
Green Belt
Slums
But where to start?
The soil around here would be perfect for planting pretty much anything. I'd probably start with spuds, to break the ground up.
Over here, where it's marshy, could be drained and cultivated as well.
Beverley Hills
Green Belt
And I'd step up production of stuff like this.
Nice catch!
And make them available in the camps.
Not just stuff with crickets.
There's other suitable mini-livestock too.
With a production cycle of around eighteen days, it's a no-brainer.
They produce top-grade fertilizer too.
Hey, I'm not stupid, you know!

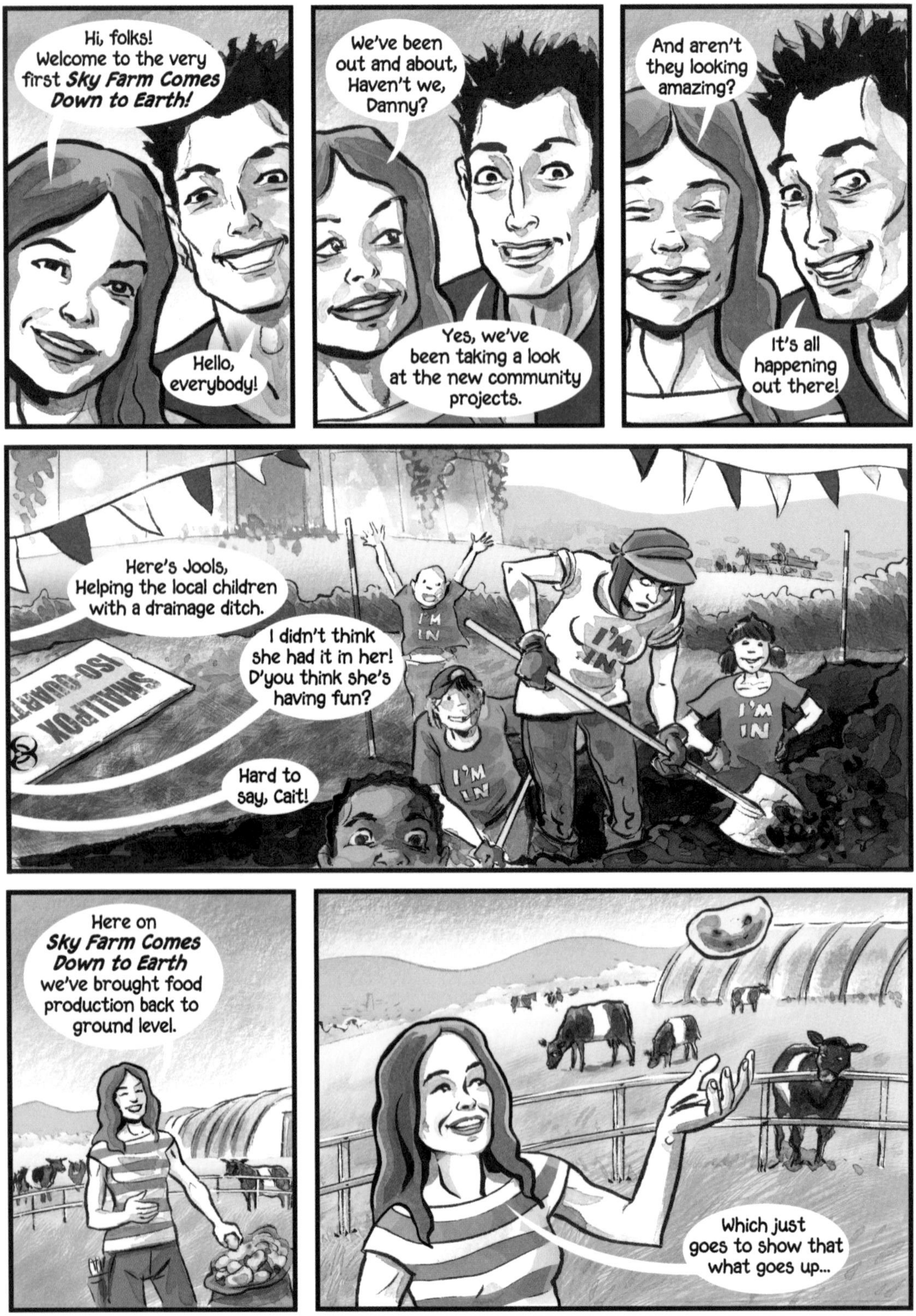
Hi, folks! Welcome to the very first *Sky Farm Comes Down to Earth!*
Hello, everybody!
We've been out and about, Haven't we, Danny?
Yes, we've been taking a look at the new community projects.
And aren't they looking amazing?
It's all happening out there!
Here's Jools, Helping the local children with a drainage ditch.
I didn't think she had it in her! D'you think she's having fun?
Hard to say, Cait!
Here on *Sky Farm Comes Down to Earth* we've brought food production back to ground level.
Which just goes to show that what goes up...

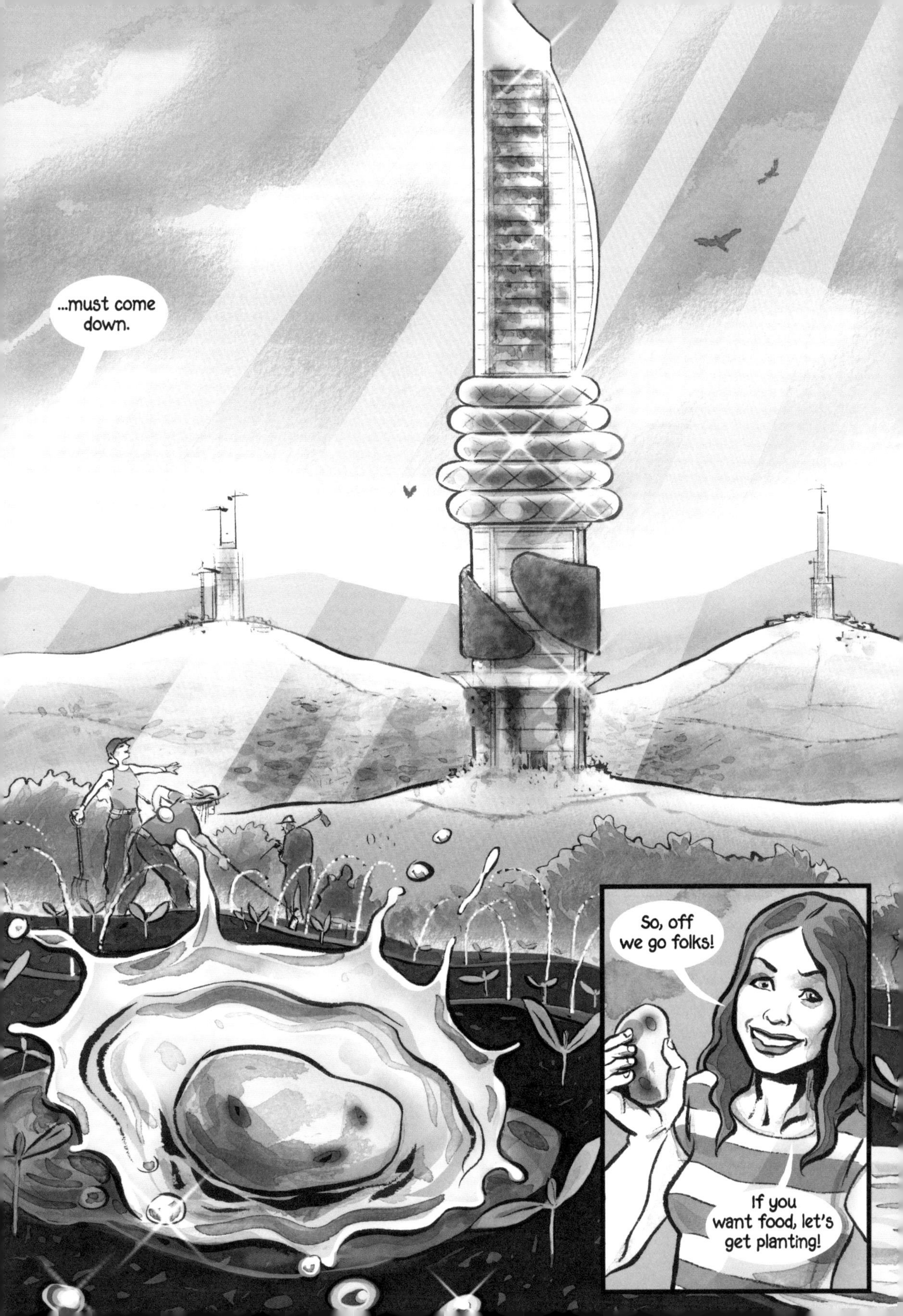
...must come down.
So, off we go folks!
If you want food, let's get planting!

About the Contributors

Barroux
Chapter 5

Born in Paris and raised in Morocco, **Barroux** studied photography, art, sculpture, and architecture in France at the famous École Estienne and École Boule. Following his studies, he worked as an art director in Paris and Montreal. While in Montreal, Barroux began illustrating by creating linocut images, and became well known for his illustrations for children's books. His work has appeared in the *New York Times, Washington Post,* and *Forbes*. He lives in Paris with his family.

Hannah Berry
Chapter 1

Hannah Berry is mostly a graphic novelist, but sometimes publishes words without pictures or illustrations without text. She is a comics teacher and editorial gun-for-hire, and was once Booktrust's Online Writer in Residence. Her first graphic novel *Britten and Brülightly* was published by Jonathan Cape in 2008, with subsequent editions all around the world. The French edition was chosen for the official selection of the 2010 Angoulême International Comics Festival. Her second graphic novel, *Adamtine* was also published by Cape in 2012. She has contributed to other graphic collections including *Above the Dreamless Dead* (First Second, US), *Hoax: Psychosis Blues* (Ziggy's Wish, UK) and *La Villa Sur La Falaise* (Casterman, France).

www.hannahberry.co.uk

Kate Charlesworth
Chapter 6

Kate Charlesworth is a cartoonist, illustrator and writer. Her work has appeared in both print and digital press, publishing and animation. Cartoon strips include the *Guardian's* 'Millennium Basin', the *Independent's* 'Lysteria Crescent', the *Pink Paper's* 'Plain Tales from the Bars' and 'Naughty Little Monkeys', *New Scientist's* 'Life, the Universe and (Almost) Everything' and the *Bookseller's* 'Font and Font'. Books include *All That: the Other Half of History* with Marsaili Cameron, *The Cartoon History of Time* with John Gribbin, *Nelson,* edited by Rob Davies and Woodrow Phoenix, and most recently *Sally Heathcote: Suffragette* with Mary and Bryan Talbot. Originally from South Yorkshire, she lives and works in Edinburgh.

www.katecharlesworth.com

Tom Kindley
Cover Illustrator

Tom Kindley was born on the 17th of May 1990 (7lbs 8oz). He has since spent much of his time working towards becoming an illustrator. He graduated from Edinburgh College of Art in the summer of 2013 and currently resides in Newcastle-upon-Tyne. Tom now spends his time as a freelance illustrator, whilst creating independent comics and zines on the side. He loves his job and is always hungry for more work. In fact, he's starving.

89

09

115

35

Dan McDaid
Chapter 4

Pat Mills
Chapter 1

Denise Mina
Editor & Chapter 5

Will Morris
Chapter 2

Dan McDaid is a comics artist and writer based in Scotland. He began his career working for Panini, writing and providing art for an acclaimed run on the Doctor Who comic in *DWM*. At the same time, he was the artist on cult favourite Image book *Jersey Gods*. He later returned to Image for art duties on Jim McCann's *Mind the Gap*. Since then, he has worked for DC Comics, Oni Press, IDW and, most recently, Dark Horse, providing the artwork for *Catalyst Comix,* written by Joe Casey; and his current book, *Vandroid*, a schlocky, psychedelic homage to eighties video nasties. McDaid was one of the artists on the futuristic thriller *Ashes/Smoke*, and wrote and drew the 1997 chapter — featuring demonic Spice Girls – of the award-winning anthology *Nelson*.

www.danmcdaid.com

Pat Mills is the creator and first editor of *2000AD*. He developed *Judge Dredd* and is the writer-creator of many of *2000AD's* most popular stories. He created the anti-war series *Charley's War* with artist Joe Colquhoun and *Marshal Law* – a critique of super heroes – with Kevin O'Neill, published by DC Comics. He recently adapted *Dead Man's Dump* by Isaac Rosenberg with artist David Hitchcock for *Above the Dreamless Dead* (First Second Books), a graphic collection of World War One poetry. His current projects include *Brothers in Arms*, a new World War One saga also with David Hitchcock.

After a peripatetic childhood in Glasgow, Paris, London, Invergordon, Bergen and Perth, **Denise Mina** left school early to concentrate on doing dead end jobs badly and rudely. Attending night school, she was accepted to study law at Glasgow University and went on to study for a PhD at Strathclyde. She has written twelve novels, three plays, five graphic novels and regularly contributes to television and radio. Her novels have won six major awards and she has been nominated for thirteen. The BBC/Slate adapted two of her novels for TV. She wrote Vertigo's *Hellblazer* for a year with Leo Manco, a stand-alone *A Sickness In The Family* with Antonio Fuso, again for Vertigo, and is currently adapting Steig Larsson's *Girl With the Dragon Tattoo* Trilogy for DC Comics.

www.denisemina.com

Will Morris is a comics creator and illustrator based in Edinburgh. He is the award-winning author of the original graphic novel, *The Silver Darlings*, a story of superstition, youthful scepticism and comradeship within a herring fishing community. He has also contributed work to a wide range of publications, including an adaptation of the Child Ballad, *Clerk Colvill*, in *Nobrow 9*, a chapter in the award-winning anthology *Nelson*, and as the artist for a chilling festive tale in Franco-Belgian comics magazine, *Spirou*, as well as a short story in *2000AD*.

You can keep up to date with Will's work online at:

will-morris.tumblr.com
twitter.com/wh_morris

Adam Murphy
Chapter 3

Dr Mary Talbot
Chapter 6

Irvine Welsh
Chapter 4

Adam Murphy is a comics artist, writer and illustrator. He is the creator of *CorpseTalk*, in which he digs up famous people from history and interviews their reanimated corpses, and *Lost Tales,* in which he re-interprets unusual or lesser-known folktales from around the world, both for the *Phoenix Children's Comics Magazine*. Other clients include the *Guardian, Linden Lab, The Times Literary Supplement* and *Talking Mats.* He has also self-published *Fever Dreams*, a collection of experimental short comics. He lives and works with his wife in Glasgow.

www.adammurphy.com

Dr Mary Talbot is an internationally acclaimed scholar of gender and language who now writes graphic novels. Her first, *Dotter of her Father's Eyes* (with Bryan Talbot; Cape 2012), won the 2012 Costa Biography Award. Her second, *Sally Heathcote: Suffragette* (with Kate Charlesworth and Bryan Talbot), came out in May 2014, also from Cape. Mary has been a freelance writer since 2009. Her recent non-fiction includes a second edition of *Language and Gender* (Polity 2010), a book that continues to be popular with university lecturers and students worldwide.

www.mary-talbot.co.uk

Irvine Welsh comes from Edinburgh, Scotland, and lives in Chicago, USA. He is the author of several novels, short story collections, stage plays and screenplays. He has lived in Scotland, England, Ireland, Holland and the United States, as well as travelling widely, and is interested in the issue of writing from a local culture within a globalized, consumerist era. As a journalist with the *Telegraph*, he was the first western correspondent in Darfur after the humanitarian crisis erupted in that region of Sudan. He also travelled to Afghanistan after the fall of the Taliban, to take part in a unique writing project on behalf of UNICEF. His number one UK bestseller, *Skagboys*, was published in 2012, and the film of his nineties number one bestseller, *Filth*, staring James McAvoy, was released in 2013. His latest novel is *The Sex Lives of Siamese Twins.*

Acknowledgements

Graphic novels are good at imagining the future. In fact, most of our classic images of tomorrow's world – silver jumpsuits, flying cars and robotic gadgets – probably originated in graphic novels or comics. So when the Edinburgh International Book Festival wanted to mark its 30th anniversary by imagining life 30 years ahead, it made sense to ask graphic novelists to help. What emerges, of course, is nothing like the science fiction visions from the 1960s and 70s, even if some of the artistic renderings in this book pay homage to their graphic style. In this book, set in futuristic New Wanlockhead, Scotland's highest village, the future looks a lot less shiny than it used to. Those enticing images from the past were driven by an underlying sense that technology offered the prospect of real progress for the human race, if only we could keep that fearsome scientific knowledge out of the hands of the baddies. Today, it's not quite so clear who the baddies might be: instead of waging war against political ideologies such as Nazism, we are now invited to indulge in a 'war on terror' – a nebulous idea if ever there was one. In practice, this book hints that the world's most intractable issues such as climate change, and the brutal expulsion of countless poorer people from mainstream society, are very much problems of our own making.

Nick Barley
Director, Edinburgh International Book Festival

This book is a partnership between Freight Books and the Edinburgh International Book Festival, commissioned as part of the Book Festival's *Stripped* programme of events on graphic novels and comics. We are grateful to the contributors who have worked in an astonishingly collaborative manner to produce the book. Once Denise Mina had created the story framework, Pat Mills worked with her to set up a series of chapter themes within the bigger narrative arc, as well as writing the opening chapter. Meanwhile Hannah Berry and Kate Charlesworth worked closely together with Denise to develop the characters, and to create the iconic design of perhaps the most evil characters in the story: the Sky Farm and its surrounding shanty town. With great sensitivity and skill, the other contributors developed the characters and brought in some imaginative new elements all of their own. Adam Murphy, Barroux, Will Morris, Irvine Welsh and Dan McDaid each took the story in surprising new directions, while Mary Talbot provided a final flourish to resolve all the story elements in the last chapter.

The book was made possible by the behind-the-scenes work of many people: Lisa Craig, Roland Gulliver, Kate Seiler, Janet Smyth and Frances Sutton from the Book Festival were central to the project, while Adrian Searle and his team at Freight Books deserve praise for being one of Britain's most courageous and enlightened young publishing companies. It was Adrian who had the idea of commissioning Tom Kindley, a recent graduate from the Edinburgh College of Art, to produce the images for the book's cover and chapter dividers. And we could not have contemplated publishing this book without support from Creative Scotland and the Scottish Government's Edinburgh Festivals Expo Fund. Above all, we thank our story editor Denise Mina, who provided the energy, dynamism, imagination and inspiration that infuse this unusual book.

Credits
Chapter 3 Adam Murphy - Colouring by Lisa Murphy
Chapter 4 Irvine Welsh & Dan McDaid - Colouring by Deborah McCumiskey
Chapter 6 Mary Talbot & Kate Charlesworth - Bryan Talbot hand-lettering font available from Comicraft

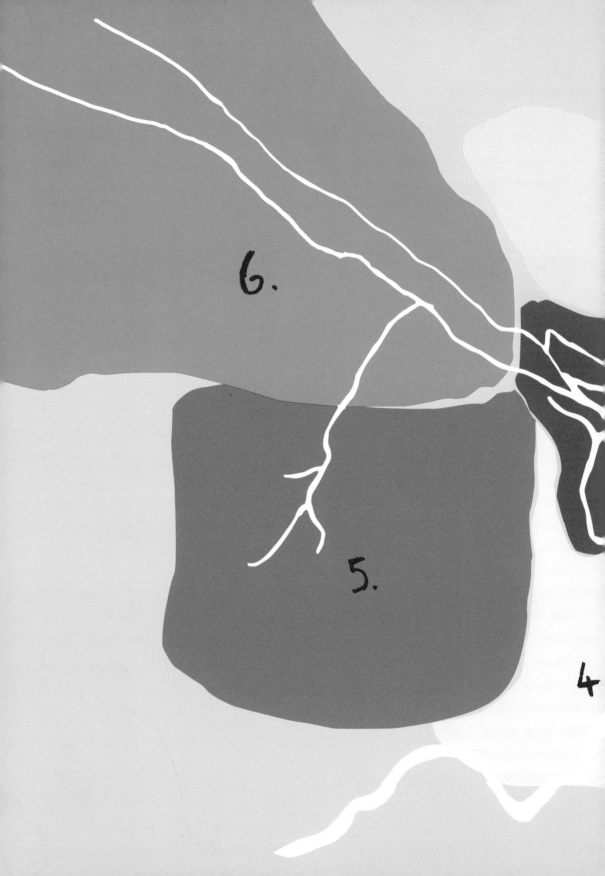